I. F. Henry Drevon

A journey through Sweden

Containing a Detailed Account of its Population, Agriculture, Commerce, and

finances ...

I. F. Henry Drevon

A Journey through Sweden
Containing a Detailed Account of its Population, Agriculture, Commerce, and finances ...

ISBN/EAN: 9783744757065

Printed in Europe, USA, Canada, Australia, Japan

Cover: Foto ©Suzi / pixelio.de

More available books at **www.hansebooks.com**

A

JOURNEY THROUGH SWEDEN,

CONTAINING

A DETAILED ACCOUNT

OF ITS

POPULATION, AGRICULTURE, COMMERCE, AND FINANCES;

TO WHICH IS ADDED

AN ABRIDGED HISTORY OF THE KINGDOM, AND OF THE DIFFERENT FORMS OF GOVERNMENT,

FROM THE

ACCESSION OF GUSTAVUS VASA, IN M,D,XXIII.

With some Particulars relating to the

HISTORY OF DENMARK,

AND TO

THE LIFE OF COUNT STRUENZEE.

WRITTEN IN FRENCH BY A DUTCH OFFICER, AND TRANSLATED INTO ENGLISH BY

WILLIAM RADCLIFFE, A. B.

OF ORIEL COLLEGE, OXFORD.

———

LONDON:

PRINTED FOR G. KEARSLEY, AT JOHNSON'S HEAD, No. 46, FLEET STREET.

ADVERTISEMENT.

THE following work is something less than an entire Translation of the Original, of which a few parts are omitted, and others abridged. The latter are, however, rather compressed than curtailed, and the omissions are chiefly of those passages which have been disapproved by an English Journalist*, whose opinion is a sufficient authority upon the subject, and whose favourable mention of the work in general first led the Translator to exert his endeavours upon it.

* Monthly Review, Appendix, June, 1789.

TABLE of CONTENTS.

LETTER I.

G*Eneral outline of the journey.—Description of Fahlun,* page 1

LETTER II.

Mine of Kopparberg—method of working it—exterior works—process of extracting rough copper from the ore, 9

LETTER III.

History of the mine.—General description of Sweden, 21

LETTER IV.

Passage of the Sound.—Helsingburg.—Journey from Helsingburg to Gothenburg.—Province of Halland.——Halmstadt.— Warberg.——Laholm. —Kongs-backa.—Inns.—Roads.—Posts.— Gothenburg, 26

CONTENTS.

LETTER V.

Description of Gothenburg.—India Company.—Internal Commerce.——Vauxhall.—Parade.—Levied Forces.—Deserters.—National Troops, page 38

LETTER VI.

Cataract of Trolhetta.—Edet.—Falkioping.—Regiment of cavalry of Westrogothia, 51

LETTER VII.

Mariestadt.—Journey from Mariestadt to Orebrö. —Arboga.—Smedby.—Castle of Gripsholm.—Troshalla.—Kumla.—Fitzia, 58

LETTER VIII.

Stockholm.—Castle.—Arsenal.—Opera.—Comedie Françoise.—National Comedy.—Queen Christina's Pavilion.—Academy of Sciences.—Repository of Machines.—Observatory.—Academy of Painting and Sculpture.—Artists, 68

LETTER IX.

Stockholm.—Isle of Admiralty.—Galleys.—Garrison.—The King.—Queen.—Prince Royal.—National dress.—Public walks.—Drotningholm, 82

LETTER X.

Stockholm.—Charitable Institutions.—University of Upsal.—Library.—Observatory.—Botanical Garden.—Cabinets of Natural History and Chemistry.—Antiquities.—Cathedral.—Old Upsal.—Antiquities,

92

LET-

CONTENTS.

LETTER XI.

Osterby.—Mine of Dannemora.—Forges, p. 106

LETTER XII.

History of the mine of Dannemora.—Workmen.—Löffta.—Suderfors.—Gefle—Cataract of Elfearsleby.—Province of Dalecarlia, 117

LETTER XIII.

Inn at Sater.—Orräs.—Gustavus Vasa.—Saterbronn, a mineral watering-place.—Mode of life there.—Sahla.—Silver mine.—Description and history of the mine.—Forge.—Process of extracting silver from the ore, 125

LETTER XIV.

Enkiöping.—Westeras, or Arosen.—Stromsholm.—Royal stud.—Kongsor.—Lake Hielmarn.—Malmar.—Mountain of Malmar.—Nordkiöping.—Manufactory of Brass.—Lindkiöping.—Floating Island.—Lake Wettern.—Wadstena and its antiquities, 136

LETTER XV.

Gold mine of Adelfors.—Carlscroon.—Post.—Dock.—Carlsham.—Christianstadt.—Province of Scania, 147

LETTER XVI.

Maglasteen.——Ystadt.—Malmoe.—Lund.——Landscrona.—Ramlos, 155

CONTENTS.   vii

LETTER XVII.

Passage of the Sound.—Castle of Cronenburg.— Queen Matilda.—Queen Dowager of Denmark.— Elseneur.—Princess Louisa Augusta.—Prince Royal of Denmark.—Revolution of 1784,   page 162

LETTER XVIII.

Comparison between the inhabitants of Sweden and Denmark,   178

LETTER XIX.

Population and agriculture of Sweden and Denmark,   192

LETTER XX.

Commerce----Navigation----Manufactures----Finances—Revenues of Sweden,   204

LETTER XXI.

Abridgment of the History of Sweden from the accession of Gustavus Vasa, in 1723, *to the death of Charles* XII. *in* 1719,   219

LETTER XXII.

Continuation of the history of Sweden from the death of Charles XII. *to that of Frederic* II, 235

LETTER XXIII..

History of Gustavus III. *from* 1771, *to* 1786, 257

LETTER XXIV.

History of Struenzee,   303

SWEDISH COINS.

1 Stiver	=	0	0	$0\frac{7}{8}$
4 Stivers	= 1 Copper Marc	0	0	$1\frac{5}{9}$
3 Copper Marcs	= 1 Silver Marc	0	0	$4\frac{2}{3}$
4 Copper Marcs	= 1 Copper Dollar	0	0	$6\frac{2}{3}$
9 Copper Marcs	= a Caroline	0	1	2
3 Copper Dollars	= 1 Silver Dollar	0	1	$6\frac{2}{3}$
2 Silver Dollars	= 1 Plote	0	3	$1\frac{1}{3}$
3 Silver Dollars	= 1 Rix Dollar	0	4	8
2 Rix Dollars	= 1 Ducat	0	9	4

A Ton of gold is a nominal sum equal to 100,000 silver dollars.

These valuations are taken partly from the original, and partly from Guthrie.

ERRATA.

		for	read
p. 2. l. 14.		through,	over.
37.	11.	capitain,	captain.
39.	22.	affords,	afford.
54.	3.	town,	city.
95.	6.	dele alone.	
112.	12.	fused,	smelted.
122.	2.	ore,	iron.
——	3.	smelted,	worked.
159.	21.	St. Vierge,	the Virgin Mary.
211.	note.	487,500 l.	900,000 l.
213.	note.	ten pence,	1s. 6d.
258.		Hats,	Caps.

A

JOURNEY, &c.

LETTER I.

Fahlun, July .... 1785.

MY DEAR FRIEND,

FROM the commencement of my journey through the kingdom of Sweden, I have not had a moment's leisure for communication; whatever time I have been able to spend in any place has been wholly employed, either in acquiring intelligence by my own researches, or in soliciting it from my friends; and the information thus obtained I have been careful to note and preserve in my journal.

Let me now, however, acknowlege the receipt of your letter, addressed to Copenhagen, which came to me at Stockholm, through the means of Mr. the Comte de R...

I now write from the depths of Dalecarlia, the place in which Gustavus Vasa was educated; and in the midst of those brave Dalecarlians, who, under his orders, freed their country from a yoke by wh ch it ha been oppreſſed for two centuries.

I arrived at Stockholm by the way of Gottenburg, Falkioping, Marieſtadt, Orebro, and Arboga, and, paſſing from thence to the northward, viſited Upſal, and remained ſome days upon an eſtate, the owner of which led me to the famous mine of Dannemora, ſo rich in iron of the firſt quality. At Loſta, the magnificent eſtate of the Baron de Geer, I ſpent a day in obſerving the different operations of the forges there eſtabliſhed. I then went to the cataract Dahl Elbe (or rather the river Dahle) which, after ſeparating into two courſes, precipitates itſelf through hideous rocks of the height of more than fifty feet. The foam of the waters, the noiſe produced by their fall, and the height of this cataract, form a grand and intereſting ſpectacle. From thence I went to Gefle, a port in the gulph of Bothnia; and thus, after a journey of two months, arrived at Fahlun.

After ſeeing the copper mines of this place, I propoſe to ſurvey thoſe of ſilver at Sahla; from thence I ſhall go to Nordkiöping, Carlſcroon, and Yſtadt, and, making the tour of Scania, ſhall return to Helſingbourg, through the oppoſite ſide of the kingdom to that by which I paſſed from thence to Stockholm.

From what I have juſt told you, and from your own knowledge of the country by the map, you will

will perceive that I did not reach Stockholm by the neareſt road; but it was not my purpoſe in viſiting Sweden to confine myſelf in the capital, or to follow the ordinary route; on the contrary, I intend to obſerve every thing curious, either in the productions of nature or in the performances of art; and to make the complete tour of a country which intereſts me both by the picturesque diſpoſition of its ſcenery, and by the activity, genius, and hoſpitality of its inhabitants. In the execution of this deſign, I ſhall give particular attention to the mines, to the works conſtructed at Carlſcroon for the accommodation of a fleet, and to thoſe of other parts deſigned for the promotion of commerce and the eaſe of internal navigation.

You would hardly imagine at how little expence I perform my journey. My Ruſſian *voiture* is tolerably light, and the roads are ſo good, that four Swediſh horſes, although their ſize is very ſmall, and their appearance bad, are every where able to draw me; for theſe I pay no more than at the rate of ſixteen pence Swediſh for each horſe per mile, which mile* is nearly as long as two common French leagues and a half.

I ſtop wherever there is any thing curious enough to deſerve notice; but, when there is no invitation of this ſort, my journey is continued by day and night.

---

* Thirteen Swediſh miles and a half are reckoned to a degree.

night. Indeed the nights, by their clearness, are as favourable to the traveller as mid-day; and, as I am seldom without the pen or the pencil in my hand, I shall be able to furnish you with some tolerably exact descriptions. For these, however, you must wait my return into Denmark; and, till then, you will attribute it to want of opportunity for writing long letters, if I send you only an account of such particulars as may occur during the course of my journey.

Let me, however, mention that Sweden consists entirely of one continued rock of granite, covered in different places, with a greater or less quantity of earth, which, though agriculture has for some years been greatly encouraged, is for the most part badly cultivated. The country is very thinly inhabited, and, in some districts, I have passed through deserts of twenty or thirty leagues in extent, where one could perceive only a few poor huts placed upon the mould which covers the rocks, and overhung by firs, of which there are some immense woods, without any mixture of other trees. To this account there are, however, some exceptions: Sudermania, which I have surveyed from one end to the other, and all the southern parts of Upland, are well cultivated. Scania, which I have yet to see, is said to be very beautiful; and the cultivation of Ostragothia is much praised. But the labours of the mines, the works which relate

to

to them, the management of the forges, and the manners of the people, are subjects for investigation, which sufficiently repay the trouble of a journey into Sweden. I have seen amongst mines of iron, the simplicity of the golden age; and though in some places scarcely any thing appears to the eye but rocks, whose bowels contain the materials of steel, I have there found men with hearts uncontaminated by any of its qualities.

The city of Stockholm is well situated, and the view of it is highly picturesque. Here, as in most capital cities, the peculiarities of the national dress are most strictly preserved, especially by those persons who frequent the court. Their habits of association are very cheerful; and the nobility, and those who are in general called good company, have manners sufficiently cultivated. People of distinction, merchants, and wealthy persons, afford a ready welcome, and shew a sort of prejudiced kindness to strangers. The common people, as in all the other parts of Sweden, make their bread but once, or at most twice, in the year; it consists of rye mixed with oats, and is called *knikkebroë* or *kakebroë*; this they form into cakes of the figure and breadth of a common plate, and of the thickness of a little finger; they then make a hole in the middle, and the peasants string them together by hundreds, and suspend them from the ceilings of their houses. The bread of this sort, although immoderately hard, is not ill tasted; and it often appears at the tables of persons of the first distinction, accompanied with wheaten bread of very excellent colour and flavour. In times of scarcity, and especially in the North of Dalecarlia, they add to the meal of rye and oats, the bark of the birch tree, well broken and pounded; and this bread becomes then so hard, that nothing but the tooth of a Dalecarlian seems able to penetrate it.

Fahlun. I arrived at Fahlun yesterday (sunday) at six in the morning, about four-and-twenty hours after my departure from Gefle: during the whole of my journey from Stockholm I had seen only woods and rocks; judge, therefore, of my pleasure when I found myself in the midst of a town so well peopled as to be said to contain seven thousand inhabitants.

After a short repose, I presented my letter of recommendation to Mr. Haldin, fiscal of the mines; he received me in the politest manner, and made me an offer of his table during my stay here, which I readily accepted. At dinner I found Mr. Haldin, his lady, his brother, secretary to the King, and a knight of the polar order, some officers of the regiment of Dalecarlia, and three young ladies, who alone did not speak French; and who, by their gaiety of manner and beauty of countenance, made me regret that I had no opportunity of enjoying their conversation. After

dinner,

dinner, Mr. Haldin and some of the officers proposed to me a walk in the town and its environs. I found the greatest part of the inhabitants of Fahlun to be miners and forgers. The houses, as in the other parts of Sweden, are of wood, but there are a few built of brick and stone. Those of the governor of the province, the superintendant of the mines, the fiscal, and a few other of the principal officers of the mines, the town-house, and two large churches, are entirely of stone. There are two paved streets, the others are covered with the *scoriæ* of copper broken and rammed. Having surveyed the town, we went to Kopparberg, where are the mines; I saw the different entrances, or wells, at the bottom of two large excavations, of which one is called the *grand mine*, and the other, which is less, *Louisa Ulrica*. From all these openings there arose a thick smoke, occasioned by charcoal fires lighted at the bottom of the mines every sunday, in the absence of the workmen, in order to soften the ore, which they also each day separate from the rock by the force of gun-powder.

Having finished our walk, we returned home with Mr. Haldin, and found at his house a numerous company, who took tea, and formed themselves into parties for play, which was succeeded by a supper; there was much gay and animated conversation; and as I had placed myself by a lady who spoke excellent French, I passed a very

delightful

delightful evening. Although much fatigued, I arose this morning at three, to have the pleasure of writing this letter to you, and I am now in instant expectation of returning to view the copper mine at Kopparberg, which is about half a quarter of a league from the town. I here propose to descend, and take a small subterraneous walk at the depth of more than a thousand feet under ground: if I should chance to hear what the Antipodes say, you may depend upon my relating it to you. I did not descend into the iron mine at Dannemora, although of less depth than this, because the machine in which it is necessary to be placed seemed something dangerous, and I perceived no disposition in myself to be so born along in the air, when I could see from the scaffold upon the edge of the excavation, every thing that was done at the bottom of the mine. The opening is there a quarter of a league in circumference, and the depth of the mine between three and four hundred feet. The descent into the mine of Kopparberg is by ladders, and I have therefore no fear.

This town, by its situation at the foot of the mountain, in which is the entrance to the mine, is liable to the inconvenience of being frequently filled with smoke, which descends upon the first application of fire to the ore: while I now write, this smoke is so strong, that the whole village appears

pears enveloped in a thick cloud, and from this issues a smell of sulphur which is scarce supportable. The inhabitants, to whom this is familiar, consider it as a preservation from the stings of gnats, of which there is an immense number throughout all Sweden; and pretend that wooden houses impregnated with these sulphureous particles, last longer than any others.

Monsieur Haldin now attends to conduct me to the mine; I therefore hasten to assure you that I am, &c. &c.

LETTER II.

Helsingburg, Sept. .... 1785.

MY DEAR FRIEND,

WHILE my passage into Denmark is prevented by a terrible storm, which will probably detain me for at least four-and-twenty hours, I am happy to employ my leisure in writing to you. You have, by this time, I hope, received a letter, which I sent to you immediately after my departure for the centre of the earth; a journey which I performed successfully by the help of some bundles of fir chips, and which abounds with wonders as much as those of the famed subterranean traveller *Klaas Klim*.

For

For four hours which I spent in the bowels of Kopparberg, and during which, partly by the help of ladders, and partly by stairs, I descended from one gallery to another, my astonishment increased at every step. Our descent was at first by a zig-zag staircase, formed in an excavation of, perhaps, two thousand feet in circumference, and three hundred feet in depth, and thus far we were able to proceed by the light of the Sun. In a corner, at the bottom of this excavation, was a wooden hut of six or seven feet in height, at the door of which stood two figures, half naked, and as black as ink, each of whom held in his hand a faggot of lighted fir, and, thus equipped, might have passed for one of Pluto's pages. Here, also, we found four entrances to the mine itself; the most convenient is that which opens into this hut; but they are each honoured with the name of some Swedish prince or man of rank. Upon our appearance at the door of this, they brought for myself and servant two dresses, entirely black, made like those of the *Heiducs*, and intended to secure our clothes in the narrow passages of the galleries. I had put on mine, when I perceived my man, terrified by the dismal appearance of my garb, and still more by the prayers which our guides were offering up for our preservation and deliverance from the mine, refusing either to put on his scaramouch dress, or to make any attempt towards

towards defcending farther. Thefe fellows during our defcent of the firft ftaircafe, had been entertaining us with ftories of falling fragments of rock, broken ladders, and fudden eruptions of water or peftilential vapours; we had alfo feen prayers offered up by every workman upon his approach to the mine; and thefe circumftances had made fuch an impreffion upon my young *Frieze*, that nothing lefs than the moft profufe reproaches of his cowardice could induce him to follow me.

At length, by paffing partly through alleys fupported by timber work, and partly under vaults felf-fupported, I arrived at thofe vaft halls, whofe tops and extremities the feeble light of our faggots could not reach. In fome of thefe halls there are forges at which they manufacture and repair the tools ufed in the mine; and the heat in them is fo exceffive, that the workmen are all entirely as naked as nature produced them. Others ferve for magazines, either of gun-powder, for the purpofe of explofion, or of cords and other neceffary utenfils; and between thefe the communication is by the alleys already mentioned. There are fome of thefe halls in all the galleries, and between each gallery are either fteps or ladders. Befides thefe, there are openings hollowed perpendicularly from the outer furface to the loweft gallery, which ferve for the admiffion of air, and through which heavy commodities are lowered in barrels, by means of pulleys
kept

kept continually moving, during the whole time of work. Horses are stationed at the top of the mountain, for the purpose of working these pulleys, and the barrels are held by iron chains, which are used instead of common ropes, on account of the destructive quality of the vitriolic and coppery vapours arising from the bottom of the mine; even the chains do not last long in these vapours, and they, therefore, often use ropes made of hog's bristles or cow's hair. On this account, and in order to prevent other accidents, the workmen are prohibited from ascending or descending by the barrels, and are obliged to use the more tedious route of the ladders. These openings also, with the subterraneous fires, and other physical causes, produce in the lowest galleries such currents of air, as in some places can be said only to resemble tempests; but without this method of purification, the air would be so unfit for breathing, that no person could exist in it for a quarter of an hour. The alleys which I have mentioned are sometimes of the height of five or six feet, and sometimes so low that it is necessary to creep along them; in these the currents of air are the most violent and dangerous, for it often happens that when a profuse perspiration has been brought on by the heat of the forges, you are met by one of these currents, which are always as cold as ice, and which even freeze the sweat upon your body.

The

The vaults, which are not supported by timber present sometimes very remarkable appearances; prisms of different figures being formed by the crystallization of the vitriol which trickles down them. Imagine a thousand pointed projections, like those in sugar-candy, but of the length of eight, ten, twelve or twenty feet, and of the most beautiful green colour, hanging from the top of these vaults, and reflecting the light from their various-formed sides over the ore with which the partitions are filled.

In a gallery seven hundred feet under the surface of the earth, they dissolve this vitriol, and force it from the mine by a curious hydraulic contrivance. The water of a considerable spring is put in motion by a machine worked by horses; this water dissolves the vitriol, and afterwards precipitates it through a trough containing some old iron, into another. The whole operation, and the labour by which it is performed, are something singular. Four-and-twenty horses, which, as well as the men, relieve each other every six hours, keep the machine at work both by day and night. The horses are kept in stables in this gallery, with mangers hollowed in the rock; and when they have once entered the mine, are never suffered to leave it, but to be exhibited once a year at a sort of review. They are then raised and lowered by pulleys and bandages, through the openings in which there are

ladders,

ladders, in the same manner as with us horses are hoisted on board ships.

My curiosity led me as far as the last gallery, eleven hundred feet under ground, and in which the copper is chiefly worked. Here, notwithstanding the excessive cold, I again saw labourers entirely naked; and though a spectator, well clothed and covered, may feel himself almost frozen, yet, such is the immense exertion used in hewing the rock, and in separating those parts where the ore is found, that these men, in pure nakedness, were entirely covered with sweat. The darkness of these subterraneous regions, the fires perceived at different distances, the sort of gloomy light which proceeded from them, the naked labourers, black as the ore at which they worked, and surrounded by sparks produced by their hammers, the noise of all this labour and of the hydraulic engines in motion, with the horrible figures which from time to time rushed past me with torches in their hands, made me doubt a little whether I had not really descended rather too near to Tartarus. Yet this scene is not to be compared with that which presented itself to me, when upon descending to the very bottom of the mine, I entered a sort of large hall, the vaults of which were supported by pillars cut in the rock, and surounded with seats of the same material. Here my two conductors enquiring if I would

not

not sit down and listen to a small piece of music, the effect of which would surprise me: "Of what sort is this music?" said I.—"It is the strange noise," answered they, "which the rocks make when, in order to lessen the trouble of breaking them with an axe, they are blown in pieces by gun-powder."

My fondness for the wonderful, and my reliance upon the prudence of my guides, made me comply, upon the condition of their remaining with me. They gave me their words for this, which they said they might the more easily keep, as this was almost the only hall in which there was no danger. One of them then left me to give his orders, and returned to our seat in a minute afterwards, where we remained wearied by expectation, and shivering with cold, for a quarter of an hour. I had scarely expressed my impatience, when a discharge struck my ears with such force as I had never before experienced; this was succeeded by a sudden light, which illumined the whole of this subterraneous territory, but in an instant vanished, and left us in total darkness, the concussion of the air having extinguished our faggots. This darkness was interrupted only by the flashes from succeeding discharges, of which the light lasted only for a moment, but the sound was long and terribly reverberated in echoes. The vaults cracked, the earth shook, and the benches

on

on which we sat trembled. I was then eleven hundred and thirty-six feet beneath the surface of the earth; and when I caught the scent of the smoke, listened to the noise of bursting rocks, and surveyed my guides, my domestics and myself, you will, perhaps, think me excusable if I own that the little hair which nature has left me rose upward with fear. This harmonious music continued for about half an hour, and left us at once to an entire silence, which, with the darkness of the place and the sort of suffocation produced by the smoke, served only to prolong my terror. I found, however, that this operation was repeated every day at noon, during the repast of the workmen, to whom the hall in which I was seated, and some niches cut in the rock, served as a shelter from the violence of the explosions.

These explosions are necessary here, because the rock is very hard, and the miners could not otherwise proceed above a few toises in a year. One of our guides having, by groping his way, obtained a light, we returned by a different passage, not more than half the length of that by which we entered. I was detained, however, to observe a chamber hollowed in the rock, containing a square table in the middle, surrounded by cushioned benches; four chandeliers illuminated with wax hung from the top of the vault, and the rock was wainscoted to the height of five feet. In this
chamber

chamber the council of the mines meets twice a year, and there is a kitchen and cellar hewn in the rock, for the accommodation of the company who dine in it upon this occasion. Here also I found a small collation sent for me by Mr. Haldin, and you may believe that I thought it a very acceptable present.

You can scarce imagine the effect of the light and air upon my emerging into the warm climate of a most beautiful day from this vast abyss, in which heat, wind, cold, and damps succeed each other in the most extraordinary manner. After a little rest at the entrance of the hut before mentioned to you, I ascended the top of the mountain, and, at the house of the inspector, found Mr. and Mad. Haldin with some ladies and gentlemen who had accompanied me thus far in my way to the mine. Here also, I was presented with a book, in which I was desired to note my name, character, and any thing either of verse or prose which occured to my recollection. This custom had been mentioned to me at Stockholm, and I had therefore, prepared some lines, containing a compliment to the ladies of Fahlun, which I immediately wrote down, and was fortunate enough to find received as an impromptu. Indeed the compliment was applicable enough, for I found the ladies to whom Mr. Haldin introduced me lively, beautiful, and of amiable manners. But my sub-

terraneous

terraneous journey had fatigued me so much, that after viewing the exterior works, especially the mechanism of the pumps, which are always throwing up water from the mine, I retired to rest at my lodgings.

These pumps are necessary to secure the mine from inundations, and are thus worked. A chain of the length of five thousand feet, composed of bars of fir, and constructed, on account of the vapours, with as little iron as possible, is put in motion by a stream of water led through an aqueduct from a lake on the top of the mountain. The chain, which is double, draws the water from the reservoir, into which it has been forced from the bottom of mine by the hydraulic engine before mentioned, and the water is afterwards conducted by a second aqueduct to the bottom of the mountain, and into a river which flows through the town. The whole mechanism of this operation is the same as that at the iron mine of Dannemora, but with these exceptions, that the wheel which gives motion to the whole, and which at Dannemora is forty-four feet in diameter, is here forty-eight; and that at this place they have contrived a bell, which rings while the machine moves properly, but stops when it is disordered by the least accident. This is the signal to those appointed to watch the machine, of whom there are always two in attendance both by day and night, through the

whole

whole year. One of thefe is ftationed in a kind of box near the middle of the chain, and within hearing of the bell; and it is his duty, with the affiftance of twelve men, who relieve each other in turn, to keep the wheels, pulleys, and axles conftantly fupplied with greafe.

This mine, although nothing is obtained from it but copper, contains fuch a quantity of iron, that the geometrician of the place is unable to make any ufe of the compafs in correcting his plans of the different works.

Having flept for two hours, and dined again with Mr. Haldin, I went to fee the different operations through which the ore paffes before it becomes rough copper. Thefe may be thus arranged and defcribed:

1ft. A pile is raifed to a certain height, containing alternate *ftrata* of copper ore and fir wood; the wood is then lighted, and thus the ore is cleanfed from the fulphur, and the rough ftone becomes feparated. When the wind fets towards the town during this operation, the fmoke and ftench are fuch as can fcarcely be borne by thofe not accuftomed to them.

2dly. It is then beaten by means of large hammers, put in motion by a wheel, which is acted upon by water, and

3dly. It is fmelted in furnaces, in order to be beaten again.

C 2   4thly.

4thly. They roast it again, in order to extract any heterogeneous matter, especially sulphur, that may still remain. And,

5thly. It is resmelted. By this last operation the *scoria* is made to pass through a hole at the top of the furnace, while the metal, running through another at the bottom, is received in moulds of sand, and formed into the shape of large bricks*. But though bricks of this sort have been for some years used in building, it is by no means certain that houses formed of them will be able long to resist the inclemency of the weather. At Dannemora they use the *scoriæ* of iron for the same purpose.

The lumps of rough copper, obtained from the ore by these operations, are sent to Avesta, a town about four miles from Fahlun, to be refined. There, silver and some very small quantities of gold have at times been extracted from them. I saw a medal of this silver, struck in the year 1758, upon the occasion of a visit to the mine from the late King and Queen, and his present Majesty, then Prince Royal. They shewed me also a ducat

---

* The original has, " *tandis que le metal qui reste au fond sort par un trou menagé dans la partie basse du fourneau dans les formes de sable, auxquelles on donne la figure de nos plus grandes briques.*" But there is probably some mistake here. In the account of the iron mine at Dannemora, the *scoria* of copper is compared with that of iron, with respect to its value when formed into bricks; it is, therefore, to be supposed that the *scoria* alone, not the metal, is used for that purpose.——T.

made of this gold, extracted at the expence of four times its value; and a very beautiful red colour, in powder, obtained by volatilifation.

My hoſt informs me dinner is ready, and I am, therefore, obliged to conclude. The ſtorm continues with the ſame violence, and has raged equally for four hours, which I have ſpent in looking over my journal, and writing to you. The Sound, of which I have a view from my window, is furiouſly agitated, and the veſſels in the roads ſhew by their motion the immenſe violence of the waves. Elſineur, the caſtle of Cronenburg, and the ſhores of Denmark, form the other parts of this moſt magnificent profpect. But the ſublime pleaſure which this ſcene produces, is leſſened when I conſider the danger of the paſſage; I tremble at the idea of encountering ſuch waves as now riſe to my ſight, and perceive that I ſhall for a long time be condemned to liſten to the clattering windows of this miſerable inn. Adieu.

I am, &c. &c.

LETTER III.

Helſingburg, Sept. ... 1785.

MY DEAR FRIEND,

THE rain and wind having confpired to prevent my walking out, I proceed to give you ſome farther account of the copper mine

mine at Fahlun. Upon this subject I have been favoured with a memoir, from which I shall extract the principal articles.

" This mine is the most ancient of all those of
" copper in Sweden, having received its privileges
" so far back as the thirteenth century, under
" the kings Waldemar and Magnus Ladislaus.
" Since the year 1581, the government has given
" particular encouragement to the working of
" mines, and has bestowed upon those of Fahlun
" all sorts of privileges, even that of affording
" protection to persons accused of crimes not
" capital.

" The mine is worked by a society or company,
" whose stock is divided into 1200 shares, and
" who pay to the crown a fifth part of their profit;
" the ore as soon as taken from the earth is sold
" by this company to the forge-masters; and each
" estate in the neighbourhood, in proportion to its
" size and value, is obliged to furnish a certain
" quantity of fuel, according to a rate settled by
" the king.

" The ore of the different mines of Kopparberg
" is by no means equally rich, some yielding only
" one or two *per* cent. of copper, and some twenty
" or thirty. Indeed, all the mines produce much
" less now than they formerly did; in the middle
" of the last century 20321 *schisp* of copper were
" annually obtained from hence, but, through
" the

"the course of the present century, the average annual produce has been only from 4 to 6 thou- sand *schisp*. This decrease is attributed to the falling in of some vaults, badly excavated by the miners of former times, the ruins of which have so choaked up the richest veins, that the workmen have not yet been able to open them.

"For some years the exportation of copper was entirely prohibited, and it is now permitted only under certain restrictions, and to a certain amount. The domestic manufactures of this article are now encouraged by high premiums, especially those of yellow brass; and thus the most beneficial means are used to lessen the exportation of it in its unmanufactured state.

"In this mine twelve hundred workmen are often employed."

Besides the mines of copper, iron, and silver, there is also a gold mine at Adelfors in Smaland; but this is worked merely for its silver by some adventurers, who are at present scarcely paid their expences, but proceed in the hope of future profit.

The silver mine at Sahla is of considerable consequence, but yields to that of iron at Dannemora; indeed this last may be called the Peru of Sweden, exceeding in value those of copper, and supporting by its produce the greatest part of the trade carried on in the country. And so barren is the surface of the soil in Sweden, that the inhabitants may be said to owe their subsistence to the riches thus contained in the bowels of the earth.

I have seen almost all the provinces, and, except Westmannia, the northern part of Sudermania, the southern part of Upland, Ostrogothia and Scania, I can pronounce them to consist only of two sorts of granite, the one reddish, and the other grey. But in this latter province the soil is fertile and well cultivated, and, notwithstanding the great number of inhabitants, they consume only half the corn produced in it, and are able to furnish the rest in traffic to their neighbours.

The provinces of Westragothia, Nericia, Gastricia, and Dalecarlia, with the northern part of Upland, and the southern part of Sudermania, are only hideous rocks and immense deserts, with gloomy woods of fir-trees of thirty or forty leagues in length. In the mountainous country there are many indisputable traces of some terrible revolution of the earth; and the rocks heaped on rocks, in many extensive places to a most astonishing height, recall the idea of the giants wars, or rather indeed seem to be certain proofs of that great convulsion of nature which many naturalists believe to have happened, although in ages so remote as to be recorded only in the marks of destruction and violence which yet remain. At least Sweden, above all other countries, seems to afford the most materials for the support of such a system.

It

It has sometimes happened that I have travelled for four-and-twenty hours through woods and rocks, in which I have literally seen no other habitations than those of the Chivergoors, a sort of peasant post-masters, who live at the distance of two, three, and sometimes of four leagues from each other, in wooden cabins, that hold themselves, their horses, and their corn, placed in a small square spot of ground, in which they plant hops. These people scarcely know the use of herbs, and eat only bread diluted with milk or water, yet with this they and their families seem cheerful and contented, and can hardly conceive a happier mode of existence than their own. They are good natured and honest beyond example, and are very robust and healthy, especially in Dalecarlia. After the age of forty, they permit their beards to grow, and this, joined to one's knowledge of their simplicity and frugality, gives them a very respectable appearance.

The storm, which I have already mentioned to you once or twice, begins to lower, and I have hopes of passing over to Elsineur to-morrow, and dining at Droningaard, an estate belonging to my friends, the C .... s. When I have a little recovered from my fatigue, I shall hasten to send you some extracts from my notes, and to communicate the information obtained in a journey which I certainly undertook with very eager hopes, and

in

in which I have tasted many varieties of enjoyment.

In the mean time I seize the opportunity of better weather to view the situation and the environs of Helsingburg, where I now remain, as at all times and in all places,

Your &c. &c.

LETTER IV.

Droningaard, Sept. .... 1785.

MY DEAR FRIEND,

THE activity and turbulence of my life for some months past, is well contrasted and rewarded by the peaceful state in which I now enjoy the kindness of my friends, and the luxuries of a delightful country:—A convenient dwelling, the charms of a cheerful and unrestrained society, and a delicious season calling forth all the beauties of variegated nature, are the principal features of this happy scene. We have here a wood separated by many pleasing walks, and well filled with stags and hinds, a noble lake, and a garden entirely laid out in the English taste, with a hermitage, shrubberies, rivulets and cascades. The hills which rise on the opposite side of the lake, in some places cultivated and laid out in pastures, and in others covered with villages, castles, and country-houses, offer such a

continual

continual variety of rural pleasures, as takes off all remembrance of my late fatigues. I have also the pleasure of your correspondence, and the satisfaction of hearing frequently from those in whose welfare I am most interested.

I shall now proceed with my account of Sweden, and, to give some order to my descriptions, begin with Helsingburg, the first town at which you arrive after quitting the dominions of Denmark at Elsineur. My journal will direct me in this correspondence, and I shall communicate to you not only what I have seen, but what I have been able to learn from good authorities among the Swedes themselves, upon subjects concerning which I was desirous of information. I had the happiness of being recommended to persons who were able to give me very exact intelligence, and who furnished me with several memoirs, containing some curious and particular details.

After dining with the rich merchants, Fenwick and Godin, to whom I had a letter of recommendation, I embarked at Elsineur, on Friday the 6th of May, every thing necessary having been previously provided by these gentlemen. The strait which separates Sweden from Denmark, is about a mile in breadth. I passed it in about half an hour in as pleasant weather as could be wished.

The embarkation at Elsineur is performed in the most convenient and ready manner; but at Helsingburg

singburg there is not even a quay to receive you; and the broken carriage in which you are obliged to truſt yourſelf, is in continual danger of breaking or falling into the ſea, even though it ſhould not be diſturbed by wind.

On leaving Denmark you are ſtruck with a proſpect, the beauties of which it is impoſſible to deſcribe: Elſineur, the caſtle of Cronenburg, with its woody heights, the roads filled with veſſels of every nation, and the ſhores of Denmark crowned with villages, country houſes, and woods, combine to produce the delightful effect of this extraordinary coup-d'œil. The Swediſh ſhore, though by no means equally beautiful, opens to you ſeveral picturesque ſituations; and there is a tower of very reſpectable antiquity, which, from the top of a high mountain, commands the town of Helſingburg, ſituated between it and the ſound.

HELSINGBURG. This town contains about twelve hundred inhabitants, who live chiefly by fiſhing and agriculture: there are, however, ſome manufactures; and the profitable neighbourhood of Ramlos, where the nobility of Scania aſſemble to drink the waters in the ſeaſon, gives a tolerably flouriſhing appearance to the place, which the continual paſſage of travellers between the two kingdoms, and the garriſon, conſiſting of a ſquadron of huſſars, alſo

contribute

contribute to improve. The season at Ramlos begins in the middle of July.

At seven in the evening, my voiture being refitted and ready, I set out for Gothenburg, where I arrived on sunday night, exactly eight-and-forty hours after my departure from Helsingburg *. In this journey I travelled day and night, and stopped only at a few small places, which scarcely deserve the name of towns, such as Engelholm in Scania, Laholm, Halmstadt, Falkenburg, Warberg, and Kongsbacka, all in Halland, a province situated along the north sea, or rather along a gulph of that sea, formed between Jutland and Sweden, and called Schaggerack or Cattegat.

PROVINCE OF HALLAND. This province, in its general aspect, presents only an hideous object to the eye, and fills the mind with ideas of some terrible devastation of nature. For the space of eight miles, the distance between the villages Morop and Ossa, I could not perceive one tree, the humble juniper alone growing upon the little moss which covers the rocks. These villages are not less wretched than the country in which they are situated; you see no habitations but those of the peasants, who are obliged to furnish horses to travellers; and meet no human being but some mi-

* The distance from Helsingburg to Gothenburg is generally computed at twenty-one Swedish miles, or fifty French leagues.

serable

ferable shepherds, whose sheep straggle among the rocks, in search of the scanty moss which is their only food.

The five miserable places in Halland, which they call towns, are now to be described.

HALMSTADT. Halmstadt, which has a manufacture of cloth, and a celebrated fishery for salmon, contains about two thousand inhabitants, and is the only one of these towns possessed of walls and gates. It is therefore honoured with the fine name of a capital, and has a garrison consisting of a company of hussars, of the same regiment with those at Helsingburg.

WARBURG. At Warberg there is also a company of hussars, and near it a fortress, which defends the entrance of a sort of port, into which small vessels run for shelter. The inhabitants catch herrings and other fish in the North Sea; and I am assured that this port, which is now only sufficient for a few small pinks, would formerly have received the largest fleets. This decrease, as upon the other coasts of Sweden, has been gradually produced; and is attributed by many learned men to the falling of the sea, which they believe to have retired from all the coasts of this kingdom. I shall perhaps take up this subject hereafter.

LAHOLM. At Laholm, where I saw the ruins of a fire, which had consumed half the town

town before my arrival, I met the Swedish colonel, Wrangel, who as well as myself, waited for horses. He told me that he had served in France in the war of 1744, and was at the taking of Bergen-op-Zoom, where he became very well acquainted with Dutch bravery. That after the peace he had taken a journey into Holland, to which country he was so much attached, that he never received a greater pleasure than when he was fortunate enough to meet a Dutchman. In testimony of this good will, he made me partake of his provisions; and we drank together to the prosperity of a country which, at the age of more than sixty, he professed himself every day inclined to re-visit. Upon our parting, he gave me some instructions for my journey, which I afterwards found very serviceable.

KONGSBACKA.
At Kongsbacka (or King's Mountain) a little hamlet at which I changed horses, two miles on this side Gothenburg, I met General Daniel, the governor of that city and of the province of Westragothia, of which it is the capital. He was going, in quality of inspector, to review some regiments in garrison in Scania. When I presented myself to his Excellency, he received me with great politeness, gave me a recommendation to the Count de Saltze, commandant of Gothenburg, and lamented that I should come into his government

at

at a time when he was unable to pay me the honours.

INNS. During my whole journey, the provisions put into my wallet at Droningaard by my friends the C . . . s were very useful; and prevented my complaining of a country which, at the places where you are obliged to change horses, affords no other sort of refreshment than some excellent milk, and bread of the sort described to you in my letter from Fahlun. I found the inns upon this road, as in all the other parts of Sweden, very miserable. The houses, being all of wood, and never washed, abound, in summer, with every sort of vermin; and the little cribs without curtains expose you to the piercing stings of a most dreadful number of gnats, while the beds themselves contain various sorts of insects, against which even the mattress that I carried with me proved a very feeble defence.

ROADS. You are recompensed, however, for the fare, and the beds at the inns, by the excellence of the roads, which, though a little rough in some parts of the mountainous country, may rival those so much boasted of in England. The bottom of these, except in Scania, where there is a good deal of sand, is a hard rock; and their breadth is such, that four *voitures* may easily pass at a time, even in the narrowest part. The bed of gravel, which they lay upon the top,

is

is also so beaten and compacted, as to have no where any appearance of a rut. This is to be understood, however, chiefly of the high roads and those they call *royal*; and upon these you may travel with great ease and rapidity, the horses, though very small, being strong and swift.

Posts. The order established in the conduct of these, is very convenient to strangers and travellers, but equally burthensome to the peasants, and highly prejudicial to agriculture. Of this you may judge from the following account. In all the high, and even in the cross roads, post-masters are appointed, (*chiverhoors*) who are also a sort of innkeepers (*gast-vry-hous*) and have under their direction a certain number of peasants. The peasants, in their turn, and according to the value of their farms, are obliged to provide one, or, sometimes, two servants, with one, two, three, four, or more horses, which remain in waiting for twenty-four hours, and are then succeeded by others. If any traveller arrives, they are paid for their time and trouble, if not, they lose both. You must perceive that these services are very oppressive, and cannot be performed without great detriment to the cultivation of estates, although they are not very rigorously demanded, especially in the time of harvest. The horses are by no means always in waiting; and unless you send forward a man and horse, you may

D be

be detained a long time for each relay. I therefore took the precaution of difpatching a *voorboode* (fo they call them) and his orders procured every thing to be in perfect readinefs. Each poft-mafter, who is commonly a peafant himfelf, and obliged to furnifh horfes in his turn, has under him an infpector *(hall karl)* who, upon the arrival of a traveller, enquires the number of horfes wanted, fetches them, and has them harneffed. He then prefents a journal *(dag bok)* divided into feveral columns, in which the traveller, immediately before he fets off, is required to write his name and character, the day and hour of his arrival, thofe of his departure, the place from whence he came and to which he is going, with the number of horfes he takes. One column in this book is appropriated to complaints, and, if the traveller makes any, there is another to receive the defence of the poft-mafter, who, at the end of each month, is refponfible to government for his conduct.

Many patriotic writers have reprefented the grievance of thefe kind of fervices, and propofed in their ftead a fmall tax upon the peafants, that, with fome affiftance from the ftate or the crown, would be fufficient for the fupport of poft-horfes, and a great relief to agriculture, which cannot be too much encouraged in Sweden. Hitherto, however, government has not regarded their complaints,

plaints, though in many other respects agriculture has been greatly attended to and promoted.

I had forgot to tell you that the use of hired voitures is unknown here, and that at no stage can you find either a chariot or a post-chaise. The traveller must, therefore, take his own voiture, or be contented in the carriage of a peasant, with two or four wheels, in which he may be jolted perhaps more than he desires. Indeed, the number of travellers in this kingdom is too small to defray the expence of proper conveniences.

GOTHENBURG. Upon my arrival here at eight o'clock at night, I was stopped at the barrier, and asked in Swedish, " Have you any thing prohibited by the King ?" but perceiving my ignorance of their language, they put the same question to me in German, and I answered " No."—— " Who is Monsieur ?—— " A Dutch officer, travelling for his pleasure."— " Has Monsieur nothing?"——" Nothing but his " night-cap and a little linen :" to assure them of which, I dropped a billet for six *daalders kooper munt*, and was immediately answered by " Pass, " Monsieur." Having got over the bridge, I came to a gate, and was addressed by an officer, " Who is Monsieur ? From whence comes he ? and " Whither is he going ?"—" I am a Dutch officer, " on my journey from Copenhagen to Stockholm." —" Monsieur will shew me his passport."—I

produced

produced it:—" Very well, Monsieur, this must be signed by the captain of the Grand Guard, and you will receive it at your inn." " Officer, your servant."—" Good night, Monsieur." A few smacks of the coachman's whip soon brought me to my inn, where I wished for nothing so much as a supper and a good night's rest, and was just stepping into bed, when I was surprised by the sound of clarinets, hautboys, French-horns, and a trumpet. I ran to the window, and my servant, whom I had sent to enquire what was the matter, brought me word that these were the musicians of the Count de Saltze's regiment, who came to welcome the arrival of a Dutch officer, or, in in plain terms, to beg by means of music. After listening to a few marches, I dismissed them with some money, and desired they might drink to the health of the Prince of Orange. This sort of serenade is common at Gothenburg upon the arrival of a stranger; but I have since past through many garrison towns without receiving such an honour, for which I have consoled myself by the possession of my *daalders* and *plottes*. The music was gone, and I had prepared to stretch out my limbs, almost dislocated by a jolting of eight-and-forty hours, upon my uncurtained bed, when a rapping at the gate again prevented me. They opened it, and admitted a hero of about two pence a day, covered with feathers, and roses of ribbands,

something

something in the fashion of Henry the Fourth's time. "My officer," says he, "I have brought "your passport signed by the captain."—"Ah, "my friend, how comes it you speak French?"— "Thank God, captain, I am a Frenchman. A "wish to see the world leads me, by turns, into "the service of many powers: when I am tired, "I desert, and, as my figure is of the military "height, I never want bread. I can, besides, dress "hair, and shall be proud of serving Monsieur the "Capitain in that way." I took the passport, thanked him for his offer, and dismissed him. He went, however, with a very lingering pace, and at last, with a certain arrangement of his fingers,—"It is usual, Captain, upon these occasions" —"I understand you, my friend, here's some- "thing for you."—"Oh! Captain, I absolutely "must enter once more into the service of Hol- "land—brave, generous Dutchmen!—but a good "night to my most noble captain." He flew down stairs by leaps of four at a time, and I stretched myself upon my crib, where, in spite of the music of the gnats, I soon fell asleep. You are now, perhaps, willing to do the same; and, therefore, I conclude, with assuring you, that, in every situation, I am, &c. &c.

LETTER V.

Droningaard, Sept. ... 1785.

MY DEAR FRIEND,

YOU will believe that I did not long delay my examination of a city so celebrated for commerce, and second only to Stockholm in point of beauty and grandeur.

Gothenburg, then, is situated upon a bank of the river Goth, which issues from the grand lake Wennern*; and, at the distance of a great league below the city, empties itself into the Schaggerack. A canal, which communicates with this river, divides the city into two parts, and, with some beautiful linden trees on each side, gives it very much the air of a Dutch town. Behind these trees stand two rows of well-built houses, and, among the latter, that of the East India Company, which is very large.

INDIA COMPANY.
This company was established in the late reign by Henry Koning, a rich merchant of Stockholm, who, in the year 1731, obtained a grant of an exclusive trade to India for

---

* The lake Wennern is the largest in Sweden, being reckoned fourteen miles in length, and seven in breadth.

fifteen

fifteen years. The grant was renewed in 1746, and in 1753 the company, which had been hitherto known under the firm of Koning and Co. assumed the name of the Swedish East India Company. In 1762, another grant was obtained for twenty years, which, however, the company did not begin to enjoy till 1766.

During the first years, they sent some vessels to India, especially to Bengal; but their real commerce is with China, whither they send annually one or two vessels, and receive from thence as many in return. The goods are generally sold in October by public auction, to which many foreign merchants resort.

INTERNAL COMMERCE.
The merchants of Gothenburg, as well as those of Stockholm, have the advantage of circulating their commodities through the interior parts of the kingdom; the first by the sluices of Edet and Trohhelta, which open to them the navigation of the lake Wennern, the latter by those of Arboga, which affords an entrance into that of Hielmarn. Besides the considerable trade carried on by the India Company, Gottenburg has many profitable branches of commerce, among which is the sole fishery of herrings for exportation. For more than a century, this fish deserted the shores of Sweden; they appeared again in 1740, and the quantity is now so great, as to form

one of the moſt abundant articles of trade. The city itſelf is inacceſſible by large veſſels; theſe, therefore, remain in the roads, and diſcharge their cargoes into others of leſs burthen, which come as far as a ſuburb, called *Haga*, very little ſmaller or leſs populous than the city. In this ſuburb are ſtocks for building veſſels, and every thing elſe relative to the maritime department of their commerce. The goods are carried from thence to Gottenburg, by means of the canal above-mentioned, and unladen at the very doors of the warehouſes in which they are depoſited.

VAUXHALL.
Between the ſuburb *Haga*, and the city, there is a ſort of orchard, which they call Vauxhall, with a raiſed orcheſtra in the middle, that nearly fills it, and a circular row of boxes, in which the company ſit and take refreſhments. The inhabitants of Gottenburg are as proud of this Vauxhall, as the Engliſh of theirs, although the difference is ſo great, that it is abſurd to make a compariſon between them.

The play-houſe, though ſmall, is pretty, and the performers, I am told, tolerably good; but of this, as they exhibit only in the winter, I had no opportunity of judging.

PARADE.
The Count de Saltze, commander of the garriſon, to whom I paid my reſpects, received me with much politeneſs,

liteness, and, after a walk to the parade, detained me to dinner. There, however, I could not help observing the unfitness of the national habit to military use, as it exposes the least defect in size or shape, and is only proper for light, well-proportioned men. The round hats, roses of ribbands, yellow and blue scarfs, with plumes of feathers of the same colours, give the officers and soldiers an air by far too theatrical. The garrison is composed of the regiment of Saltze, which makes part of the levied forces.

The army is divided into levied forces, and national troops.

LEVIED FORCES. These are always marching regiments, and are garrisoned in the towns situated upon the Schaggerack, the Sound, the Baltic, and the Gulph of Finland, and in some fortresses of the frontiers and Pomerania. They are composed of deserters from all nations, and of apprentices and servants of bad conduct, whom, as well as vagabonds, they enlist by force. These form nine regiments of infantry, including the foot-guards and the artillery. There is also a regiment of hussars, and a body of light-horse. The regiment of guards is divided into two battalions, each battalion containing eight companies of musqueteers, and one of grenadiers, and each company 100 men. The whole number of these forces is as follows:

The

	Men
The regiment of foot-guards, 2 batt. 18 comp. — —	1800
The regiment of artillery, 3 batt. each batt. 1000 men — —	3000
Three regiments, each 1200 men -	3600
Four regiments, each 800 men —	3200
A corps of chasseurs — —	400
A regiment of huffars, 2 squad. each squad. 150 men — —	300
Light-horse, 4 comp. 100 in each —	400
	12,700

 The regiments of guards and artillery are clothed once in two years, the others once in three. The whole is done by contract, at the expence of the crown, which also pays to each soldier 32 *daalders silber munt* annually. They are likewise lodged and fed, and have one pair of shoes in a year. The troops in garrison in Pomerania have something more pay.

DESERTERS. As there is no cartel of exchange between Sweden and Denmark, deserters are enlisted in each kingdom. When the Sound is frozen over they generally find some means of escaping, notwithstanding every precaution used to prevent it. At that time piquets from the garrisons of all the ports in Sweden and Denmark, are stationed upon the ice

at

at proper diftances. They go out at the dufk of evening, form large femi-circles round all the places at which the foldiers can efcape, and return when the day appears. Immediately after the fhutting of the gates they vifit the quarters of the men; this is repeated every two hours, and as foon as a man is miffed, they give notice by the difcharge of a cannon; upon this fignal, the piquets gradually approach each other, and the poor criminal, thus furrounded, is immediately taken away to certain flavery. But the attempt is generally made in very dark nights, when it is common for the deferters to pafs through the piquets, and fo efcape. And fometimes the piquets themfelves defert, with the inferior officers by whom they are commanded.

NATIONAL TROOPS. The national troops are divided into 21 regiments of infantry, not containing equal numbers, but amounting in the whole to

	23,000 men.
Seven regiments of cavalry —	7,000
And four regiments of dragoons	3,000
	33,000

Thefe men are levied from the lands belonging to the crown, the holders of which are obliged to contribute, not only to the fupport of the troops, but

but of a great part of the clergy, and civil officers. The estates *(hemmans)* are divided into *rottes*, and each *rotte* is charged in a settled proportion, the best with the support of cavalry, the others with that of infantry.

An estate of fifty *daalders silber mundt*, annual rental, is called a *rustholl*, or hemman charged with the equipment and support of a horseman; and an estate of forty such *daalders* constitutes an *haaste-hemman*; or estate charged with the support of a horse. There are other estates *(foerdels hemmans)* which contribute only a certain proportion of pay, and some, called *foermedlins hemmans*, which are liable to be charged in both respects.

They ought, in general, to furnish each soldier with a chamber and stove, a barn, a stable, a small spot of ground for the growth of cabbages and hops, with hay and straw for the support of a cow, and a certain quantity of wood and charcoal. This sort of estate is called a bostelle. The soldier is, besides, entitled to an annual payment of ten *daalders silber munt* for a great coat, and receives, every three years, one pair of shoes, and one of stockings.

When new uniforms are wanted, the crown supplies the cloth and materials, but the expence of making is discharged by assessments upon the estates; and, on the promotion of a soldier to the rank of an inferior officer, the *rotte* to which he belongs is obliged to supply another.

This

This whole fyftem, being intended chiefly for the encouragement of agriculture, each poffeffor of a *boftelle* is enjoined,

1ft. To attend to the cultivation of the fields.

2dly. To clear annually, and for a ftipulated price, a certain quantity of uncultivated land, if there is any fuch in the neighbourhood of the *boftelle*.

3dly. To grow, if poffible, a limited number of hop-poles. And,

4thly. To encreafe each year, if it can be done, the quantity of meadow ground.

Every third year, and upon each change of a tenant, the eftate of the *boftelle* is furveyed by infpectors, who make deductions from the pay of the occupier for any wafte that may have been occafioned by negligence; and when there is no uncultivated ground to be cleared, the foldier is obliged, at a fettled price, to affift his landlord in the labours of the field.

The *boftelles* of the officers are of different value in proportion to their rank; the colonel has his in the center of the divifion, and that of each captain is fituated amongft thofe of the officers in his company. The pay of a Colonel of Infantry is 600 *daalders filber munt*, and of one of cavalry 1500; of a Captain of Infantry 200, of Cavalry 300. An ordinary horfeman or dragoon has 15, and a foot foldier 10 *daalders filber munt*.

The

The regiments are, in general, filled with Swedes and compofed of very handfome fellows; the *rottes*, from which the levies are made, always chufing their ftouteft and beft proportioned men, who are afterwards fubmitted to the colonel, without whofe approbation they are not received.

In diftricts where the *boftelles* are not very remotely difperfed, the foldiers affemble by companies every funday, to be exercifed by their officers and ferjeants. The whole regiment is brought together, once a year, in the fpring, and is then encamped for three weeks in its own diftrict. In every third or fourth year, encampments of feveral regiments together are formed in fome province, which is generally the center of many diftricts; and, for the reft of their time, thefe military hufbandmen, who are inrolled for life, employ themfelves in the ordinary labours of cultivation. They are, however, frequently vifited by the officers and ferjeants, who infpect their clothes, arms, and military accoutrements.

The cavalry has no pike-men; their duty being performed by the inferior officers, who alfo teach the troops to ride; and each foldier is obliged to drefs and exercife his own horfe.

Befides the feven regiments of cavalry, there is a corps of horfe in garrifon at Stockholm, fupported by affeffments upon the divifions of the eftates.

estates. This corps escorts the Royal family, and contains 150 men, who have each the rank of cornet.

In time of war, these divisions also contribute by certain taxes to the supply of forage, transports, and provisions: the remainder of the expence is defrayed by the crown.

Allotments or divisions of the crown lands were first planned by Gustavus Vasa, and the scheme was adopted and proposed by several of his successors; but Gustavus Adolphus and his daughter Christina, having by sales, mortgages, or gifts, alienated the greatest part of their domains, in rewards to the nobility, the execution of the plan was for a time impossible. At length, Charles the eleventh, having recovered, by different compensations, many of these estates, and distributed *bostelles* to his officers, added several other *hemmans* and *rottes* for the soldiery; and in 1697, the whole affair of *indelnings-werket*, or allotments, was finally settled.

A patriotic writer* undertakes to prove that these allotments, so far from being favourable to agriculture, are upon the whole highly detrimental: " For the farms or *bostelles*, being held by persons who consider them only as temporary possessions, every advantage is drained from them for the present, although by means which in the end may

* M. Faggot.

prove

prove destructive to the land." He therefore proposes " That, instead of allotments, quit-rents shall be established, which the crown shall levy, and apply to the support of the army."

To this it is replied, " That the great attention given to the superintendance of these *bostelles* renders the abuse of them very difficult; that the soldier, being, by this plan, rendered a landholder, considers himself as a citizen of his country, and may be supposed to feel the greater zeal for its defence; that this army, which forms the strength of the state, being never upon the march or collected in bodies, but when necessity requires it, not even appearing in regiments more than once a year, is much less expensive than if supported upon the footing of levied or garrison troops; and that, therefore, the advantages of the present method are much greater than the evils proposed to be remedied." They also urge the advantages derived from the present practice, on the score of population, the soldier being now enabled to marry and propagate colonists, for districts yet uncultivated.

The *corps de genie* is divided into six brigades, residing at Stockholm, Gothenburg and Carlscroon, and in Scania, Finland and Pomerania. In each place, the fortifications are entrusted to their care, and each brigade contains,

A Colonel of Brigade,

Quarter Master,

Lieutenant

Lieutenant General,
Captain Mechanist,
Captain for tuition,
Lieutenant Designer,
Lieutenant Modeller, and some Conductors.

The whole body is commanded by two Directors General, one for Sweden, the other for Pomerania, each of whom has an Aide de Camp. A professor belonging to the corps resides at Stockholm.

An honourable and comfortable provision has also been made for military men, by a pension bank, instituted in 1757, the subscribers to which, paying annually six *per* cent of the value of their appointments, after twenty-five years of service, and subscription reckoned from the 20th year of their age, are entitled, upon retiring from the army, to their full pay for life.

The whole arrangement and management of the National army, is admirably adapted to a country in which troops are wanted chiefly for defence. The soldier who has cultivated the soil is its best and most natural defender; the enemies to his country he esteems as enemies to his person; and, having a mutual interest in the preservation of the kingdom, with every other inhabitant of it, he knows that when he exposes his life for his king, he is taking the most effectual means to preserve his family and his property. Indeed, the kingdom of Sweden, in whatever light we consider it, seems much better suited for defence than conquest; and this feudal distribution of the land should be valued as a circumstance above all others tending to promote its interest.

I return from this digression to

The whole defence of this city GOTHENBURG. on the southern side, where the port is situated, consists of a wall of free-stone, fixed and cemented upon the rock itself, and surrounded with a large ditch, into which they have contrived to bring the water of the *Molndal*, a river which empties itself into the Goth. The rest of the city is built chiefly upon two rocks, and the entrance of the port is defended by a guard-ship, and a fort of some strength, called Elsbourg.

Among the acquaintance which a residence of eight days at Gothenburg, enabled me to make, I cannot omit to mention Mr. de Lisle, the French Consul, and Mr. Aelstroom, a rich merchant. I had letters to them both from my friends the C . . . . s, and found in the former a man of great information and amiable manners, who, by his readiness to afford me a sight of every thing remarkable, and his communications upon a variety of interesting subjects, contributed much to my enjoyments at Gothenburg. The latter, an intelligent man of business, gave me an open invitation to his house, where I met with a very hospitable reception.

It

It is now time that I should conclude, by assuring you how much I am, &c. &c. &c.

LETTER VI.

Droningaard, Oct. ... 1785.

MY DEAR FRIEND,

TROLHETTA. I quitted Gothenburg at the opening of the gates, on Monday the ... of May, and partly by following the northern direction of the river Goth, near a chain of rocks, whose horrid aspect was singularly contrasted by the beauty of the opposite shore, partly by climbing over these rocks themselves, upon the sides of some very terrible precipices, I arrived at nine o'clock at night at the famous fall of the Gothe, at Trolhetta. This spectacle, which it is so much more easy to conceive than describe, is formed by the separation of the river into two parts, of which one takes its course over a declivity of an hundred or an hundred and fifty feet; and the other, falling perpendicularly, forms a cataract of thirty-two feet in height. At the distance of some paces from the fall, a saw-mill is turned by a part of the water; and the foam which, arising from the fall, spreads itself to some distance, the spray from the innumerable cascades of the other

other half of the river, the gulphs and whirlpools formed at the bottom, with the noise occasioned by this mill, and by so many falls of water, present a terrible and magnificent scene, in the midst of which some rocks arise, from whence you have an opportunity of viewing the whole at once. This cataract interrupts the navigation of the grand lake *Wennern* by Wennersburg, a small market town situated upon the straight, through which the river Goth issues from the lake, in its course towards the Scaggerrak, below Gothenburg. Above Trolhetta, the navigation is performed by means of some confiderable sluices, which very well deserve attention.

In this journey from Gothenburg to EDET. Trolhetta, I passed through the small village of Edet, where the river precipitates its whole flood, but in a fall of inconsiderable height, and by no means so beautiful as that of Trolhetta. The village is, however, remarkable for a canal which they are now hollowing through the rock, in order to give a passage, by means of sluices, to a part of the river. Six or seven hundred men are employed upon the work, which, with the Suices at Trolhetta, form part of a grand plan for joining the Baltic with the North Sea, by means of a communication cut through the kingdom. These sluices, which yet want much of being finished, will afford an uninterrupted navigation

gation from Carlſtadt in *Wermeland*, at the northern extremity of the lake *Wennern*, to *Gothenburg*; and if ever the difficulties which oppoſe the junction of this lake with that of *Hielmarn* by *Orebro* ſhall be overcome, they may then, by the communication of the latter with lake *Malern*, through the ſluices of Arboga, tranſport all kinds of merchandiſes, in one veſſel, from Gothenburg to Stockholm, and thus open a paſſage between the North Sea and the Baltic.

Having remained at Trolhetta about two hours, obſerving the ſpectacle of the cataract, which I could not willingly quit, I again betook myſelf to the voiture; and, after a moſt haraſſing journey of that night and the next day, arrived about 10 in the evening at

A ſmall town of Weſtragothia. FALKIOPING, The croſs roads by which I travelled, lay over the moſt difficult mountains and rocks, and the continual jolts of my voiture effectually prevented ſleep; I therefore thought Falkiöping a comfortable place of refuge, although, of all the towns of Sweden, this is perhaps the worſt. You are to imagine a large unpaved ditch, in which they have ſtuck a row of wooden huts, with coverings of turf or mofs, and doors four feet high. The *chiverhous*, or inn, at which I lodged, was the beſt houſe in the place, to which they have given the name of

a city,

a city, though it has neither walls nor gates, and is furrounded only by an enclofure of rotten juniper trees. To prove, however, that it is a town, they make you pay for a double poft upon your departure.

After fupping upon boiled eggs, the only food to be obtained in the place, I ftretched myfelf upon a bed, or rather crib, with all my ufual clothing, and the additional envelopement of my *fchantz looper*. I was awaked about three in the morning by a moft tumultuous buzzing of gnats, flies and other infects, iffuing from the convenient receptacle of my crib, from which they foon drove me, to employ myfelf in writing, till the arrival of my horfes delivered me from this kind of purgatory.

I took the road to Maricftadt, fituated upon the lake Wennern, and there, at feven o'clock at night, again entered upon the great royal road, which runs from Gothenburg by Trolhetta to Wennerfburg, and from thence, after coafting the lake, reaches Stockholm through Orebrö and Arboga. I had quitted this route at Trolketta, to gratify a curiofity which I was foon made to repent by the inconveniences of crofs-roads. From Falkiöping, however, though ftill upon one of thefe roads, my journey was fomewhat more eafy, and I was again gratified by the fight of a level country, diftributed into beautiful meadows and well cultivated fields.

REGIMENT OF CAVALRY OF WESTROGOTHIA.

At *Kloftret*, a ftage four miles from Falkiöping, I heard of an encampment of this regiment, near *Bolum*, a village about half a league diftant. There I arrived about nine in the morning, and, leaving my voiture and fervant upon the high-road, walked alone towards a large plain, where the encampment was formed, and the regiment at that time drawn out to be manœuvred. I was in uniform, with a white hat, my fword under my arm, and in boots, but without fpurs. After about a quarter of an hour, an officer on full gallop rode up, and, politely accofting me, enquired who I was. I defcribed myfelf as a Dutch officer, who, travelling from curiofity, and hearing of the encampment, came to fee it on his way.—" Would Monfieur choofe to ride?" I thanked him for his politenefs, and as he rode away, his cane difcovered him to be the adjutant. In a minute afterwards he returned with another officer, the Major, to whom I paid my refpects, and who made me the fame offer of a horfe. Having neither the proper hat nor any fpurs, I would willingly have been excufed; but the Major's politenefs prevailing, he conducted me to the Colonel, and, after a formal introduction, prefented me a horfe. When I had followed the regiment through all its manœuvres, the colonel gave me an invitation to dine with some officers, a pleasure which I could not accept, having dispatched a *courier* with orders for horses at all the stages as far as *Morixstadt*. The Major attended me to my voiture, and just before my departure enquired my name and rank. He then gave me his name, the *Baron de Cicors*; and added, that he had been particularly intimate with Mr. *de Heeren*, during the residence of the latter at Stockholm, as Envoy Extraordinary from the States General.

You are without doubt curious to know something of this regiment. It is national, that is, raised from the allotments, and contains a thousand men, which, as in most of the other regiments of cavalry, are divided into eight squadrons. The manœuvres were, in general, by no means brilliant, and the soldiers, though of good appearance, were badly mounted; yet, considering the length of their front, they went through some changes of the line, and developements of the column, with tolerable execution. When about to retreat, the flanking parties are ranged in two lines upon the flanks, where they remain immoveable, continually loading and discharging their pistols, while the regiment retires along their lines. But their grand attack was neither spirited nor regular; and indeed very little skill is to be expected in troops, who,

who, except during their encampments of three weeks, are never brought together in arms, nor accustomed even to the mounting of a guard.

Monsieur the Major and myself having exchanged assurances of remembrance, I pursued my journey, and, as the distance from Falköping increased, found the roads more even, and the rocks and precipices less tremendous. At length, at about two leagues from Mariestad, the soil became an entire flat, and I passed through one of the most beautiful plains I had ever beheld, covered with a delightful crop of rye.

During this whole journey, as in the preceding, I should have been condemned to preserve a perfect fast, but for the wallet which my friends had so well furnished in Denmark. *Knäckebröd*, milk, and sometimes eggs are the only provisions to be found in the houses of the peasants, where even the use of wine is unknown, its place being supplied by a sort of bad beer brewed by themselves. But the wild strawberries, which were then ripe, often made a part of my repasts: these, though small, are well flavoured, and the woods contain them in such quantities, that at every stage the children for a trifle are ready to bring you a basket full.

I am, &c. &c.

LETTTER VII.

Droningaard, Oct. .... 1785.

MY DEAR FRIEND,

MARIESTADT. MARIESTADT is a pretty town, situated, as I have already told you, uponthe Lake Wennern. It was built by Charles IX. who gave it the name of Marieſtadt, in honour of his queen, Anna-Maria. The ſituation, which is very beautiful, is the moſt remarkable thing to be told of it, except, indeed, that there I paſſed a comfortable night. Having viewed the whole neighbourhood at my leiſure, I ſet out on the afternoon after my arrival, and reached Orebrö, the capital of the province of Nericia, between four and five the next morning. The diſtance is eleven miles.

The road from Marieſtadt to Orebrö is the great royal road, and my journey upon it was very agreeable.

Some miles from Marieſtadt, at a ſmall village called *Howa*, you enter the province of Nericia. Here I was detained by the aſtoniſhing perſeverance of an officer, who refuſed a bribe of ſeveral *daalders ſilber munt*, and perſiſted in unpacking my cheſt and portmanteau.

There

There is some hardship in being thus searched at the entrance of every povince, after having passed through the same ceremony upon the frontiers of the kingdom. The provincial officers are, however, seldom rigorous, and the affair generally ends in a bribe of a few daalders, which I found a sufficient protection in every other part of my journey. Prohibited commodities having been circulated in the interior parts of the kingdom, they take this method of checking a traffic, which, by the inflexibility of a few such officers as that at Howa, might indeed be soon annihilated. But I have been informed that he expected a good seizure. Whether I am indebted to my countenance or my voiture for exciting suspicions of smuggling, I know not.

OREBRÖ. Orebrö is a town of considerable size, and built, like all those of Sweden, entirely of wood. The houses are painted of a reddish brown colour, and uniformly covered with roofs of turf, which are sometimes mowed and ornamented with flowers, so as to give one a notion of the gardens of Semiramis. The utility of such roofs, in checking the progress of fire is very obvious, and on this account, in parts where turf is not to be had, the houses of the peasants are covered with moss, thatch being every where rejected, as too dear and dangerous. But before the turf or moss is laid on, they spread over the timber-work of the roofs large squares of birch bark, which prevents the rain from penetrating into the houses. In all Orebrö there is but one house covered with tiles. This is an ancient seat, built of freestone at one corner of the town, and in it the governor of the province resides. A small river runs before it, and empties itself into the lake Hielmarn, upon the bank of which the town is situated. From the top of a fine stone bridge, built over this river, there is a view of a fall, at the distance of some toises, down which it pours its whole breadth; and from the tower there is another charming view, comprising the parterres upon the houses of the town, the lake, a rich plain covered with cottages and standing corn, and the heights behind, crowned with woods, and closing the horizon. In the population of this plain, the traveller finds some recompense for the continual solitudes which he passes through to arrive at it.

Such scenes, indeed, occur but too seldom in Sweden, there being at least four leagues of wretched deserts, for one of a populous and well cultivated country.

The whole country from Marieftadt to Orebrö is almost entirely covered with wood, but there are some intervening and uncultivated spaces, filled with herbs of spontaneous growth. The grounds in the neighbourhood of Marieftadt and Orebrö are well cultivated; and, for three or four leagues round

round each, there were crops of wheat, oats, and flax, with rye as high and as copious as I had ever seen any. About some villages, and upon the banks of the rivers, I saw also very beautiful pastures; and it is not to be doubted that Sweden, with more inhabitants, would shew a much greater quantity of cultivated ground, notwithstanding the rock of which it so much consists.

It was my intention to remain at Orebrö one whole day, both for the sake of resting myself, and of viewing a place so much recommended by the beauty of its situation, and its own remarkable neatness. But, upon the arrival of my horses according to orders, the next morning, I was seized with an illness, produced by fatigue and some other causes, which made it impossible for me to proceed. Here, however, in a poor and miserable inn, I had the happiness to find an host whose care and attention I shall for ever remember, though I may perhaps never be able to forget the wretched soup he continually made me. Goose broth, garnished with raisins, currants, peas, garlic, and apples, was the omnipotent restorative which he prescribed, and administered with an honest zeal, always to be recollected with gratitude. A bottle of excellent wine, the remnant of my Droningaard provisions, had, however, a much better effect than the inn-keeper's remedy; and in the afternoon, I was able to dress myself and walk out. Upon my

return,

return, juft as I was about to make myfelf fome tea, a gentle tapping at my door introduced an officer in the Swedifh drefs, with the blue fcarf, yellow feather, and little order of the fword at his button-hole. He approached me with a lively air, and, as I rofe, faid in very good French—that being informed there was a Dutch officer detained at an inn by ficknefs, he had thought it his duty to come and offer thofe fervices which all military men ought to render each other. I anfwered this civility as well as I was able, and he proceeded—
" You are going to drink tea, Monfieur, and by
" the little cheft, I perceive the tea is your own—
" a Dutchman's tea muft be good; permit me,
" therefore, to introduce fome company, to whom
" fuch will be very acceptable." He ran out, and in a moment after returned with two agreeable young ladies. I had feated them, and was proceeding to make the tea, when he interrupted me—
" There is an old lady in a coach below, very much
" afflicted with the gout, but who is, notwith-
" ftanding very defirous of becoming acquainted
" with Monfieur and his tea. How fhall we ma-
" nage this?" I propofed that we fhould take the table to the coach door, and there drink our tea together. Immediately the Chevalier took the teapot and cream-jug, the ladies the cups, myfelf the tea-cheft, and my fervant the table. We flew down ftairs, laughing like mad folks, and in an inftant

stant seated ourselves round the table by the side of the coach, in which sat the good lady, very much diverted to see us in the open street, surrounded by all the gaping blackguards of the town. My company however, soon drove away; the ladies with their servant in a coach and six, and Monsieur, the Lieut. Colonel de Lejonanker in a chaise and four, accompanied by a man whom I took to be his valet-de-chambre. I was informed that they came from Stockholm, and were travelling to their estates; but the inn-keeper having told them that he had a Dutch officer in his house, detained by sickness, the Chevalier immediately ran up stairs to make his compliments, and offer me his services. The good old lady, in return for my tea, invited me to pass some time at her seat, a favour which I was obliged to decline, having yet a very long journey to make. They then gave me some recommendations to their friends at Stockholm, which I afterwards found very useful.

From what passed at the encampment in Westrogothia, and from this adventure with the Lieut. Colonel and his family, you will be able to form some opinion of Swedish politeness and good humour, of which I have yet some more traits to give you. Being now infinitely better, and very able to continue my journey, I set out on the morning after this visit, intending to proceed only to Smedby,

distant

distant seven miles and a half, where they told me I might sleep at one of the best inns in Sweden. On leaving Orebrö, the road lies through a populous and well cultivated plain of two leagues in extent, after which it runs entirely through the woods as far as Fallingbrö, a large post-house, and the first place in Westmannia. I here met the old Count de Scheffer, with his lady and a grand suite, upon a journey to their estates. While their horses were changing, I had a wish to be presented to his Excellency, and for this purpose applied to a large well-looking man, who soon informed me he was the family cook, and very graciously consented to perform the office of chamberlain.

The Count and his lady received me with great politeness, and assured me of their wishes to be serviceable to me at Stockholm. They enquired for whom I had letters, and recommended me to a sort of private lodging-house, where the accommodations were much better than at the inn to which I had been directed. The Count de Scheffer has a very majestic air, and is, I am assured, much regretted both by the King and the nation, whose councils he for a long time wisely directed. He retired from office last year, and now resides upon his estates in the country, universally beloved for his attachment to the King, and his concern for the welfare and prosperity of the people. His

place

place is now held by the Count de Creutz, formerly the Swedish ambassador in France.

ARBOGA.
My second stop was at *Arboga*, the residence of the governor, and government of Westmannia, of which it is the capital. The town is famous for some considerable sluices, communicating with the lakes Hielmarn and Mälern, the latter of which extends as far as Stockholm. It is, however, a very mean place, consisting of low wooden houses, arranged in very narrow streets. That of the governor alone is built of stone.

I soon left Arboga, and arrived in very good time at Smedby. The whole province of Westmannia is very beautiful. Rocks and woods there are, indeed, here, as every where in Sweden; but in many considerable districts, grain of all sorts, especially rye, flourishes admirably, and upon the whole this may be reckoned one of the most populous and best cultivated provinces.

The peasants, in general, wear the *frieze* habit, large hats, large breeches, and short jackets, all black, except the little facings upon the sleeves.

At Smedby, three miles from *Arboga*, I passed the night. This is only one very large house, stone-built, and entirely insulated in a charming valley, in the midst of many beautiful landscapes. The inn is the best and handsomest in Sweden.

The next day, at about half a league from Smedby, I entered *Sudermania*. Several well cultivated

tivated plains appeared from the road, and at Sudertalia, a small town upon the lake Mälern, about four miles from Stockholm, I saw a tolerably beautiful country. But from thence you find only rocks and deserts, even to the very gates of the capital.

CASTLE OF GRIPSHOLM.
I went a league out of my way to see *Gripsholm*, a royal seat, pleasantly situated near the little town of *Manfred*, and upon the bank of a small lake, which communicates with the Mälern. It is of great antiquity, and surrounded by four towers, but is best known in history as the prison of the famous Eric the XIVth, son of Gustavus Vasa. Here the court sometimes resides in the Spring, and there are some very elegant, well ornamented yachts, by which they arrive and return.

TROSHALLA.
At the little village of Troshalla I stopped to observe a magnificent fall of water. A river which passes there, running with amazing rapidity amongst large fragments of rock, makes, in the space of three or four hundred feet, above a thousand cascades of two, three, four, and even six feet in height, of which there is a perfect view from a bridge of six arches, built about the middle of the fall.

KUMLA.
Kumla, where I arrived at night, is a small neat town, built upon an eminence five miles from Stockholm, at

whic-

which I confoled myfelf for the miferable inn and meagre foup, by the hope of an ample recompenfe on the morrow. My meal was indeed fomething animated by a conteft between myfelf and a fwarm of flies, as formidable as thofe which attacked Gulliver at Brobdignag. Thefe infects are, perhaps, larger and more numerous here than in any other part of the world, and their buzzing is abfolutely terrible. An uncurtained crib, to which I was fhown, afforded a poor profpect for the night, but my fatigue at length procured me a few hours fleep.

I fet out at four in the morning, and, having changed horfes at Sudertalia, I bid adieu once more to the beautiful part of the country, and began my journey through the rocks and deferts, eight leagues of which feparate Sudertalia from the floating bridge that brings you into Stockholm.

Half way along this road, there a little affemblage of three or four houfes, at which you change horfes. This they call Fitzia, and it is fituated upon the bank of a fmall lake, round which the picturefque arrangement of woods and rocks, forms one of the moft romantic views I ever beheld. Here the inhabitants of Stockholm come upon fifhing parties in the fummer, and live upon the produce of the lake. Before, however, I defcribe the capital of Sweden, let me conclude this letter, by affuring you how much I am, &c. &c.

LETTER VIII.

Copenhagen, Nov. .... 1785.

MY DEAR FRIEND,

HAIL, rain, snow, frost, and shortened days have obliged us to change the country for the town, and we are now established at Copenhagen for six months. Assemblies, concerts, shows, and meetings for play, have taken place of walks, sailing parties, hunting and fishing. Libraries, cabinets and manufactures succeed to the culture of flowers, trees and plants. Each mode of life has its use, and it is well that each has also its turn. In the country, the beauty and grandeur of nature fills the mind, and an independence analagous to the primitive state of man aggrandizes our ideas. Imagination rises from the earth, which we cultivate, to that infinity of matter, where all that our feeble eyes can perceive convinces us of the existence of that Great Being, who connects us with himself by an everlasting chain, the links of which are far more perceptible amongst country occupations, than in a round of tumultuous pleasures that check or extirpate the powers of thought. In the city, however, we study men, their knowledge, their industry and manners; and

observe

observe the contrasted effects of regulated and unrestrained passions.—But no more philosophy.—You are impatient to accompany me to Stockholm. —In my last letter I brought you to the floating bridge;—it is now time that you should pass it. This I was not permitted to do till my baggage had been very strictly searched for contraband goods.

STOCKHOLM. Count Scheffer had directed me to the Dutch quarter of the city *(Dütske Buë)* exactly opposite to that by which I entered it. I therefore traversed its whole length, which is about a league, besides passing through a large suburb, where the rocks and houses seem to contend for pre-eminence. The buildings, which were at first entirely of wood, improved as I advanced towards the heart of the city, and at length, instead of these, I could perceive only houses of brick or free stone, covered with tiles, slate or copper, and arranged in broad straight streets.

At *Dütske Buë* I found the house recommended by Count Scheffer; and a very portly handsome hostess, who graciously told me in bad German, that her husband being from home, she could not promise me a lodging there. She, however, asked me to walk in; and her husband, when sought for, was soon found. This was a little ugly toad-looking fellow, who, having surveyed me once or twice

twice from head to foot, began the following conversation in German.——" Well, Sir - your servant—what would you please to have?"——" I want lodgings."——" Ay, but there are none empty." I then expressed my disappointment, the Count de Scheffer having mentioned them as very worthy people. " The Count de Scheffer?"——" Yes, the Count de Scheffer."—The Count is a very worthy man, but it is impossible he can know whether I have any room for lodgers." I was upon the point of going somewhere else, when I thought of saying, " His cook also told me so." Upon these words they both exclaimed " The cook!—what, our best friend the cook?—O! Monsieur, without doubt you shall be accommodated" He then called for valets, lacqueys and hostlers; one took my portmanteau, another my trunk, and he shewed me in triumph into a large and splendid chamber, where I was admirably lodged, and soon became very well contended with my hosts. The Count, however, would be diverted to find how much more is to be done by his cook's name than his own; but would, perhaps, soon discover that the cook and the landlord keep up their intimacy at his expence.

The morning after my arrival, my first care was to see Monsieur the Baron V ... D ... G ... our minister. This nobleman interested himself in my welfare with something more than politeness,

ness. He proposed to have my baggage brought to his house, where he would have had me lodge, and, when I would not permit that, offered me the free use of his table, whenever I was not obliged to dine elsewhere. He also presented me to all the foreign ministers, to most of whom I had letters from those of Copenhagen, shewed me every thing worth seeing in Stockholm, and gave me an introduction to several select companies.

Of all my letters of recommendation, that for Mr. Wahrendorf, a very considerable merchant, was the most useful to me. His daughter is married to Count *Rosen*, master of the horse to the Queen; and besides the numerous civilities received from his family, and the many valuable acquaintances which I acquired through his means, he furnished me with directions and recommendations for all the mines and forges, and for several towns where I proposed to stop. By his introduction, I became known, amongst others, to Messrs. Grill and Pyll, the principal owners and workers of the famous mine at Dannemora, at whose estate, after my departure from Stockholm, I passed several days.

The derivation of the word Stockholm has been sufficiently discussed by travellers; and the foundation of the capital is already so well known, that I shall not trouble you with any repetition of the story.

story. The city is built upon several heights, formed into islands by rivers, or rather arms of the sea, and connected together by floating bridges. From many points of view the scenery is highly picturesque; rocks, houses, trees, water and shipping being frequently collected together in the same coup-d'œil, and producing a very extraordinary and pleasing effect.

A canal of twelve miles in length, formed naturally in the midst of rocks, joins the Baltic Sea and the lake Mälern, and makes in the centre of the city one of the most beautiful ports imaginable. The Baltic shore is covered with an immense number of islands, or rather rocks, which they call *scheeren*, and by which the navigation is often rendered very dangerous: on this account, although between the islands there is sufficient depth of water for the largest men of war, the whole business of the Admiralty has been transferred to Carlscroon, where the port is larger, and the entrance very commodious. A single frigate guards the entrance of these *scheeren*, but in the port of Stockholm there is a fleet of fifty galleys.

By the canal, just mentioned, the city is separated into two districts, of which the northern *(Nordermalm)* is situated in Upland, and the southern *(Sudermalm)* in Sudermania.

The palace, which is square and very large, stands upon the highest part of an island in the midst

midſt of this canal, and commands the whole city. It is at preſent a modern building, the old one having been burnt and rebuilt in 1743 and the following years. A large rough baſement, hollowed in the ſhape of caverns, ſupports the ſingular union of the Ionic and Corinthian orders, with that ſort of figured columns called *caryatides*. It exceeds in ſize the palace of Copenhagen, but yields to it in magnificence of furniture and elegance of internal decoration.

ARSENAL. An intereſting ſpectacle is here formed by an amazing collection of trophies of all ſorts, of which thoſe of Narva alone fill one entire hall. Such monuments to the bravery of Guſtavus Adolphus, Charles Guſtavus, and Charles the Twelfth, fill the mind with a ſort of emulous admiration of their glory, which is ſoon loſt when we remember, that all theſe colours, drums and ſtandards are but the records of victories, obtained at an expence of blood and treaſure, of which the loſs is ſtill viſible in the poverty and deſolation of Sweden. Yet I could not look without veneration upon the ſtuffed ſkin of the horſe that carried Guſtavus Adolphus at the battle of Sutzen, in which he was ſlain; or upon the coat, hat, gloves, ſword, belt and boots worn by Charles the Twelfth upon the night of his death. The ſpots of blood upon the right glove and ſword belt ſtill remain, and prove

him

him to have put his hand firſt to the wound, and afterwards to his ſword. The cloth of the coat is ſcarcely ſo good as that now worn by a corporal. Here alſo is a curioſity of another ſort, and which excites a very different kind of admiration; this is a ſmall ſloop built by Peter the Great at Sardam, with his own hands, and taken by the Swedes upon the road to Peterſburgh.

This relic immediately produces a compariſon, in which the Swediſh heroes ſoon yield to the ſuperior character of the Ruſſian Prince. The former, ſparing neither the blood nor treaſures of their ſubjects, gratified their ambition by a few temporary conqueſts, while the latter ſought in foreign countries the means of improving a barbarous people, whom he afterwards eſtabliſhed among the rank of reaſonable beings.

In a large hall, to which they next led me, there is a repreſentation of all their kings, from Guſtavus Vaſa, completely armed according to the faſhion of their times, as large as life, and each mounted upon his favourite horſe, the ſkin of which is preſerved and ſtuffed. I felt ſome awe upon the ſight of this ſingular cavalcade, which they render more intereſting, by aſſuring you that the faces are all exact likeneſſes, having been moulded from the originals after their death. A ſimilar ſpectacle to this you may probably remember in the tower of London, but there is this difference

difference between them, that in the latter the horses are of wood, and were all made in Holland.

In another room are the dreſſes, ſaddles and bits uſed at coronations from time immemorial; they are, as you may ſuppoſe, much decayed, and, indeed, very little better than rags and rubbiſh.

The churches of Stockholm are all inferior to the cathedral at Upſal, except the palace chapel, which is very large, and abounds in marble. They are, in general, very full of monuments, of which the moſt remarkable are thoſe of Deſcartes, in the church of St. Claire, and of the celebrated General Steinbock. The Kings and Royal families are all interred in the Knights church, upon the iſland of the ſame name, except Guſtavus Vaſa, who lies under a ſuperb monument at Upſal. This iſland *(Ridderholm)* forms one of the quarters of the city.

OPERA. The Opera houſe is a magnificent building, entirely new, and raiſed at a great expence. The company is ſaid to be a good one; but as they never perform in ſummer, except upon extraordinary occaſions, I had no opportunity of aſcertaining their merits. Their firſt man, *Kaſlen*, whom I have heard at a public concert at Copenhagen, is a Swede. He has a good perſon and an agreeable voice, with ſome taſte and muſical ſkill.

COMEDIE

COMEDIE FRANCOISE. At the *Comedie Fran-çoise* I was much pleased. The King has been at great expence for performers, and their first actor, Monvel, is no doubt known to you by several pieces of his own composition. His figure is far from good, but is fully recompensed by his talents. His Majesty, with whom he is a favourite, has bestowed upon him the office of reader, and the privilege of wearing the court dress. Here, also, I saw our old heroine Madame Prevot, whom you may recollect at the Hague in the first line of tragic and comic characters. She is here doomed to personate old women, while her husband, Mr. Baptiste, plays the violoncello in the orchestra; and to such a size is she grown, that I did not know her till she was pointed out to me, when I at length discerned the well-known features through the load of fat by which they are oppressed. Their daughter adds to the musical and theatrical talents of her father and mother, a very extraordinary agility in dancing; but, notwithstanding this, and the excellence of her figure, the girl has the misfortune to be more ugly than I thought any woman could be. A little while after my arrival, Mademoiselle Baron, who left the theatre at the Hague about three years ago, in endeavouring to avoid a coach, fell under the horses, and was so much bruised as to survive only a few days. The accident happened

pened juft as fhe was upon the point of making a brilliant fortune by her connection with a very rich Swedifh nobleman. This theatre is a bad one, and reminded me of nothing fo much as our dear *Cafuariftraat*.

NATIONAL THEATRE.   The National playhoufe is tolerably pretty. Of the acting, I was unable to judge, having no knowledge of their language; the company, however, feemed to praife it. The firft actrefs is a Danifh woman, called Walter, the daughter of a common failor, and educated at Copenhagen by a private perfon. She is handfome, and has many admirers, whom fhe delights herfelf with tormenting by a variety of caprices. A very fingular inftance of her infolence is told here. Thinking herfelf not fufficiently paid for her performances, fhe petitioned for an increafe of falary, and one day fpoke to the King about it with rather more fpirit than ufual. His Majefty bid her be content with the prefent payments, and told her very pofitively they fhould never be increafed.—
" Very well; then I demand my difmiffion."—
" You fhall neither be difmiffed nor better paid."—
" O! then I fhall make my efcape—fly from the
" country—and never fet my foot in it again."—
" You may try—but will probably not find it very
" eafy to efcape from the kingdom if I forbid it."
A little while after, notwithftanding the watch kept

kept upon her, she did escape, and at the last port wrote in the *dag-bok*—" Sire, it is much easier to "escape from your kingdom than you suppose.' She desired this book might be shewn to the King, and, as a curiosity, they sent it. She then went to Denmark, and settled herself at Copenhagen, where she was known, and received with great applause, when the King made her proposals to return. At first she treated them with disdain, but, having at length obtained the sum demanded, she returned to Stockholm, to enjoy the triumph and congratulations that awaited her. Besides these three exhibitions there is a fourth, similar to that of the Boulevards, at Paris, where they perform only detached scenes of small operas and farces. This is open only in summer, the actors being drawn from the inferior part of the French company. They perform in a pavillion built by Queen Christina, in the midst of a large garden at a corner of the town. Here she is said to have diverted herself in secret with her favourites; and as it was originally dedicated to pleasure, it has never been perverted from the purpose of its institution. They exhibit twice a week, during the nights on which there is no performance at the theatre. The company assemble in the walks towards night, and when they are wearied, retire into the pavilion, where they purchase refreshments, and are entertained with songs and humourous representations.

ACADEMY

ACADEMY OF SCIENCES.
The Academy of Sciences was inftituted in 1739 and holds its meetings at Stockholm. Their memoirs, as the celebrated tranflator obferves, prove them to have directed their attention " to " every thing that could contribute to the good " of their country." Agriculture and mechanics, two fciences eminently interefting to this kingdom, have been the chief objects of their refearches. The depopulating wars of preceding centuries had prevented all progrefs in the former, and the ignorance of the inhabitants, nearly approaching to barbarifm, was to be conquered only by vigorous and able endeavours. For fome years the moft beneficial effects have arifen from their exertions: and feveral individuals, encouraged by the prizes of the " Patriotic and Agricultural Society," have given great affiftance to the general defign.

REPOSITORY OF MACHINES.
This collection contains an immenfe number of models of new or improved inftruments and machines, and proves the fociety to have made fome laborious and fuccefsful advances in the fcience of mechanics. Befides thofe of agricultural inftruments, here are many models of very curious machines ufed in the operations of the mines. One *Polheim*, an able engineer and mechanift, has rendered himfelf very eminent throughout the kingdom for his ingenious inventions of this fort.

And

And another mechanist, called *Thunberg*, a man now above eighty years old, has invented many mills and curious hydraulic machines, both for agricultural purposes and the services of the mines. The stupendous works at *Carlscroon*, which I hope soon to describe to you, are under his direction.

THE OBSERVATORY. The Observatory is a lofty and beautiful building, raised upon a rock at the extremity of the city, and furnished with a great number of excellent astronomical instruments of all sorts. Here the Academy of Sciences hold their meetings.

ACADEMY OF PAINTING AND SCULPTURE. This academy was instituted by Count Tessin in 1739, and an exhibition is every year made of their performances. I saw many paintings which had obtained the premiums, and which appeared to me tolerably good; but my admiration was most excited by some pieces of sculpture, executed by a Swede named *Sergel*, who forms his taste by studying the chefs-d'œuvres of antiquity at Rome, and those of modern times in France. The King took him last year to Italy, that he might perfect himself by a second view of those remains of antiquity, which had more than once served him as models. He is the pupil of a Frenchman, named *Archeveque*, who has left at Stockholm two fine specimens

specimens of his performances; the one a pedestrian statue of *Gustavus Vasa*, in the ancient habit, and with a long beard, placed before the hotel of the knights of the equestrian order; the other an equestrian statue representing Gustavus Adolphus in the Roman habit. Both these are of bronze, and the last, which I saw in the workshop, is intended to be placed in the center of a large square fronting the palace. Of this square, which is not yet finished, the opera-house will form one side, a palace, which they are now building for the princess Albertina, another, and a third will be formed by the castle, separated from it by a canal with a bridge of several arches.

But, however elegant these statues may be, the connoisseurs speak much more highly of an equestrian statue in the square of the four palaces, so called because each side is formed by a single palace. This is a bronze statue of Frederic the Fifth, father of the present king, erected at the expence of the India Company, and modelled by a French sculptor, named Sally, brought hither to execute it at a great price.

Their most esteemed painters are a young man, named *Pasch*, who succeeds tolerably well in portraits; and Mr. Rosaline, who by a long and laborious study at Rome, has raised himself much above the rank of common artists. He gives a great deal of grace to his figures, and a charming colouring to the whole; but his chief excellence is in the draperies. The portraits of the Royal Family, done by his hand, rather give one an opinion of his skill as a painter than of any fortunate power of obtaining a likeness.—The paintings of an old man, whose name I have forgot, are also much commended.

In an apartment of the castle I was shewn busts of the King, Queen, and Duchess of Sudermania, all great likenesses, and a Venus done after that of Medicis, by the *Sergel* whom I before mentioned. The Venus has this singularity, that the head is a portrait of one of the finest women in Stockholm.

A curious miniature painted by Hoyer, a Dane, ornaments the King's private cabinet. It represents the interview between his Majesty and the Empress of Russia in Finland in 1783. The whole composition was designed by the King, and the figures are said to be perfect likenesses.

I am, &c. &c.

LETTER IX.

Copenhagen, Nov. ... 1785.

MY DEAR FRIEND,

AMIDST the business and diversions of this place, I am happy to find opportunities of writing to you, in continuation of
those

those accounts which you have already favoured with so flattering a reception.

The quay which lines the port of Stockholm is of extraordinary breadth, and about a quarter of a league in length. It is bordered by many beautiful houses, and by one side of the castle, while an immense number of vessels, ranged along its sides, and the Isle of Admiralty, of which there is a view, contribute to make it a very interesting scene.

The island is considered as a part of the city, and contains a dock-yard, docks and magazines for the reception and equipment of the galleys, caserns for the corps of marines, and the elegant houses of the Admiral *North-Anker*, commander of the port and dock-yard, and of the other principal officers. On one side of it is a very high rock, upon the top of which stands an old castle, formerly the defence of the port, but now suffered to remain in a very ruinous state, a new one having been built at the entrance of the Scheeren. My friend Monsieur V... D... B... introduced me to Admiral *North-Anker*, a very meritorious officer, to whom the marine is indebted for several excellent regulations, and for an able work printed at Stockholm in 1774, entitled, " A Treatise upon the necessity " of supporting a Navy, and exercising the Sea- " men." He permitted me to take a view of every thing remarkable in the island, and appointed an officer who had served in our navy, and spoke, Dutch to attend me.

The galleys are used upon the lake Malërn, amongst the rocks called *Scheeren*, and on the coasts of Finland. They are safe only in favourable weather, as they can by no means bear a high sea or a strong wind. Their principal use is in transporting troops, who are frequently exercised and instructed to row them, the number of slaves being far from sufficient. The model upon which they are built was brought from Russia, and they are so constructed as to be taken in pieces by the sailors, and placed on board men of war, in order to be launched in shallow seas, and parts where the navigation is rendered dangerous by rocks. I went on board one, which had sometimes carried the King in his voyages to Finland. This was made for fifty oars, and was then in the dock-yard to be refitted. The others were in their separate docks, and, I therefore, did not see them; but they are of 28, 32, 36, 40, and 44 oars, of which the largest carries a twenty-four pounder in the bow, and the smallest a twelve pounder. They are in all 58, and four of them are so constructed as to serve either for frigates or galleys as occasions require. To the whole fleet belong several prames armed with cannon, a couple of brigantines, a bomb-ketch, and some sloops for the purpose of reconnoitring.

General

General Count Erentwärd, so well known for his fortifications in Finland, suggested the structure and use of these galleys, which he has admirably adapted to the difficult navigation of the Swedish coasts.

They shewed me here a yacht, called the Amphion, in which the king makes his passages to Finland or Carlscroon, when galleys are not to be used. It is a beautiful vessel, something resembling our *Buyten-yatchts*, but without the raised awning: the dining-room, bed-room, and writing closet richly ornamented, and furnished with an elegance very uncommon.

The garrison is by no means strong at Stockholm, being composed only of the foot-guards, light-horse, a part of the regiment of artillery, and a corps of horsemen selected from the younger branches of the first families, two of whom always escort the royal family. In this capital, as in all cities at which courts reside, shows, balls, assemblies, and gaming prevail in the winter. Notwithstanding the shortness of their summer, the Swedes are very fond of the country, and delight much in the picturesque appearance of their provinces, to which they fly from Stockholm as soon as the season permits. On this account, I saw only few people of fashion, the greater part having retired to their estates, or to some of the mineral waters with which Sweden abounds. A large party of the nobility were this summer at Medivi, a place celebrated for its waters, where the Princess Albertina then resided for the benefit of her health.

The King, when at Stockholm, lives very familiarly with his subjects, frequenting the assemblies of the nobility, and even of the *Bourgeois,* and visiting in all respects like a private person, in which character, upon these occasions, he is desirous of being received. No expence is, however, spared to render the court brilliant. His Majesty gives particular encouragement to public spectacles, and there is an opera now in preparation, entitled Gustavus Vasa, composed upon a plan suggested by himself. The music is by *Nauman,* master of the chapel to the Elector of Saxony, and a painter has been obtained from Italy to execute the decorations.

The Queen is a perfect Danish beauty, with a fair complexion, blue eyes and blond hair. Her person is stately, and there is no resemblance between her and her brother the King of Denmark. As she sees no company during the absence of the King, I had not the honour of being presented; but I saw her at the comedy, surrounded by the whole court in the national dress, and have frequently met her upon the promenade, accompanied only by one lady, and followed by a lacquey. Her manners appeared to be very amiable, and she is certainly much beloved.—I was presented

sented to the Prince Royal, then about seven years old. He is of a very weak constitution, but appears to have made considerable advances for his age. Our conversation was in French. He was dressed in the national habit, which sat very becomingly upon him. The Baron de Spaar, his governor, is a very well-bred man, and has the reputation of possessing all the qualities requisite for the education of a prince destined to the throne. A young prince whose robust make seemed to indicate a longer life, died much regretted, in the last year. Since his death, the Prince Royal alone remains to the hopes of the nation, the Duke of Sudermania having no children, and Prince Frederic being unmarried. These two brothers were upon a journey into the country, and I had, therefore, no opportunity of seeing them.

The habit of the court, both for gentlemen and ladies, is black, with facings of flame coloured satin. On gala days every body appears in satins of this colour, and white; but those who do not go to court, or have not been presented, wear any colour indifferently. No ladies of Stockholm wear the national habit, but those who rank with nobility, or have been presented at court by virtue of the employments of their husbands. All the others are dressed in the French fashion, as in the other parts of Sweden. This national dress is constantly worn only by the men; the women have laughed at the decree,

decree, and the habit, if adopted at all, has since been generally rejected.

There are some public walks at Stockholm, in which the gay world assembles towards evening. Besides that of Queen Christina, there is another of great beauty, being formed of large alleys and arbours of linden trees, under the shade of which a vast number of people are continually passing without distinction of rank. Along these alleys parterres of flowers of all sorts offer their scents to the passengers, and, those who are weary of the crowd, may enjoy the retreats of many shady bowers, enlivened by the songs of numerous birds. The nightingale alone, of all the birds known in Holland, is not found here: her visit extends no farther than Scania, and even there, the song is by no means so spirited as in more southern countries.

In an inclosure of a suburb on the outskirts of the city, the King has a small pleasure-house, delightfully situated upon the bank of a canal, connected with the lake Mälern. Here the woods are divided into charming walks, terminating in picturesque points of view. The admirers of rural scenery are much attracted to this spot, which the King has permitted to be opened for the reception of the public. It is called *Carsberg*.

I must not forget to mention a superb park at the gates of Stockholm, in which also the inhabitants enjoy some charming walks. It is upon the banks

banks of one of the canals of Scheeren, and between the trees you catch a tranfient view of all the veffels entering or going out of the port, which are obliged to double the points of thefe iflands. Here there are feveral houfes of entertainment, at which dinners, and all forts of refrefhments are to be had. The park is very large, and planted with trees of various kinds, the roots of which feek their nourifhment in the fiffures of the rocks. In an inclofure of this park is a pavilion, or rather pleafure-houfe, the ufe of which the King has given to Mr. de Sprengporten, who fo much diftinguifhed himfelf in his favour, at the head of the Finland corps, on the day of the revolution; he is aged and infirm, but has two brothers [*], one in the fervice of Holland, the other envoy extraordinary to the court of Denmark.

At the extremity of another fuburb, there is a mineral fpring, to which they attribute fome good qualities. I faw feveral drinkers, who were apparently of the inferior claffes, and unable to bear the expence of more diftant remedies. You would be furprifed to find how much a cool fituation is fought after here, and will fcarcely believe me, when I tell you, that in the months of June and July, the heat is almoft infupportable. At that time the fun is almoft always above the horizon,

[*] The firft is now in the Ruffian fervice, and the latter received the appointment of ambaffador in 1788.

and

and the natural warmth of his rays is increafed by reflection from the rocks. But, notwithftanding the heated ftate of the atmofphere in the day time, the nights are exceffively cool, and, I think, colder in proportion to the heat of the days. The obliquity of the fun's courfe at this elevation of the pole, occafions him to remain long about the limits of the horizon, and then the air begins to cool.

Such is the clearnefs of the nights, that during the whole time of my remaining at Stockholm, I could have read by midnight the fmalleft writing; a fort of continued day, which is of great affiftance to thofe who are induced to traverfe the country at this feafon of the year.

DROTNINGHOLM. The King, when in Sweden, ufually paffes the fummer at *Drotningholm,* a feat about two miles from Stockholm, upon the banks of the lake Mälern. The voyage is made in fmall failing boats, there being no accefs but from the lake, which is here very narrow, at moft not above a quarter of a league in breadth. This fhort navigation, however, in windy or rainy weather, excites a great deal of difcontent among the foreign minifters, and others who are obliged to pay their attendance at court two days in a week. In order, therefore, to fpare them this inconvenience, a bridge is conftructing at immenfe expence and trouble.

The road is to be made by blowing away rocks, and muft afterwards be fecured from the waters, by large dikes.

The feat is very beautiful, and contains many richly furnifhed apartments, In it are a library, a cabinet of natural hiftory, another of ancient and modern medals, with a collection of original Flemifh, Dutch, and Italian paintings. The whole was brought together by the Queen's mother, fifter to the great Pruffian Frederic; a Princefs who united an hereditary elevation of foul, with a fondnefs for the ftudy of the fciences, and a tafte for the fine arts. At a confiderable expence, fhe made feveral elegant and complete collections, and inftituted an academy of belles lettres, which, during her life, held its meetings at Drotningholm.

The gardens are large, and the walks well laid out, though with fomething too much attention to uniformity. In one quarter, called *Canton*, the Chinefe manner has been exactly imitated. A large pavilion, furrounded with a dozen fmaller ones, each fitted up, and deftined for fome feparate ufe, has very much the air of a Mandarin's refidence. One of thefe contains a compleat forge and workfhop, with the neceffary apparatus for making locks, an art in which the late King was faid to excel, and which, with fome of his favourites, he frequently exercifed here. The other pavilions are furnifhed as bed-rooms, or rooms for fupper, dancing,

dancing, or cards. The furniture was brought from China, and is the most splendid that could be obtained. Here the King sometimes gives fêtes, and then the valets, pages, and lacqueys are dressed entirely in the Chinese taste.

But what struck me as most admirable at Drotningholm, was the singular contrast of trees and flowers, with the barren rocks by which they are surrounded.

I am, &c.

LETTER X.

Copenhagen, Nov..... 1785.

MY DEAR FRIEND,

THE charitable institutions established at Stockholm do honour to human nature. They boast two houses for the reception of orphans, a foundling hospital, and one for gratuitous inoculation. Of the first, one was founded in 1732, at the expence of the city, and the other in 1755. That for foundlings was established in 1753, by the free-masons. There are also two lying-in-hospitals, of which one was founded in 1774, by *Ramstrom*, a physician, but was soon after adopted by the patriotic society, who have charged themselves with its support; and the other,

in

in imitation of so good an example, by the magistrates of the city. In these a certain number of women are received during their illness, and care is taken of those children whose mothers are unable to nurse them. Besides these institutions, there is another, called the College of Medicine, whose general utility and benevolent purposes can never be sufficiently praised. It was established by government in 1698, and is composed of a president, six assessors, three professors, two assistants, a syndic and secretary, who all reside in the capital. Forty physicians, deputed by this college, and paid by the state, are sent into the different provinces, in order to give attendance to the poor *gratis*. The fund for the support of this institution is raised by a small excise upon wine and brandy, and a custom duty upon the importation of coffee. Out of this fund all necessary medicines are supplied, and, in general, the whole expences of illness defrayed. An establishment, formed in 1774, for the benefit of those afflicted by the Cyprian disorder, is not to be passed over without its share of praise. Mr. Halman, one of the physicians of the court, is appointed to the care of patients of this class, and three apothecaries are engaged to furnish medicines at cost price. Stockholm has also its hospitals for the cure of the usual disorders, and some houses for the relief of the poor.

Your observations upon the hospitality of the Swedes are exceedingly just. This country, on account of its soil, situation, and climate, is not likely to become the residence of strangers, or, indeed, to be often visited by travellers. A journey into Sweden, undertaken for the mere purpose of viewing the country, is almost a phænomenon; on which account they are very little subject to be the dupes of those adventurers so common in places of public resort. Hospitality is one of the first virtues of mankind, and can never be destroyed but by treachery and distrust. It is here universally practised, and amongst people of distinction is rendered still more pleasing by their agreeable easiness of manners and great natural politeness.

You have, indeed, some ground for supposing " That the barrenness of the country must take " much from the pleasure of travelling." At first, the unusual breadth of the roads, the forests of lofty firs and enormous birch-trees through which they are cut, and the frequent views of woods, lakes, rocks, and rivers, strike the imagination, and raise the mind; but the tedious length of these forests, the perpetual sameness of verdure and solitude, and the prospect of a desolate uninhabited country soon substitute sadness for sublimity, and make you seem as if you was alone in the world. Although these forests, especially those of *Dalecarlia*, abound with wild animals, I

saw

saw very few in my journey: the elks, bears, and foxes, to avoid the attacks of the hunters, remain in the higheft and moſt inacceſſible places; but herds of hinds, and ſtags are ſometimes ſeen at a diſtance, feeding between the trunks of the firs upon the ſcanty moſs which alone grows upon the rocks. Twice alſo I ſaw ſome foxes, nearly white, and ſome hares of the fame colour.

I left Stockholm about three o'clock in the afternoon, having firſt dined with Mr. V... D... B... who, to ſave me the trouble of being examined as a traveller, politely took me in his carriage beyond the barriers of the city.

PROVINCE OF UPLAND. UPSAL.
That night I ſlept at Upſal, the capital of Upland, and the feat of a celebrated univerſity. It ſtands at the diſtance of ſeven miles from Stockholm, and the road to it lies through a cultivated country, in which great quantities of excellent corn, eſpecially barley and rye, are annually grown. I arrived there at about eleven o'clock at night, and happily avoided a terrible ſtorm which came on immediately afterwards. At my inn I found a good bed and ſupper, provided for me by Mr. V... D... B... who had ſent an expreſs from Stockholm to order it.

I had a letter to Mr. *Menanderhielm*, profeſſor of aſtronomy, from Monſieur *Muſchin Puſkin*, the

Ruſſian

Russian minister in Sweden, whom you knew at the Hague, and whose son is a student in the university; to Professor *Linnæus*, son of the celebrated *Linnæus*, Mr. *Afzelius*, experimental lecturer in chemistry, and the librarian Mr. *Vilenius*, I had also letters from Mr. *Wahrendorf*, Mr. *Grill*, and other persons.

I had much pleasure, on entering *Upsal*, to think that I was then in a place which had been honoured by the residence of the celebrated Linnæus; and from which, as from a center, the rays of his knowledge expanded over the whole circumference of the globe. In this there was also a mixture of national feeling. I recollected how much my country had contributed to the perfecting this great man; and that under the famous Boerhaave he had studied all the plants and herbs of Holland, Mr. Clifford having furnished him with the opportunities and conveniences of study. On this account, I persuaded myself that the Swedish nation in general, and this university in particular, must feel a sort of gratitude which would ensure a favourable reception to every Dutchman who should arrive at Upsal.

The morning after my arrival, I dispatched my letters, and desired to know when I might pay my respects to the several gentlemen. Mr. Afzelius and Mr. Menanderhielm, jun. came to me immediately. Mr. Afzelius politely assured me that his time

time and endeavours were at my fervice; and Mr. Menanderhielm told me that his father, being indifpofed, had taken the opportunity of a vacation to drink the mineral waters at *Saterbronn*, in the mountains of *Dalecarlia*. He then joined with Mr. Afzelius in offering me his fervices, and they began by conducting me towards the library. We had before fent a meffage to Mr. Vilenius, the librarian, with the rank of profeffor, by whom we were met and conducted into two large apartments, in which the books are depofited.

LIBRARY. This, according to Mr. Vilenius, contains 40,000 volumes, diftributed into claffes, of which that of philofophy is the moft complete. At the two ends of thefe apartments, are placed the ftatues of Guftavus Adolphus and Charles the Eleventh, the principal reftorers and protectors of this univerfity, which was firft founded in 1478. After receiving fome endowments and privileges from Guftavus Vafa, it had been neglected for feveral fucceeding reigns, but was at length reftored by Guftavus Adolphus, who prefented it with the libraries taken in his wars, which he always carefully preferved from the pillage of the foldiers. From Charles it alfo received fome benefits and privileges.

In a large coffer, filled with manufcripts, I was fhewn the *Codex Argenteus*, fo called becaufe the letters upon the parchment are all filvered. This is a

H manufcript

manuscript of the fourth century, and contains a translation of the four evangelists into the Gothic language, by bishop *Ulphilus*. Here also is preserved the manuscript journal of Eric XIV. son of Gustavus Vasa, who was imprisoned and poisoned by his brother in the castle of *Gripsholm*. His superstition, which increased almost to madness, is fully recorded by this journal, where, at the head of each day of the week, he has placed some signs of the Zodiack, and several hieroglyphic figures. The first book printed in Sweden, dated anno 1483, is shewn here; and a fine cabinet made at Ratisbon, which that city presented to Gustavus Adolphus. It is composed of inlaid work, and the workmanship, considering its date, appears to be well executed. In it is a fine agate, curiously painted on both sides, and some curiosities, which would be more properly preserved in a convent than in an university library. Such are Judas's purse, one of the pieces of silver received by him for betraying our Saviour, and the slippers of the Virgin Mary. Remarking my surprise to the librarian to find such things in such a place, he laughed, and confessed the circumstance was ridiculous enough; but, says he, these things were received in the cabinet, and, therefore, cannot well be separated from it. He then took from a little drawer a carved cherry-stone, containing a coach with six horses, a coachman, postilion, and lacqueys, and two persons seated in the inside;

inside; a work entirely executed in ivory by the famous general Baner*. The apartments are ornamented by a complete historical collection of Swedish medals in cabinets, and by several portraits, amongst which I distinguished that of Archbishop Trolle, the strenuous opposer of Gustavus Vasa.

OBSERVATORY. During the absence of Mr. Menanderhielm, the Observatory, than which none was ever worse furnished, was under the direction of Mr. *Prosperin*, who has the title of Observator. A pendulum by Graham, a quadrant, a Gregorian telescope, and a perspective of twenty feet in length by Dollond, are the only instruments to be seen here, except three tin tubes used by Messrs. Maupertuis, Celsius, Outhier, &c. in the famous operation of measuring a degree of the meridian at Tornes. They are preserved here in memory of these great men, who, by using them in an important and difficult discovery, have entitled them to some degree of veneration.

BOTANICAL GARDEN. My two guides introduced me to Mr. *Linnæus*†, to whom I presented my letter. He received me with much politeness, and led me

---

* The pronunciation is generally *Banier*.
He died in the course of the same year.

into the garden, the arrangement of which, he said, was the same as in the life of his father. Having very little knowledge of botany, I was unable to estimate the merit of this collection; but as the plants are all preserved as in the time of the late professor, its value is probably very great, and recompenses them for the uncommon attention they bestow upon it. Most of the plants which live abroad with us, are here kept in green-houses, and never exposed to the open air.

The garden is entirely laid out in the Dutch taste, being surrounded with linden trees, and *neatly* divided by hedges properly cut. It is about twice the size of the botanical garden at the Hague. Of the present professor *Linnæus*, I have not much to say; he was in Holland about two years ago, and you probably saw him. He is here thought much below his father in abilities; but there is a sister who studies botany, and has published some observations that are highly spoken of.

Near the botanical garden is the cabinet of natural history, which is in great disorder, and very ill furnished.

CABINET OF CHYMISTRY. This collection was made by Mr. Bergmann, the late professor of chemistry, whose death is much lamented here. It is very curious, and worthy of its author, whom the Swedes

Swedes deservedly praise, and place amongst the first rank of learned men. I heard much also of Professor *Menanderhielm*, whose acquaintance I afterwards obtained at *Säterbronn*.

Upsal, when I was there, contained about seven or eight hundred students, amongst whom I perceived many Russians; the number varies in different years; and, as in all other universities, depends much upon the character of the professors.

Of the three universities of Sweden this is the chief; the others are *Abo* in Finland, and *Lund* in Scania; the latter chiefly celebrated for theological studies. I visited this in my journey through Scania, and propose to give you some account of it hereafter.

The antiquities of Upsal and its neighbourhood are very remarkable. Till the 13th century, this was the residence of the Swedish kings; and upon a height in one corner of the city, are the ruins of a palace, which appears to have been of considerable size, and was probably in the days of its erection a monument of gothic taste and magnificence. Great part of it was accidently burnt in the beginning of the present century; they have rebuilt one side with stone, and in this is the residence of the provincial governor, as well as some dungeons used for prisons.

The cathedral, which is the finest church in Sweden, well deserves notice. Formerly the ceremony

remony of coronation was performed in it, but Ulrica Eleonora, younger fifter of Charles the Twelfth, was the laft who received a crown here. Her hufband Prince Frederic of Heffe, was the firft king crowned at Stockholm. Amongft the vaft number of tombs with which the church is decorated, I obferved that of Guftavus Vafa, who is reprefented in an ancient habit reclining between his two wives. Here alfo are the tombs of the celebrated chancellor *Oxenftiern* and of Catherine of *Jaquellon*, daughter of a king of Poland, and wife of John the Third, fon of Guftavus Vafa. The afhes of Eric the Ninth, furnamed the Saint, repofe in a filver fhrine reprefenting the cathedral, and placed on the right hand of the altar behind a large iron grate. He was flain in a battle with the Danes near Upfal, *anno* 1160, and was at firft interred at *Gamle Upfala*, which I fhall foon defcribe to you, from whence his bones were removed to this cathedral.

An old trunk of a tree, refembling rather a club than a ftatue, was fhewn me as the image of Odin, who was formerly worfhipped in Sweden under the name of Thor. It was brought here, after having fallen from a niche in the fteeple of the church at *Gamle Upfala*, and is a mere block of wood, carved at the upper part into the refemblance of a face.

I looked

I looked long and anxiously for some monument expressive of the respect due to the memory of Linnæus, and, not perceiving any, enquired of my conductor where it was. He told me there was no monument, and he did not know in what part of the church Linnæus was buried. We, however, began to search for it, and read all the inscriptions upon the pavement. At length, upon a small stone, half hid by a bench, we discovered, " *Hic jacet* " *Linnæus Professor.*" There was no characteristic epitaph or historical inscription, and the grave was not to be distinguished from that of a common *bourgeois*. Happily, however, his fame is already diffused by his works, and neither monument nor epitaph are necessary to prolong it: a consideration in which I lost the pain at first occasioned by such gross neglect.

OLD UPSAL. *Gamle-Upsala,* or Old Upsal, (*Gamle* being the Swedish word for *old*) is at the distance of a league from the city. I went thither in a small country calash drawn by one horse, the driver of which places himself behind. About twenty peasants houses compose the village, which is situated upon an eminence surrounded by an immense number of round *tumuli* * of different sizes, and no doubt formed by the hand of man. The tradi-

* The original has *monticules*.

tional

tional account of these *tumuli* is, that some contain the bones of their ancient kings, and others were used as places of sacrifice to the gods. A village, the residence of these kings, is also said to have existed there before the birth of Christ; but there are no vestiges to confirm the report. About a century before the Christian æra, these countries were subdued by Odin, at the head of a people issuing from the banks of the *Don* or *Boristhenes*: a low square tower, built of common stones, which still remains, is attributed to him, and to this a church is added of the same materials, but of more modern construction, having been built so late as the eleventh century.

In a field, at the distance of half a league from thence, I saw another monument of antiquity, called *Morasteen*: this is a heap of broken stones, upon which the ancient kings stood to harangue the people, who bore them upon shields from thence to their palaces. The stones are now preserved in a hut, and upon them are the half obliterated marks, which you are told, formerly expressed the names of these kings, and exhibited their coats of armour.

In the church of *Gamle Upsala*, I was shewn the place from which the bones of Eric the Saint were removed to the cathedral of Upsal. Near this place, they shew you upon a wall under a vault, an ill-shaped statue, with some old gilding upon it, it, said to be an ancient representation of this sainted king, but which I should have taken for some *chef d'œuvre* of modern awkwardness, rather than the production of ancient devotion. Here also I was shewn the niche from which fell the curious image of *Odin*, before mentioned to you.

It is now time that I should give you some account of the city of Upsal itself. This is soon done. It has neither walls, ramparts, nor gates, and all the buildings are of wood, except only the churches, the Observatory, the town-house, and the houses of the archbishop, and a few others. It is small, containing, perhaps, three or four thousand inhabitants, and is situated in a beautiful, well cultivated plain, upon the banks of the small river *Fyris*, by which it is divided into two parts, the northern called *Upsal*, and the southern *Fierding*. Having no trade, it is indebted to the university, the governor and the colleges which form the government of Upland for its support. Two very remarkable customs prevail in it: one is, that, as a resource in case of fire, the inhabitants are obliged to keep on each side of their doors, a large barrel filled with water, the freshness of which is preserved by the continual soaking of fir branches, whose verdure gives a cheerful appearance to the town. The other, that through the whole day as well as night there is a man walking upon the top of a tower, to give the alarm upon the first symptoms of fire; and that he may be known to be upon his post, he is obliged to announce by a speaking-trumpet, every hour and half hour, as struck by the clock. An excellent precaution in a country where the houses are of wood, and the progress of fire so terrible and rapid.

Having satisfied my curiosity at Upsal, I set out for the mines, of which I propose to give you an account in my next letter.

I am, &c.

LETTER XI.

Copenhagen, Dec. ... 1785.

MY DEAR FRIEND,

AFTER leaving Upsal, I took the road for *Osterby*, an estate, and forge about eight miles from the city, belonging to Messrs. Grill and Pyll, from whom I had received an invitation. I arrived there at seven in the evening, and, leaving my servant and voiture at the inn, walked to the manor-house, in which Mr. Pyll resides. He received me with much politeness, insisted upon sending for my voiture and servant, and introduced me to his lady, whom I found engaged at tea, with about twenty persons of both

sexes

sexes entirely dreffed in black. Thefe I was informed, were fome of the officers and perfons employed in the mines, who, with their wives, came every Sunday in this ceremonial drefs, to pafs the day with their *Patron**. After tea, Mr. Pyll led me to the apartment intended for me, and from thence to the garden, in which I found all the company affembled. There I was furprifed to fee in chefts, the moft beautiful orange-trees, citron-trees, and other productions of warm climates, which, however, I was told were only thus expofed for about fix weeks of the year, being preferved at other times by the artificial heat of green-houfes. The garden is very beautiful, and the Dutch tafte has been exactly imitated in the arrangement of it; but I could perceive neither peach nor apricot in the open air. The gardener, who, like moft of thofe of Sweden, had learned his trade in Holland, told me that, by heating the green-houfes in winter, it was eafy to preferve them, and even to make them bloffom, but that no means had yet been found of obtaining the fruit. The fupper was cheerful, and an air of good-nature prevailed, highly preferable to the artificial politenefs and

---

* *Patron of the Mines*, is a name given in Sweden to any individual, who, with a fhare in the mines, has alfo a forge eftablifhed upon his own eftates. It is alfo fometimes beftowed as a title of honour, and fuch are the terms *Fifcal of the Mines*, *Counfellor of the Mines*, and fome others.

elegance

elegance of higher ranks. You know I have some reliance upon my skill in physiognomy, and I confess to you, that, though my ignorance of their language prevented my taking a part in the conversation of these miners, I had no scruple to believe them amongst the worthiest of mankind. They were cheerful, and I thought the goodness of their hearts made them also happy. The minister of the place spoke German, and his wife a little French; I was seated between them, and they joined in giving me a most enthusiastic description of the happiness of these good people, which they attributed to the paternal attention of their lords and patrons, in such a manner as to afford me the highest idea of my hosts. When the clock struck ten they all retired, Mr. Pyll telling me that the next morning at seven, the hall in which we had then supped, would be the general *rendezvous* for breakfast. I slept, as you may suppose, very well contented, and at the appointed time was received by Mr. and Mad. Pyll, with a gentleman who has the rank of counsellor of the mines, and his son.

Mr. Pyll politely accompanied me in his voiture to the mine of Dannemora, which is about a mile distant. Here the first object which struck my notice was, the wheel of an hydraulic machine, used to secure the mine from inundations. Of this the diameter is forty-four feet, and the fall of water by which it is acted upon, only one. It moves a fir chain of 6000

6000 feet, which, after drawing the water from the mine, forces it through an aqueduct 5000 feet long.

The mine is entirely open at top, and through the aperture, which is nearly a quarter of a league in circumference, one may view every transaction at the bottom, though at the depth of more than 300 feet. The whole opening is surrounded by machines, each of which is furnished with pivots and pulleys, and is put in motion by four horses. These are intended only to raise and lower the utensils and necessary materials, but the work-people, both men and women, generally use this mode of conveyance, although the barrels are liable to frequent accidents, and staircases, as well as ladders, have, on this account, been formed for their protection. It is, indeed, so familiar to them, that they never place themselves at the bottom of the barrel, but remain upon the rim, holding the rope with one hand, and using the other to prevent the barrel from being broken or caught by the rock, which might otherwise overturn it. To me, however, the very sight of people thus suspended between heaven and earth was terrible; and, notwithstanding my curiosity to examine the bottom of the mine, I could not be prevailed upon to risk the danger of the passage. A story which I had just heard increased my fears. Not long before my arrival, a young girl attempted to afcend by the ufual way; being alone, and unable to direct the barrel, it was caught and overturned by a point of rock, and the girl, thrown off it, fell upon the edge of another rock, where she was fufpended at the height of an hundred feet. There she remained for half an hour, in a fituation where the leaft motion muft have precipitated her to the bottom. She had, however, fufficient prefence of mind to preferve exactly the fame attitude; and was at length delivered by ropes and ladders prepared for her affiftance by the workmen. The common number of perfons who afcend by thefe barrels is three, but there are often four, and fometimes five; and as the barrel is always full of ore, it has happened that the rope has proved unequal to the weight, and the wretched paffengers have been dafhed in pieces. Thefe accidents are by no means unfrequent, yet the labourers are not at all deterred, and the ladders, which require a little more time and trouble*, are ftill unufed. Thofe who work at the bottom of the mine, are expofed alfo to other evils. In a defcent of three hundred feet, the fmalleft ftone, detached from the top, acquires confiderable force, and becomes an inftrument of deftruction. Broken limbs, and even death, are fometimes the effect of accidents of this fort, which even the

* The perpendicular afcent is ufually performed in about four or five minutes.

cripples

cripples who have suffered by them seem not much to apprehend.

The labourers appeared contented and cheerful, although their pay is exceedingly small, being in some instances so low as 7 *sols per* day. Lodging, however, and a certain proportion of bread and brandy are provided for all. On sundays there is no work performed in the mine, but fires are lighted to soften the stone and facilitate the labour of the other days. Explosions of gun-powder are used every day at noon, during the repast of the workmen, to separate the rock at the bottom of the mine.

Round the top of the opening, scaffoldings, or bridges of some feet in length have been made to project, for the convenience of receiving the ore, and to assist the workmen in their ascents and descents. From one of these I saw distinctly every transaction at the bottom of the mine, and was also witness to the strange effect produced by an explosion of gun-powder. At this time the abyss resembled the entrails of an inflamed volcano; the scaffolding upon which I stood shook, the whole mountain trembled, and I seemed to be surrounded with stones, flame and smoke. The shock was succeeded by the long rollings of subterraneous echoes, which, with a sound like that of thunder, repeated the crashes of the rocks and the noise of the explosions. I now trembled for the workmen, who

who were eating their meal at the bottom of the mine, but was assured that care had been taken to provide them with apartments, by retiring into which, they might avoid the danger. The operation itself is absolutely necessary, no tools being able to penetrate the rocks, which by these means are easily blown into pieces. The ore, when obtained from the mine, is piled up in large heaps in places appropriated for its reception; there it remains till winter, and, when the surface of the earth is well covered with snow, sledges are used to transport it to the forges, at which it is fused, and the other necessary operations performed.

Twelve hundred men are daily employed, either in the mine, or at the different exterior works.

The mines are worked at the joint expence of many individuals, but the forges are private property. In the latter the metal is entirely finished, and rendered fit for its removal to magazines, where it is deposited for exportation or home consumption.

Fifteen forges, most of which belong to Messrs. Grill and Pyll, or to the Baron *de Geer*, are supplied with ore by the mine of *Dannemora* alone. Each forge employs a vast number of men, that of *Osterby* alone requiring fifteen or sixteen hundred labourers, and several officers.

Upon our return from Osterby, we again walked in the garden, where, notwithstanding the rigour of

the

the climate, I saw melons and *ananas*, as fine as any produced in Holland.

Dinner was soon announced, and I expected we should immediately seat ourselves in the parlour where it was served. A little ceremony, however, which I could well have dispensed with, was first to be gone through. They led me into an adjoining apartment, in which stood a sideboard, well covered with glasses, and plates of bread and butter, a slice of which, with a glass of brandy, was taken by each person before going into the dinner parlour. The custom is common throughout all Sweden; but in the houses of persons of high rank, *liqueur* is sometimes substituted for brandy.

After dinner my host conducted me to the forge, and explained every operation with great patience. Under this name *(frälse brük)* are comprised all the buildings erected for the different operations through which the mineral passes, before it is formed into the lumps which they call *gucuse*. It comprises also all the houses of the workmen and officers, which, with the buildings, form a village distributed into several straight streets, each ornamented with a row of beautiful trees. The village is called *Osterby*, and it is a very pleasing, cheerful place, containing perhaps two thousand inhabitants. The houses of the workmen are small neat habitations, arranged between those of the officers, which are larger, and built at the extremities of the ſtreets. At the diſtance of half a gun-ſhot from the village ſtands the manor houſe, which, like all the others, is a wooden building, but has a ſtone foundation and a handſome cupola. Two wings contribute to the noble appearance of the whole; the one containing a ſet of apartments for ſtrangers, and the other a very beautiful church. If my curioſity was gratified by a view of the different works carried on at the forge, I had a ſtill higher pleaſure in obſerving the good-humour, candour, and friendſhip, with which Mr. Pyll treated his people, and the confidence which, in their turn, they repoſed in him. At the workſhops, he appeared like a father paying a viſit to his children, rather than a maſter ſuperintending his workmen. The little tour which I took with him raiſed my ſpirits, and filled my heart with admiration.

After tea we went to ſee the iron formed into pigs; an operation which is performed at ſtated times, when all the heterogenous matter has been ſeparated from the metal. It is then made to run from the furnace in which it has been ſmelted, iſſuing like a torrent of fire through a hole opened at the bottom, into moulds of ſand prepared to receive it. Great care is taken to keep the moulds dry, as the leaſt damp makes them liable to ſplit; and before the metal is permitted to run, they ſeparate from it the *ſcoriæ*, or groſſer parts, which riſe in a foam

foam above the liquid mafs. Through another hole, contrived above that by which the metal paffes, the *fcoriæ* is made to iffue from the furnace; and it is then formed by moulds into the fhape of bricks, inftead of which it is afterwards ufed by builders.

The next morning I accompanied the gentleman, whom I before mentioned as a counfellor of the mines, to fee the preparations making for a wall, to be conftructed between the mine of Dannemora and a lake about a quarter of a league diftant. The water that turns the great hydraulic wheel is obtained from this lake, which there is fome reafon to fear may one day penetrate through the interftices of the rock, and drown the whole mine. To guard againft this evil, they have made, partly by explofions, partly by hewing the rock, an excavation of an aftonifhing depth, in which they intend to place a wall made of *fcoriæ* piled up and mixed with lime. The walls of this fort are thus made. When the *fcoriæ* are piled up, and the moiftened lime has been properly intermixed, the wall is preffed between planks fo placed, as to form a fort of double inclofure of the height and diftance defired; the compofition is then left to dry between the planks, and when thefe are removed the wall is finifhed. The garden of the manor-houfe is enclofed by fuch a wall, and Mr. Pyll affured me, that by experiments made for several years, the *scoriæ* of iron are proved to be more proper for this purpose than those of copper.

I remained at *Osterby* that day and part of the next, employing myself in viewing a second time the operations of the forges, of which I took a very exact account. My hosts strove to detain me with them for several days: but the mines of *Fahlun* and Sahla, the dock of Carlscroon, &c. were still unseen, and I recollected that I had yet a long journey to make. On this account I refused myself the pleasure of a longer stay.

A few miles from *Osterby* there is a foundery of cannon, belonging to Mr. Wahrendorf. From thence our republic received a great quantity in the last war, and I saw there an officer of our artillery, who was still employed to examine and receive them.

I left Osterby on the third day after my arrival, and parted with great regret from my worthy hosts, whose kindness I can never forget, and whose attention to my convenience extended beyond the time of my stay amongst them. Without my knowledge, they had placed in the boot of my voiture, some bottles of excellent wine, and a variety of good provisions, by which for several days I was kept from lamenting the miserable fare of the inns.

Just before my departure I dined once more with Mr. and Mad. Pyll, and some of their neighbours,

bours, whom I found very cheerful, amiable, and well educated. I arrived foon after at Löffta, an eftate and forge belonging to the *Baron de Geer*, to whom I had been recommended, but who was unfortunately from home, upon a vifit to his brother at fome eftates poffeffed by the latter near Stockholm.

Of Löffta, however, I intend to give you fome account in my next letter. In the mean time I remain, &c. &c.

LETTER XII.

Copenhagen, Dec. ... 1785.

MY DEAR FRIEND,

I have yet fomething to tell you of the mine of Dannemora, in addition to what you have already read upon the fubject.

You are aware that nature has enriched this kingdom with a vaft number of mines of iron, which metal, even in its pure ftate, is alfo found in many of the rocks of Sweden and Lapland. The richeft of all thefe mines is that of Dannemora, which often yields at the rate of 60 *per cent*, while the others afford only 30. The iron obtained from it is known in Europe under the name of *Oeregrund* iron, (a port of the Baltic Sea in the north

north of Upland) and is chiefly used by the English, who manufacture it into the steel so celebrated for its elasticity, strength and beauty of polish, which they alone know how to give it.

The mine was first discovered in 1470, and the ore was then sold in its rough state, and unsmelted, to the merchants of *Lubec*, who fetched it in their vessels. Forges and hammer-mills were afterwards constructed under the reign of Gustavus Vasa.

The iron obtained from Sweden undergoes three principal operations.

1st. The ore is extracted from the mine.

2dly. It is smelted in the great furnace; and,

3dly. The iron is perfected by the labours of the forge.

Large quantities of wood and charcoal are consumed in these operations, which could not be carried into effect, or even subsist together in the same country, but for the abundant supply of its forests. The persons concerned in working the mines, are for the most part able to smelt the ore, and form the metal into pigs; but this they are never permitted to do, unless their own forests are sufficient to supply them with fuel. Even those forges, which do not belong to the proprietors of mines, are obliged to receive their iron in *pigs*, only from the mines to which they are assigned, and to make into bars no more than a certain

quantity

quantity proportioned to the wood they are able to obtain.

These pigs are oblong masses, the weight of which is limited to three *schifp* *. The annual produce of all the iron mines is computed at 400,000 schifp, of which a tenth part, or 40,000 schifp, is said to be furnished in bars by that of Dannemora alone.

The whole quantity is forged and hammered by 566 hammer-mills, and 1007 of the smaller forges. Three hundred thousand *schifp* are annually exported, and the remainder consumed in domestic manufactures.

The mines, smelting-furnaces, and forges, afford employment to 25,600 men. Of these

    4,000 are employed in digging the ore, and in the internal labours of the mines.

10,800 in felling, cutting, and carrying wood, and making it into charcoal.

    2,000 in smelting the ore at the furnaces; allowing 250 days, or forty weeks for smelting alone.

    1,800 in removing the iron from the smelting-furnaces to the forges.

      600 in the carriage of sand, gravel, and timber.

---

* The schifp is a Swedish weight, which is greater or less in proportion to the substances weighed. That here meant is equal to 16 lb.

4,000 in the carriage of 1,400,000 lasts of charcoal, made from 1,260,000 cords of wood.
2,400 in forging the iron.

25,600 *

At Löfsta, which is five miles to the northward of Osterby, I arrived about midnight, and found a tolerably comfortable inn. The landlord had been *maitre-d'hotel* to *Mr. de Geer,* whom you knew at the Hague in quality of Envoy from Sweden, and he here added to the employments of innkeeper and post master, that of sub-inspector of the forges. He addressed me by name immediately upon my arrival, gave me an excellent supper, professed a great esteem for the Dutch, and shewed me by his bill the next day, that he had at least an equal fondness for their money.

Throughout all Sweden, but especially in the northern provinces, apartments are appropriated in the mansions of the nobility for the reception and accommodation of travellers recommended to their care. Even the absence of the owners does not at all prevent visitors of this sort from taking up their residence in these apartments; and they are at those times received and supplied with necessaries by an

* These accounts are all taken from an Academical Discourse, written by the senator Count *Storkenstrom,* entitled *Om Suenska Jaernbruks-nœringen.*

intendant, called *verwalter*. This cuftom was obferved at Löffta, where, on the day after my arrival, I was invited to lodge at the family feat by the intendant of Mr. de Geer.

The houfe is inferior in appearance to that of Ofterby, but the gardens, which are the moft northerly of Europe, are much larger and more magnificent. Moft of the fruits are obtained by artificial heat; and even the mulberry-tree, the marfhmallow and virgin's bower, which with us endure the cold of the whole year, are here preferved in orangeries during the fummer, and in the winter in hot-houfes. Yet the verdure was very pleafing, and there were fome beautiful flowers, fuch as I was aftonifhed to fee in a country, which, for eight months of the year, is covered with fnow. Adjoining to the gardens is the village or forge, exceeding in beauty any that I faw in Sweden, except that of Ofterby, which is larger. It confifts of one long ftreet, and is entirely inhabited by the workmen, clerks, and directors of the forges.

Here, as well as at Ofterby, the iron is worked and formed into bars, in a manner practifed by the Walloons, a colony of whom have been eftablifhed at both places for above two centuries. The German method, which is ufed at moft of the other forges, is lefs expenfive, but the iron is faid to be of inferior quality,

At Suderfors, an estate belonging to Messrs. Grill and Pyll, there is a forge at which the ore of Dannemora is smelted, and a considerable manufactory of anchors carried on. The village, though inferior to the other two, has some beauty, and, like them, is entirely inhabited by the workmen. The manor-house, which, as well as all the others in this country, is built of wood, is large, commodious, and well furnished; and has a small tower, or cupola, at the top, with a very extensive and charming prospect. Mr. Grill, jun. and his lady, here passed a part of the summer, and afforded me a very gracious welcome.

From Suderfors I went to Gefle, situated on the gulph of Bothnia. The port is a very good one, and the town, which is the capital of Gastricia, is the residence of the provincial governor. To arrive at it you are obliged to pass the river Dahl, at a ferry about two leagues from the town, half a league above which, near a small village named Elfearsleby, the river makes a superb and picturesque fall. Of this a very accurate and able description has been given by Mr. Wraxall, who erroneously made this the extent of his tour, leaving the copper mine at Fahlun, and the works of Carlscroon unseen. It is formed by a large rock, crowned with high firs, which, occupying the middle of the river, occasions the waters to rise in two spouts, or cataracts, that afterwards

terwards unite and fall into the gulph, a few leagues below Gefle. One of thefe has a defcent of about fifty feet, and the other, though of lefs perpendicular height, precipitates its waters from rock to rock by a thoufand cafcades, of which the foam is fo copious, and rifes to fuch a height, as to be perceptible even at the diftance of a league. In the middle of the perpendicular fall, a black rock projects itfelf, and, with the fingle fir-tree which grows upon it, increafes the effect of this very fingular view.

Salmon is taken here in great quantities, efpecially about the ifland or rock which feparates the river into two parts. Thither, however, the fifhermen never venture but at the rifk of their lives, the lower part being inacceffible on account of the agitation of the waters, and the upper, to which they are obliged to have recourfe, expofing them to be precipitated over the rocks by the current, whenever accident or neglect brings their veffel within its reach.

The river Dahle, which is the largeft in Sweden, has its fource amongft the mountains of Norway. From thence it runs through the whole length of Dalecarlia, and, after watering one part of Weftmannia, and dividing Gaftricia from Upland, falls into the gulph of Bothnia near Gefle.

At Gefle, where I went unprovided with any letter of recommendation, I had a frefh inftance

of

of Swedish hospitality and politeness. I arrived during the night, and the next morning at breakfast received a visit from an officer of a provincial regiment, who offered me his services in the most obliging manner, and conducted me over the whole town. In this ramble I saw a considerable repository of iron in bars, intended for exportation to England, and by him I was introduced to one of the first families, who gave me an invitation to dine and sup. Gefle is situated upon a small gulph within that of Bothnia: the little river Hazuna runs through it, and, pouring its waters into a large and deep canal, affords an entrance for vessels into the town and dock. A dreadful fire, which happened in 1778, destroyed two-thirds of the place, and the inhabitants have not yet obtained money enough to repair the damage.

PROVINCE or DALECARLIA.
At a little distance from Gefle I entered the province of Dalecarlia, of which *Fahlun* is the capital. The inhabitants are distinguished by the names of black and grey Dalecarlians, the former of whom are also sometimes called iron Dalecarlians, from the number of iron nails in their shoes. These inhabit the northern and mountainous parts of the province, where the number of inhabitants so much exceeds the means of subsistence, that they are seen departing in troops for the more cultivated provinces, in

search

search of labour and food. Their peaceful irruptions are usually made about the time of harvest, and, as they are accustomed to live with great temperance, they often return into their own country, with some fruits of their labour and œconomy. The Dalecarlians make good soldiers, and are, in general, an active, brave, and laborious people, jealous of oppression, and much attached to their ancient customs and constitution.

I am, &c. &c.

LETTER XIII.

Copenhagen, Dec. . . . 1785.

MY DEAR FRIEND,

IN my journey from Fahlun to Avesta, which I expected to finish in a few hours, I was delayed by the want of post-horses, and obliged to stop, about two hours after midnight, at a small town called Sater. At the inn I found the doors open, and the rooms empty; and, being unable to rouse any person by my shouts, I stumbled from one chamber to another, and at length discovered the landlord and his wife, fast asleep upon a crib, and without any clothes or covering but their linen. The woman, who arose upon my first entrance, appeared much astonished, and to my
questions,

questions, expressed to her in German, replied with a torrent of words, which I took for Dalecarlian abuse, but luckily did not very well understand. At length we began to comprehend each other's meaning, and she put on a sort of underpetticoat, while her husband remained upon the crib, and, having once opened his eyes and surveyed me, turned himself round, and again fell asleep. With the landlady, however, I soon made my peace, and was shewn by her into a small room, where I spread my mattress upon the floor, and got a comfortable nap of two hours.

The emptiness of the house was owing, it seems, to the hay-harvest, which, at this season of the year, employs all the servants both by day and night. But through the greatest part of Sweden, especially to the northward of Stockholm, the doors of the houses, and even those of the inner-rooms, are thus left open during the night, both in the towns and in the country; an instance of confidence and security, in which the inhabitants are very well justified by experience, thieves being unknown in Sweden, except in garrison-towns, and amongst the regiments of raised troops.

Half way between Fahlun and Säter, I visited a place celebrated for the protection which Gustavus Vasa there found in the house of a clergyman, after escaping from the treachery of a Dalecarlian gentleman, named Peterson, who intended to deliver

liver him into the hands of Chriftiern *. He was
faved by the wife of this gentleman, " who, touched
" by compaffion, or, perhaps, by a yet more ten-
" der motive, fent him in the night in company
" with a domeftic and two faithful Dalecarlians,
" to the houfe of this clergyman, from whence he
" was conveyed and hid in the church. The fe-
" cret was faithfully kept, and the Danes, by thefe
" means, loft all traces of Guftavus †."

The place is called Ornäs, and is entirely infu-
lated amongft mountains and woods, at the diftance
of half a league from the great road, upon the
banks of a fmall lake. The church has been
fince converted into a houfe, of very fingular ftruc-
ture and appearance, the ftair-cafe being on the
outfide. It ftands confiderably above the reft, and
is at prefent inhabited as a country refidence, by
an officer of the mines at Fahlun.

A large hall upon the fecond floor, is confe-
crated to the memory of this event. There they
have erected a fort of throne, with a canopy of
blue filk, worked with golden *fleurs de lis*, and
under it is placed a ftatue of Guftavus of the natural fize, armed completely from top to toe, and in
the very armour which he wore upon his arrival at
Ornäs. By his fide ftands a figure of his domeftic,

* A. D. 1520.
† Vertot's Revolutions of Sweden: vol. i. p. 113 of the French edition.

in complete armour, and the door is guarded by his two faithful Dalecarlians, habited according to the fashion of their country, and adorned with long beards. Each holds in his hand a crofs-bow, and at his fide has a quiver filled with arrows. They are alfo provided with fabres of a tremendous fize, and the whole room is ornamented with pieces of ancient armour, ufed by Guftavus upon different occafions, and prefented by him to his faithful hoft. Amongft feveral little articles of furniture is fhewn his watch, which is made entirely of thick copper.

On my journey from Avefta to Säter, at the diftance of feveral leagues from the latter, I went to the mineral watering-place called Säterbronn, where profeffor Menanderhielm of Upfal then refided. This is nothing more than a little hamlet of wooden houfes, built, like thofe of the common peafants, of the trunks of fir-trees laid horizontally upon each other, and joined at the interftices by layers of mofs. In a large fquare, formed by fuch houfes, I was received by a number of curious perfons, who furrounded my *voiture*, enquiring my name and bufinefs at the place. From them I learned, that with refpect to lodging and food, the whole hamlet was under the direction of a medicinal profeffor from Upfal, who foon after affigned me a lodging for the night in one of thefe little houfes, which was fortunately vacant. My refidence contained

tained two very neat chambers for my own ufe, and a clofet for my fervant, a fmall bed without curtains, four chairs, a table, a looking-glafs, and a bureau with drawers. I had fcarcely taken poffeffion before I was vifited by a nobleman, decorated with the enfigns of an order, who, in quality of grand huntfman to his Majefty, the Baron Oxenftiern, came to do the honours of the place. He welcomed me to Säterbronn, and, when he found I had a letter for Mr. Menanderhielm, infifted upon my ftaying a couple of days with the company, to whom, as well as to Mr. Menanderhielm, he offered me his introduction. As I arrived after the ufual time of dinner, I was ferved in my own apartment, and, afterwards, this gentleman conducted me to the general promenade, which confifts of one large alley of linden-trees, elms, and poplars, bordered on both fides with meadows and paftures, beyond which the view terminates in fome woods of fir-trees. The mineral fpring rifes in a beautiful faloon at the top of this alley, where we found many walkers, who all lamented the effects of fome diforder, while their countenances wore an appearance of health which belied their complaints. Mr. the Baron introduced me to the whole company, and particularly to Mr. Menanderhielm, whofe converfation made my ftay at Säterbronn highly agreeable. Our walk continued till the clock ftriking fix gave the fignal for prayer, when we all

affembled

assembled in a hall furnished with benches, where the minister was waiting for us in a small pulpit about four feet high. After a hymn, he gave us a discourse for a few minutes, and a prayer; another hymn concluded the service. We then returned to our walk, from whence, at seven o'clock, the sound of a bell summoned us to supper, which was served in three small wooden houses, the price of eating differing at each. I supped in the best of these with the Baron, and Mr. Menanderhielm, who both spoke French, and with some very pleasing Swedish ladies, whose conversation I unfortunately could not understand.

The use of wine is prohibited, but was permitted to me, as a stranger, by the Professor, who has here the government of the company. At eight o'clock the same professor announced that the hour of refection was expired, and each person immediately arose to enjoy the beauties of the evening. At nine the sound of a bell gave notice to the water-drinkers that it was time to retire, the efficacy of the waters depending much upon a due observance of regimen. I was somewhat fatigued, and, therefore, very gladly conformed to the same rule.

At four o'clock, I was roused by the sound of a bell, which had been before noticed to me as the signal for opening the spring to the peasants and poorer people, who are not permitted to mix

with

with the better sort. At five the same bell warns them to depart, and the company then issue from their cabins, each taking the dose prescribed under the direction of the Professor, who is present. After this, each person walks or returns home as he pleases, and, an hour afterwards, when the dose is supposed to have taken effect, breakfast is served in the several cabins. The bell is not heard again till twelve, when the company assemble to a frugal dinner, which Mr. Professor almost reduces to the standard of a Baratarian repast. I was, however, very glad to stay another day in a place where I was received with great politeness by persons whose conversation and manners were highly agreeable.

The next morning at five I repaired to the spring, to take my leave of the company, and with an intention of discharging my share of the expences; this, however, the Professor would by no means permit me do, adding to the many other civilities shewed me here, his thanks for my visit, and a pressing invitation to prolong it.

The mode of life at this watering-place, is uniformly such as I have described it; their days are not diversified by play or public spectacles, but the company are, at the same time, free from sharpers and dupes, each person resorting thither for the cure or prevention of some disorder, not with a desire of increasing his fortune. Nearly the same fame manners and habits prevail in all the mineral watering-places of Sweden, except that at Medivi, plays are reprefented, during the refidence of the King's fifter, or of any branch of the royal family.

Dancing, which Mr. Profeffor confiders as promoting the effect of the waters, is the only amufement to be enjoyed at Säterbronn, and this is permitted but once in a week, between the hour of dinner and feven o'clock in the evening. On that day the hall, which in the morning ferved for a church, is in the afternoon prepared for a ball-room, and the pulpit exchanged for an orcheftra.

When all the company have retired for the feafon, the public and private buildings are fhut up, the Profeffor takes the keys, and the place is abandoned till the next year, when, a few weeks before the commencement of the feafon, the Profeffor takes thither a number of workmen, examines what repairs are wanted, and takes care that the whole place is rendered habitable and convenient. This is always done at the expence of the province, and is a very great public benefit.

From Avefta, where I arrived in good time, I fet out for the mine of filver at Sahla. On the road I changed horfes, and obferving a very fteep defcent, at the bottom of which was a floating bridge, over an arm of the river Dahl, I was unwilling to be driven down it by the intoxicated

beaft

beast who was allotted me for a coachman, and, therefore, directed my servant to take the reins. By some accident they fell from him, and the leaders, harassed and provoked by the shaft-horses, soon threw the feeble postilion, a child of ten or eleven years old, and the whole set flew down the descent with a velocity which I cannot now recollect without horror. At one moment the carriage seemed ready to rush into the river, towards which the road at first directs itself, but the horses with great dexterity turned the corner, and passed the bridge, exactly in the middle, with the swiftness of lightning. The bridge, which was composed only of the trunks of fir-trees, bent beneath the action and weight of the carriage, while the ruggedness of the flooring increased the chance of an overturn, and the paltry railing, which ran along it, seemed a very slight defence against any kind of accident. A steep ascent on the other side of the river considerably checked the fury of the horses, and, with the assistance of the coachman, whom the fright had sobered, I soon restored every thing to its proper place. In the mean time we were joined by our little postilion, who had received only a slight contusion from the fall.

Sahla, a town of a moderate size, is built entirely of wood, in straight streets, which all issue from a large opening in the center. It is, however, a very dirty, disagreeable place, and the streets are so over-run with grafs, that, every evening, before the shutting of the gates, cattle are drove in to feed till the morning. The town is celebrated for having been the refidence of the royal family, in the year 1710, while Stockholm was ravaged by a peftilential diforder, which carried off 20,000 perfons.

SILVER MINE.
In a fmall mountain, at the diftance of half a league from the town, is the famous filver mine. The defcent into it is at firft by ladders placed in an opening of about ten feet in diameter, there being no large excavation, as at Dannemora or Fahlun. In one of the firft galleries, at the depth of about fifty-feet, you arrive at the bottom of thefe ladders, and the defcent by buckets begins. Here, however, the exceffive cold, and the danger of this mode of travelling, checked my progrefs. The buckets are worked in the fame manner as the barrels at Fahlun and Dannemora, and the mechanifm of the pumps is exactly fimilar, except that there are here two large wheels, each of the diameter of 44 feet. This mine, which is the moft ancient and the richeft of all thofe of filver in Sweden, was firft worked in the year 1188, and through the whole of the fourteenth century yielded 24,000 marks *per* annum. In the fifteenth century the annual produce funk to 20,000 marks, and under the reign of Charles the Tenth to 2,000; at prefent the quantity is ftill lefs, the ore yielding

so

so little as two lots of pure silver *per* quintal. The principal gallery, from which the richest ore is extracted, is entirely fallen in, and they are at present employed in making new openings, in order to arrive perpendicularly upon the vein. Formerly the lead used in precipitating the silver from the ore was brought from England, but the mine itself now affords enough for the operation.

Half a league from the town is the forge, under which name is comprised a large town inhabited entirely by the workmen and those employed as inspectors. Here the ore is brought from the mine, and the silver is obtained by the following process.

1st. They pound the ore, in order to separate from it those parts which are mere stone, and they afterwards wash it in a tub, over which they spread a coarse linen cloth.

2dly. The mass, thus cleansed, undergoes a sort of calcination in a vaulted furnace, the heat of which makes it unite and form one body, but is not sufficient to produce fusion.

3dly. They add to this calcined mass, some secret matter or preparation of their own, which has the property of attracting the silver and lead contained in the mass, while the sulphur is made to evaporate; both bodies are fused before they are suffered to cool.

4thly. The scoriæ, which contain iron, are taken off, and the lead, united in fusion with the silver, runs through a hole made for that purpose.

5thly. This mass *(werkbly)* is afterwards refined in the refining furnace *(trib-herd)* and sent in lumps to the moneyer's office in Stockholm.

The mine was formerly worked for the sole profit of the crown, but in the year 1682 it was undertaken by a society, whose stock is divided into 200 shares.

At the house of the inspector, I was shewn the buckets in which the kings Charles the Tenth and Eleventh descended to the bottom of the mine, and also three others used by his present Majesty, when Prince Royal, and his two brothers. The dresses worn by them in their descent are also preserved; they are made of black silk, and fashioned entirely like those of the miners.

It is now time that I should conclude this letter, with assuring you how much

I am, &c. &c.

LETTER XIV.

Copenhagen, Jan. ... 1786.

MY DEAR FRIEND,

My journey from the mine to Carlscroon carried me through Enkiöping, a wretched town, worse even than Sahla, and into which

which cows, sheep, hogs, and geese, are drove from the country every night to graze upon the herbage that over-runs the streets. It is, however, celebrated for its antiquity, having been one of the residences of the kings, before the times of Odin, and is very well situated upon the lake Mälern, which enables it to carry on some traffick in the interior parts of the country.

Westerås, or *Arosen*, the first place in Westmannia, is a very ancient city, the residence of an archbishop and of the governor of the province. It is situated upon the mouth of the river Swarta, which, after dividing the city into two parts, falls into the lake Mälern. Of this situation its name is said to be descriptive; *Ar*, signifying a river or lake; *os*, a mouth, and *Westra* relating to Upsal, which is sometimes called *Oester-aros*. The cathedral is remarkable for its beautiful tower, and for a number of tombs, amongst which is that of Eric the Fourteenth[*], and those of many archbishops: and the city is celebrated in the annals of Sweden, the government having here been changed from an elective to an hereditary monarchy[†].

Störnsholm, a royal seat at the distance of a few leagues from Westerås, is a very ancient and rui-

[*] Eric XIV. after an imprisonment of eight years at Gripsholm, took a draught of hemlock in 1577, by command of King John, his brother.

[†] The crown of Sweden was declared hereditary A. D. 1544, in favour of the male descendants of Gustavus Vasa.

nous building, which the king never ufes except by dining in it when he comes to view his ftud. The ftallions are much boafted of, but I faw only fix, of which two from Spain, one from Tartary, and another from Denmark were the fineft. The brood mares and foals were then at grafs at Kongfor, a village at the diftance of a few leagues, where there are fome beautiful pafture grounds upon the banks of a canal, running from the lake Mälern to Arboga. They were all fhewn to me by the perfon who has the care of them, and I faw none that formed an exception to my general remark, that the Swedifh horfes, although ftrong and hardy, are by no means beautiful, and are, in general, liable to the fpavin.

In the afternoon I embarked with my voiture in a large boat, in order to make the paffage of the lake Hielmarn. A perfect calm foon made it neceffary to row, and the oars were plied by two men and four women; the firft in rags and half naked, the latter covered only by their fhifts and fhort under-petticoats. Indeed the exceffive heat made fuch fort of clothing a luxury; and though I was fheltered from the fun by the hood of my voiture, and had a moft delightful profpect of the veffels and iflands upon the lake, I could not avoid longing for the moment of landing, when I might enjoy the fhade of the woody mountains, which bounded the profpect on the oppofite fhore. The

paffage,

passage, however, was not made in less than four hours*, and it was night before I arrived at *Malmär*, a village composed of about a dozen huts, at the foot of a mountain called *Malmär baka*, or mountain of Malmär.

I had been warned of the danger of passing this mountain, which abounds with heights and descents, bordered by steep rocks and horrid precipices. But the other road makes a circuit of four miles, and, therefore, after taking the precaution of ordering some peasants to follow me in a waggon, I began my ascent of the mountain, and arrived at the top about half an hour before midnight. The sun was already below the horizon, and though the moon shone very clearly, the enormous wood of fir-trees through which I travelled, was almost impervious to its feeble beams. As the peasants had exerted themselves considerably in the ascent, it was necessary to stop, and afford them some refreshment; I had excellent brandy and knikkebroë, which soon restored their courage, while the promise of a farther reward, revived the industry of those who, already wearied with the undertaking, began to talk of returning home. We then commenced the descent, which was of so much difficulty and danger, that some of the peasants were obliged to walk upon the edge of a precipice, supporting the carriage with their shoulders,

* The lake is there about two leagues in breadth.

and

and others were employed in restraining the fury of the horses, who, provoked by the continual jolting of the carriage against their hams, could scarcely be prevented from exerting their speed. While I was thus travelling, for a great part of the time, in utter darkness, my voiture every moment likely to be dashed to peices by a rock, or hurled down a precipice, I added to the real evils which surrounded me, the pains of apprehension; I knew myself to be in the power of the postilions and peasants, who might have robbed and murdered me without danger of discovery; and, notwithstanding my endeavours, I found my fears upon this account unconquerable, till the rising sun shewed me the beauties of a more level country, with the towers of Nordkiöping in perspective. At length we arrived at the bottom of the mountain, and I rewarded my peasants for their honesty and labour.

NORDKIÖPING.
A magnificent road, making part of that called the royal one from Stockholm to Nordkiöping, conducted me to the latter place, where, after a few hours rest, I delivered my letters to Mr. *Shäff*, a merchant, who received me with great hospitality, and shewed me every thing remarkable in the city. Nordkiöping is situated upon a gulph, called *Brawiken*, making part of the Baltic Sea, into which the river Motala, after traversing the city, pours its waters. It is one of the largest and most mercantile

mercantile places in Sweden, having a manufactory of articles in brafs, and a confiderable commerce with France, of which thefe are the chief fupport.

Brafs, you know, is made by fufing copper and lapis calaminaris together in large crucibles, from which the melted mafs is made to run into flat moulds formed in the fhape of double tubs. After this, the plates of metal are here cut into ftripes by fciffars, and thefe ftripes are drawn, by means of ftrong pincers, through five different holes, under which rollers are kept continually turning, in order to give the wire its proper fhape. The fciffars, pincers, rollers, and hammers, by which the plates are rendered more perfectly flat, are all put in motion by an immenfe wheel, that turns feveral others, and is itfelf acted upon by the river, the primum mobile of the whole. By this means alfo the large bellows ufed at the furnaces are worked.

Befides this manufactory, which is the property of an individual, there are others of guns, cloths, paper, &c.

Nordkiöping, though not the capital of Oftrogothia, is by far the moft confiderable city in the province, both with refpect to its buildings, and the number and riches of the inhabitants. Its extenfive commerce gives it an air of activity and opulence, which alfo appears in the furniture

of

of the houſes, and the magnificence of the entertainments. From Nordkiöping I went to Lindköping, the capital of Oſtrogothia, and the reſidence of the governor of the province, ſituated upon the river *Stäng*. It is one of the moſt ancient cities in Sweden, but very ſmall and ill-built. The moſt remarkable object is the cathedral, which, after that of Upſal, is the largeſt in the kingdom. In it are ſome very handſome tombs belonging to the families of Blieke and Löwenhaupt. The houſes, as in the other towns of Sweden, are of wood, but badly conſtructed, and with a mean appearance. The town-houſe, the chancery-office and the caſtle, or ſeat in which the governor reſides, are the only ſtone-buildings.

Not far from this city is a ſmall lake, of which a very extraordinary circumſtance is related. It is ſaid that from time to time a ſmall iſland appears upon the ſurface of the lake, which, after remaining viſible for, perhaps, the ſpace of a year, ſuddenly diſappears, and is not ſeen again for four, five, and often for ſix years afterwards. It is covered with herbs, ſtones, and the roots and trunks of trees. The phænomenon, whatever may be the cauſe of it, has been ſeen by the King, as I was told by the commandant of a marine regiment at Carlſcroon, who aſſured me that he had walked with his Majeſty upon the iſland.

I went

I went four miles out of my road to view the celebrated antiquities of Wadftena, a fmall city, fituated upon the banks of the lake *Wettern*. There I arrived about night, and, after a wretched fupper, which very well correfponded with the appearance of the inn, I wrapped myfelf in my *Schantfloper*, and endeavoured to get a nap upon my mattrefs. From reftlefs flumbers, and the company of a whole brood of infects, I was very glad to be roufed by the rays of the fun, which, with the delightful appearance of the morning, invited me to walk and view the town. A fine alley of trees led to the lake, upon which the fun now rofe with all his fplendour, while its furface reflected the bright clouds that fwam lightly through the atmofphere, and a beautiful ifland, rifing in the middle, formed an amphitheatre of meadows and cultivated grounds. Unwilling to quit fuch a fcene without a full enjoyment of it, I feated myfelf upon a little eminence, which commanded the whole, and there involuntarily fell afleep. I fhould not have mentioned this circumftance, if it was not rendered extraordinary by the total want of recollection and abfence of mind which enfued upon my waking. I found myfelf ftretched upon the earth, entirely ignorant of my fituation, unable to remember even the name of the place, and without any knowledge of the circumftances which brought me thither. Whether my late fatigues fufficiently account

count for it, I know not, but I remained in this state for a quarter of an hour, and it was only by repeating frequently to the paffengers the word *chivergoor*, that I was able to obtain a direction to my inn.

While I was breakfafting upon fome bad coffee and *knikkebroe*, I was vifited by four gentlemen, who, after bowing very refpectfully, began to accoft me in the Swedifh language, of which, in a few words that I had learned to repeat upon fuch occafions, I foon informed them I was ignorant. They then went away, and in about half an hour returned with an officer, who by his grey hairs, and the order of the fword, with which he was decorated, appeared to have feen fervice. He told me, in very good French, that the gentlemen, his companions, were members of the regency, who had commiffioned him, a lieutenant-colonel of engineers, to exprefs their good wifhes, and make me a tender of their fervices during my ftay at the place. I expreffed to lieutenant-colonel Eillehok my fenfe of this politenefs, and, after accepting an invitation to dine at the houfe of one of thefe gentlemen, I was conducted by him to fee the curiofities of the place.

The cathedral was built by St. Bridget in 1348. Near it ftands a building, the remains of a monaftery eftablifhed by the fame perfon, but now converted to a more ufeful purpofe, having been endowed

dowed by Queen Chriſtina, with a fund for the ſupport of wounded and aged ſoldiers. Mr. Eillehok has at preſent the ſuperintendance of this inſtitution, which admits only a limited number. In the cathedral the ornaments of the altar, the crucifix, the ſtatues of male and female ſaints, and that of St. Bridget herſelf, are exactly the ſame as in her time. A ſon of Guſtavus Vaſa, known in hiſtory by the name of Duke Magnus, lies interred here. Of feeble intellects from his earlieſt childhood, his father aſſigned him a reſidence in a large gothic ſeat, that ſtill remains entire, the façade of which is a beautiful ſpecimen of this ſort of architecture. It is built of ſtone, and ſtands cloſe to the town, upon the bank of the lake. The inſide is now entirely deſtroyed, and has been fitted up for a diſtillery of brandy, and a manufactory of linens.

After viewing the cathedral, Mr. Eillehok conducted me to another church, of leſs ſize, but tolerably handſome, where were depoſited the reliques of St. Bridget. She died at Rome, and ſome Pope, I know not who, ſent her bones hither, where they lay in a fine coffin, covered with red velvet, and ornamented with inſcriptions upon plates of ſilver. A ſmall chapel, in which they are placed, receives the viſits of the curious and devout.

From this diſmal ſcene I was very glad to be ſummoned to dinner, where the lady of the counſellor did the honours of the table, and, by her politeneſs

politeness and attractions, interested me much more than all the venerable antiquities which I left behind. Afterwards we walked towards the lake, which I was assured, sometimes exhibits a phænomenon still more curious than the appearance and disappearance of the island near Lindkioping. In the stillest and most delightful weather, it becomes on a sudden, violently agitated, and the waves rise to such a height as to make navigation dangerous. The physical cause of this effect has been long sought for, and that to which it is now attributed is very singular. It has been observed, that the lake is never thus agitated without an apparent cause, except when that of Constance in Switzerland is disturbed by some tempest, and, *vice versa*, that whenever the wind raises the waters here, those of Constance are moved in the same sudden, and wonderful manner. From these circumstances a communication has been supposed to exist between the two lakes, and the conjecture is further supported by the appearance of some plants in each lake, known to be peculiar to the neighbourhood of the other. At Wadstena they make no scruple to account for the phænomenon, by attributing it to such a communication; but you will consider how far a circumstance so improbable is proved by the facts here mentioned.

I am, &c. &c. &c.

LETTER XV.

Copenhagen, Jan..... 1786.

MY DEAR FRIEND,

I LEFT Wadſtena at ſix o'clock at night, and, after a continued journey of two nights and a day, arrived at Carlſcroon. My road lay through Smoland, three-fourths of which conſiſt of immenſe woods and barren rocks, ſometimes ornamented with heaps of ſtones that ſeem to have been piled up by the hand of man, but very ſeldom exhibiting any ſigns either of inhabitation or culture. There are, however, ſome mines, and, amongſt them, one of gold at Adelfors; but this is chiefly remarkable for the ſpirit which induces the adventurers to continue their operations, notwithſtanding the unprofitable labour and expence at preſent beſtowed upon it.

The inhabitants of Smoland are large and robuſt, and have the reputation of being deſcended, with leſs corruption than thoſe of the other provinces, from the ancient Goths. They always intermarry with each other, and from time immemorial no ſtranger has been known to ſettle amongſt them.

Carlscroon, the capital of the province of Bleking, and the residence of the governor, is situated upon the shore of the Baltic sea, and built upon a large insulated rock. The road to it is over two other islands, which are joined to the main-land by three large bridges, and contain two suburbs of considerable size, but dirty and ill-built, being inhabited only by the lower sort of people. The city takes its name from its founder, Charles the Eleventh. The houses, though mostly of wood, are very well built, and many are raised to the height of three stories, ornamented with sculpture and colonnades, and painted so as to have a very beautiful appearance. A handsome church, which is now building at one of the extremities near the dock-yard, is intended to form the center of a large square, composed of many elegant houses. While I was there they were employed in levelling the ground for the scite of this square, by frequent explosions of gun-powder, an operation which was also performed in several streets, where the rock rose in pointed projections so as to make walking inconvenient, and travelling in a voiture impossible.

The inhabitants of Carlscroon consider *Bleking* as the finest province in the kingdom, and, although I was not quite of the same opinion, it must be admitted that the country is in many places very fruitful, and contains many fine estates and seats of

the

the nobility. The province supports no soldiers, but is obliged to furnish a regiment of marines; a sort of militia, which, when the whole number is mustered from the different estates, amounts to 13,000 men. Of these seldom more than a thousand are employed, except in time of war, and during their meetings to exercise. The garrison of Carlscroon consists of 1,600 men, divided into three companies.

I had two letters of recommendation, one for Mr. Pylgardt, a rich merchant, honoured with the title of Patron of the mines, the other for Vice Admiral Chapman, director of the dock-yard, a man of very superior talents, to which he owes his fortune, and much esteemed among the Swedes. He has particularly distinguished himself in naval architecture, having invented a new section, and executed a model upon which the fastest sailing vessels in the Swedish service are said to have been built. A work written by him upon the subject of the navy, is also well known and received.

The next day I was conducted by an officer, who had been in our service under Mr. Dedel, to the port. This is very large and convenient, being almost surrounded with docks, and having a long bridge, on the two sides of which vessels not in use are kept at moorings. I reckoned here twenty-eight vessels of the line, and frigates, amongst which were one of 100 guns, one of 96, one of 84, two of 74, and several of 60 and 50 guns. The whole fleet, including five vessels now equipping, consists of 37 vessels of the line, and 9 frigates. The five vessels thus fitting out, and four others, which were in the water, but unrigged, were built in the course of four years. There were several upon the stocks, either wholly, or almost in skeleton, and I was shewn one of these vessels, which was constructed in six weeks, all the parts having been prepared before-hand. The plan of reviving and increasing the naval force was concerted about four years ago; one part of 1782 was spent in preparing and collecting the materials, and in 1783 they began to build. It is intended to build four vessels annually, till the fleet shall be restored to a respectable situation; and, to defray the expences of this plan, the King has suspended the execution of half the works at the new dock. These works are, indeed, stupendous, and exceeded all the high-wrought expectations which I had conceived from the accounts given of them. Twenty-nine years have been already spend in forming them, and they yet want much of completion. At the entrance is a bason hollowed in the rock, of about fifty feet in depth, and surrounded by quays of free-stone, at which four men of war may at the same time receive or discharge their stores. From this bason canals of communication are formed, that, by means of large locks, afford a passage for

each

each vessel into its own dock, of which there are twenty for ships of the line, and ten for frigates.

One of these separate docks, with its canal and lock, is entirely finished. The bottom is composed of free stone, joined and cemented with pouzzolane, a sort of cement, brought for that purpose from Italy, and laid in a bed, which has been hollowed in the rock, exactly of the shape of a ship's keel. Along the whole length of this dock, they have contrived two stair-cases * of stone, by means of which they erect the beams or scaffoldings, when the vessel is rendered entirely dry, in order to be repaired. The walls, which support the roofs and separate the docks from each other, are formed of the same free stone and cement, and are at least of the thickness of twenty feet up to the height of the vessel's upper deck. There platforms are constructed for the reception of the guns of each vessel, which are delivered and received through large arched openings communicating with the platform, and with the inside of the dock.

The roof is of timber, plated on the outside with iron, and so contrived as to bear all the levers used in loading and unloading the vessel. When the dock is to be rendered perfectly dry, the water is suffered to run through a vent in the bot-

---

* Galleries are probably meant. T.

tom, which they open by a machine prepared for that purpose; it is then received in a bason hollowed immediately under the dock, and from thence is forced, by means of a windmill, into the other bason before mentioned.

These covered lodges, when the plan is perfected, will form a large semi-circle; but the second is yet unfinished, and, from the immense expences of the undertaking, it seems doubtful whether the whole number will ever be completed. At present they are chiefly employed upon the improvement of the ancient dock, which will, probably, be not less useful than the new one. Indeed, it is by no means certain that vessels can be preserved by this method longer than by those now in use; and, even if this is admitted, it will still remain to be enquired, how far the millions expended in forming the docks, sluices, basons, and canals, are likely to be repaid by the savings proposed.

This new dock was begun in the late reign, upon a plan suggested by one *Thunberg*, now a very old man, who has the direction of the works constructing upon the river Gothe. The ancient dock, which is a sort of canal of 350 feet in length and 30 in depth, was hollowed in the rock, and entirely completed between the years 1715, and 1724. It was planned by Polheim, and is situated between the port and the new dock, communicating, on one side, with the dock-yard and port, and, on the other, with the sea, by means of two canals of such size as to admit the passage of first rate men of war. Both canals are enclosed by very large flood-gates, and before that which opens towards the sea, they have placed a moveable dam of very ingenious construction, in order to protect the sluice from the violence of the waves. When a vessel has entered the dock, in order to be calked, they shut the gates, place the dam before them, and an immense pump is put in motion, either by men, or horses, which in twelve hours renders the dock entirely dry.

The port of Carlscroon, which is very deep, and easy of entrance, is capable of containing an hundred ships of the line. It is defended by two strong forts, whose fires cross each other, and are undoubtedly able to sink any fleet that should attempt to force a passage. They are both built upon rocks in the sea; the one called *Kongsholm* (King's Island) the other *Drotnings-kiar* or Queen's Rock.

Within a quarter of a league of Runneby, a large and flourishing town three miles from Carlscroon, is a mineral spring, at which the nobility of Bleking, and the polite inhabitants of Carlscroon, assemble for their health and amusement. The season had expired before my arrival, but I was received by the physician, who has the care of the place, and saluted, as strangers usually are, by a

battery

battery of six pieces of cannon. From thence I went to Carlsham, a place of considerable trade, and a fort of the Baltic, which exports great quantities of iron, and is defended by a fort built upon a rock in the open sea. The town is very irregularly situated, and, in some parts, the inhabitants on one side of a street, have their view of the opposite houses intercepted by high and steep rocks.

In my road to Christianstadt, I passed through a small and wretched hamlet, called *Hembrohult*, which attracted my notice, as the birth-place of Linnæus, whose father here executed the duties of a parish priest for forty years. A complete collection of indiginous plants formed by him, first excited in his son a taste for botany.

Christianstadt is a fortress situated upon the small river Helga, which, after supplying the ditches of the fortifications with water, falls into a lake that communicates with the Baltic. The bridge and ramparts, at that time, furnished employment to a party of criminals, consisting of deserters, and of persons whose sentences have been changed from death to slavery. These unhappy wretches are chained together in couples, and each couple, upon their route to and from their cells, is fastened to a long chain; one, or, sometimes, two overseers, armed with staffs, guard the whole party, and drive them forward rather like beasts than men.

Each

Each criminal is allowed for his support five Swedish sols *per* day.

The town has a manufacture of gloves, much esteemed for the softness of the leather and the neatness of the workmanship. It is a well fortified place, built in the form of a long square by Christian IV. King of Denmark, in 1614. In the wars between the Swedes and Danes it has often been besieged and taken, and is now a garrison town, defended by a part of the King's own regiment.

Scania, both in appearance and value, much exceeds any of the other provinces in Sweden. Its gentle hills and luxuriant vallies produce every sort of grain, and afford pasture to numerous herds of cattle; while the many well-built towns and elegant houses, prove the riches and activity of the inhabitants. In a subsequent letter I propose to give you an account of the principal places, and in the mean time I remain, &c. &c. &c.

LETTER XVI.

Copenhagen, Jan. . . . 1786.

MY DEAR FRIEND,

My journey from Christianstadt to Ystadt, lay through a sandy plain of four miles, which the extraordinary dryness of this year

year rendered so very heavy, that six horses could scarcely draw me through it in a day. But this slowness is very unusual in Sweden. The presents, by which in France, Germany, and other countries you urge the postilions to get forward, should here be employed only in moderating their ardour, and preventing their galloping down the descents of mountains, with the reins thrown upon the horses necks, and the wheels of the carriage unlocked. Their dexterity, indeed, is very great, but a stranger is at first alarmed by such uncommon rapidity, which seems more dangerous from the youth and apparent incapacity of the postilions, who are often boys of thirteen or fourteen years old, and, sometimes, especially in the season of harvest, only women or girls.

Near *Trollebo*, or the Sorcerer's nest, I stopped to examine a stone of very remarkable size, which stands by the side of the road. It is called *Maglasteen*, and is twenty feet in height, twenty-four broad, and thirty in length. The country people believe it to have been placed there by some dwarf sorcerers on the day the first church was consecrated. At the seignorial estate of *Luingsby*, not far from this stone, a horn is preserved, said to have been taken in 1490 from these dwarf sorcerers, who, on the nights immediately preceding Christmas, used to raise the stone upon pillars, and dance under and around it. The whole story is written upon

parchment,

parchment, and preferved among the archives of Luingſby, with the veneration due to an evangelical writing. The horn is fomething leſs than that of a cow, and, in the feaſts of former times, has probably ferved the warriors as a drinking cup.

The exiſtence of a fubterraneous people is believed in many parts of Sweden, and in fome iſlands of the Baltic, amongſt which is that of Bornholm. This iſland belongs to the Danes, and I was aſſured by fome of them that the inhabitants rely much upon the aſſiſtance of a warlike and forcerous people, who are ever ready to protect them againſt their enemies.

Yſtadt is a fmall, but well-built town, fituated upon the Baltic Sea, and diſtant, in a direct line, about fourteen German miles from Stralfund, the capital of Swediſh Pomerania, with which place a communication is conſtantly kept up by packet-boats.

Malmoë, the capital of Scania, is fituated upon the Sound, oppoſite to Copenhagen, and at the diſtance of about four miles. It is well built, and is faid to contain about fix thoufand inhabitants. A company of artillery, another of huſſars, and a part of the Queen's regiment compofe the garrifon; and in the center of a large fquare ſtands a very fuitable building, which is uſed as a grand guard room. The cathedral is leſs than thofe of Upfal and Linkiöping, but is of fome beauty, and ornamented with a marble pulpit. One of the pillars is hollow, and the perfon who ſhews the

the church assures you, that a monk was formerly immured in it for life, as a punishment for adultery. " Through that hole," says he, " eggs and " water were conveyed to him, to prolong his ex-" istence and his sufferings, and his skull still re-" mains at the top of it, to prove the truth of the " story." Wraxall mentions the circumstance in his travels, and appears to have no doubt of its truth; but it is clear enough that what they call a skull is nothing more than the remains of an ancient pot, which once held the holy water. The tower of this church commands a fine view of the country, the straits, and the distant spires of Copenhagen.

In the town-house, which is a very handsome building, there is a large chamber, called the hall of Canute, where a religious society, consisting of many persons of distinction of both sexes, holds its meetings. It was incorporated by Canute IV. or the Saint, and bears his name. The hall is ornamented with the portraits of many kings and queens of Sweden and Denmark, who have become members of the society, and honoured its meetings with their presence. The presents of the different sovereigns are also preserved, and amongst others are three crane-necked bottles of immense size, made of silver, elegantly carved and gilt. The largest was given by Frederic II. of Denmark.

The

The city, on the land fide, is defended by ramparts, baftions, and ditches; and towards the fea, by a fquare fort with two ditches and a double rampart. The exterior inclofure is guarded by a detachment of artillery; and the interior, in which there is an old caftle, now ufed only as a prifon, by one of infantry. The latter rampart has alfo four orillons of ftone, which formerly, no doubt, were a confiderable defence.

Lund, Is a fmall city, chiefly remarkable for the univerfity founded there by Charles IX. in 1666. It is moftly reforted to for theological ftudies, but they have an obfervatory, an anatomical theatre, and a botanical garden, of which the firft is inferior even to that at Upfal, and the latter very fmall and badly preferved, the orangery being occupied by fome women employed in winding filk for a manufacture eftablifhed here. The cathedral is large, but without any object much worthy of notice. Among the many relics, they fhow you a fhift worn by St. Vierge, long *Virgin* enough to make a night-gown for the largeft grenadier in the Pruffian fervice.

Under the cathedral is a fubterraneous church, fupported by rows of pillars, between which are the tombs of the ancient archbifhops. I defcended into it, and was fhewn a well, the water of which is conducted into all the houfes in the city, and alfo two iron gates, opening into a gallery, which

runs

runs under ground as far as Dalby, a small town, at the distance of a mile from Lund. The church and gallery are said to have afforded a refuge to the catholics in times of persecution. At this university Linnæus acquired the elements of his botanical knowledge, and from the ramparts of the city collected the plants described in his Flora Lundensis.

From Lund I went to Landscrona, a very ancient town, situated, like Malmoë, upon the bank of the Sound. Adjoining to it they are building a new town, upon a plan first begun by the late king. Many elegant houses are already finished, and strangers, especially those who build, are invited to reside here by the concession of some considerable privileges. The superb barracks for the garrison, and a magnificent hospital founded by the late queen, make two sides of a square, in which they are now constructing a handsome church, intended to form the center of the new town.

A port is also intended to be established here, and, to defend it, a fortress is building at a small distance in the sea, founded partly upon a rock, and partly upon piles. The undertaking, if it succeeds, will certainly be very detrimental to the Danes, by inviting many vessels to lie for shelter on this side of the Sound. But they consider its success as very doubtful, because the shores are
rendered

rendered dangerous by fands, which the ftillnefs of the fea permits to accumulate, while thofe of Zealand, being cleanfed by continual currents, always afford a fufficient depth of water. The new town, however, and its fortrefs may be confidered as one of thofe vaft and fpirited undertakings, in which the Swedes exercife their genius and induſtry, under fo many difadvantageous circumſtances both of nature and fortune.

The garrifon at Landſcrona confifts of the regiment of Lieutenant General Sprengporten, commander of the order of the Sword, and Envoy Extraordinary to the Court of Denmark *. It contains 800 men, who, for figure and difcipline, are confidered as the flower of the Swedifh army.

While my paffage over the Sound from Helfingburg was prevented by a ftorm, I went to fee Ramlös, a mineral watering-place, much frequented by the nobility and the opulent inhabitants of Scania, who ufually affemble here in July, and choofe fome popular nobleman to do the honours, and direct the amufements of the place. The well-known politenefs of the Swedes to ftrangers, the beauty of the fituation, and the falubrity of the climate, attract here a great deal of company from Denmark for the feafon; and the balls, which are always held on a Sunday, are attended by the

* He received the appointment of ambaffador in 1788.

M   nobility,

nobility, foreign minifters and many other perfons from Copenhagen. At Helfingburg I concluded my tour through the kingdom of Sweden, and embarked for Denmark, of which country I intend fhortly to fend you fome particulars. In the mean time I remain

Your &c. &c.

LETTER XVII.

Copenhagen, Jan. . . . 1786.

MY DEAR FRIEND,

IN my voyage from Helfingburg to Elfineur, the waters, agitated by the ftorm of the preceding day and night, ftill rolled tumultuoufly along, and the little bark, to which I had committed myfelf, rofe and fell at the impulfe of every paffing wave. By degrees the clouded atmofphere yielded to the influence of the dawn, and, at length the fun arofe in all his glory, contrafting by the brightnefs of his beams the darknefs of the turbulent fea. Surrounded by thefe great objects, in which nature feems to exprefs and exert her powers, my mind rofe to that degree of abftraction at which the thoughts fix upon one fet of objects, and are wholly withdrawn from the reft of the world. In this reverie, as I confidered the different degrees of happinefs or mifery, which I
had

had either experienced or witnessed, I thought nothing so much resembled the variety and inconstancy of human life, as the waves of a stormy sea, agitated by continual conflicts, and mutually destroying, and destroyed by each other.

At length we approached the shores of Denmark, and a view of the castle of Cronenburg put an end to my reverie. This ancient castle, surrounded with towers and ramparts, fills the mind with a melancholy awe, and excites one's pity for the unfortunate Queen, who here passed four months and a half, in all the fluctuations of fear, hope, grief, and despair. Within a few years afterwards, another Queen, retiring * from the world, took up her residence in a neighbouring castle, and dedicated her life to acts of charity and devotion. Ever since the Prince Royal obtained the presidency of the council of state, Queen Julia has withdrawn herself from all concern in the government, and resided at the castle of Friedensburg. But her tranquillity is, perhaps, sometimes interrupted, when, from the hills of Friedensburg, she views the distant towers of Copenhagen, and recollects the catastrophe of the night between the 18th and 19th of January, 1772, in which a young, beautiful and amiable Queen, born with all the qualities that might entitle her to happiness, but enthralled by the fatality of circumstances, and

* Or driven. T.

misled

misled by the openness of her own disposition, was roused from her bed, after the pleasures and fatigues of a brilliant fête, and torn away from every thing she held most dear to her.

The unfortunate Matilda, after being forcibly seized by Count Rantzau, and some other officers, was conducted to a coach and six, in which a captain of horse with his drawn sword, an inferior officer, and one of the women of her chamber, immediately placed themselves. Thus accompanied, and escorted by 24 dragoons, she was taken to the castle of Cronenburg, whither the Princess Augusta, then a child of six months old, followed her in another coach, with a guard and one lady.—Queen Julia, in the stillness of her present retreat, may frequently recur to the dangers of that memorable night, when the obstinacy of a valet, in refusing the keys of the King's bed-chamber, the tender and variable disposition of the Count de Rantzau, the attachment of a number of courtiers to Matilda, the affection of the King for his wife, and his friendship for Struenzee, formed a series of obstacles which nothing less than the most perfect courage and address could surmount.

But to return to my own situation. In the roads we passed through a fleet of three hundred vessels of all nations, and after many tacks, which gave us a full view of the whole, arrived at Elseneur. There I was detained four hours for horses, and

might

might have waited much longer, but for the obliging attentions of Meffieurs Fenwick and Godin. In this town, frequented as the grand thoroughfare between Sweden and Denmark, the pofts are fo badly regulated, that ftrangers are frequently obliged to wait four-and-twenty hours.

In the mean time I went to fee the caftle of Cronenburg, which is feparated from Elfeneur, only by an alley of linden-trees. After fome cuftomary ceremonies, we were permitted to fee it, the officer of the guard having obtained the leave of the governor, Major General de Beffel. I defired to be fhewn the apartments formerly occupied by the Queen; and the manner in which I was gratified, fhewed the requeft to be by no means unufual. The fuite now forms the refidence of the governor, and confifts of feveral commodious chambers, very fimple, and plainly furnifhed, which interefted me fo much, on account of their late inhabitant, that I could fcarcely withdraw myfelf from them. The reft of the caftle attracted my notice but little, though there were fome paintings reprefenting the wars of Chriftian V. by Carl van Manderen, and a portrait of Admiral Tromp by the fame hand*. I, how-

---

* Carl van Manderen, born at Harlem about the latter end of the fixteenth century, was appointed painter to the court of Frederic the Third of Denmark, and executed a portrait of that Prince, which Vondel has celebrated in a dozen good couplets.

The father of Carl van Manderen was both a painter and a poet.

ever, admired the immense subterraneous works, used as casemates by the soldiers, and a battery level with the water, constructed upon an abutment raised in the Sound, with which they pretend they can reach the opposite shore. It has to endure the efforts of a very heavy and tempestuous sea; but the undertakers seem not at all to doubt the strength of their work.

Hirsholm, a castle situated in a delightful valley, half-way from Elseneur to Copenhagen, was given by the King to Matilda before their separation. Here she frequently retired with select parties; and, freeing herself from the artificial restraints of ceremony, participated in those social delights, which the openness of her disposition, and the goodness of her heart so well qualified her to receive and communicate. But her fondness for pleasure, the ready influence of persuasion over her mind, and the unsuitable circumstances of her marriage, afforded her enemies an opportunity of exciting suspicions, which might have been easily dissipated by a little more caution on her part, or a little less ambition on the part of Struenzee.

Having thus filled my mind with the remembrance of the circumstances attendant upon the fall of this unfortunate Queen, permit me to give you some account of her children, and of the measures by which the powers of government have been
wrested

wrested from those who obtained them by the destruction of Matilda.

The Princess Royal, with talents which do honour to the education she has received, very much resembles her late mother in beauty of countenance, liveliness of disposition, and innate excellence of heart. The Prince Royal is, in person, much like the King, but his eye-brows are very thick, and his hair almost white. He has a serious and pensive air, speaks little in public, and seems much attached to the army, which he frequently exercises, and has conciliated, by an augmentation of pay, and by appearing constantly in a military uniform. Those who approach him most nearly speak highly of his abilities, and declare their expectations of his attaining a very superior degree of knowledge in the difficult science of governing; while his only ambition seems to be that of affording happiness to a people, whose liberal concession of absolute power so well entitles them to the gratitude and attention of their monarchs.

On the 28th of March, 1784, this Prince, being then 16 years and two months old, was confirmed in the chapel of the castle, in the presence of the nobility, foreign ministers, chiefs of the different departments and other persons of distinction, who were invited. He was examined as to the principles of religion by Mr. Bashholm, first chaplain to the court, and for three hours together replied to every question with admirable presence of mind, acuteness, and propriety. After this ceremony he was declared of age, and a day appointed for his taking his seat at the council, in the presidency of which he was to succeed his uncle Prince Frederic. Mr. Gulberg, formerly preceptor to Prince Frederic, afterwards secretary to the cabinet, and at length minister of state; Mr. Rosencrone, minister of foreign affairs; and Mr. Stehman, minister of the finances, were then added to the council, and Mr. Sporon, sub-governor to the Prince Royal, was appointed secretary to the cabinet. On the 28th of the preceding January, being the birth-day of the prince, several pensions had been augmented, and eight new Knights of the Holy Ghost were made, amongst whom was Mr. Moltke, steward of the household to Queen Julia.

At length the great day arrived, which was entirely to change the face of affairs in Denmark. The Prince Royal, seizing the moment, when, on account of relieving the guard, a part of the garrison were under arms, gave orders that no persons should quit their post till they had received permission from him. The council were then assembled, and the Prince with a paper in his hand, entered the King's apartment, where he found his uncle considerably surprized at his appearance. In a firm but respectful manner, he addressed the King, under whom, he said, the laws now called

upon

upon him to govern, with the affiftance of a council, which he was defirous fhould be compofed only of perfons worthy of his confidence. To this end, he faid, he had projected a change of members in the actual council, and had prepared a memoir upon the fubject, which he hoped his Majefty would give him permiffion to read, and would afterwards honour with his approbation and fignature. His firmnefs overcame the attempts made to intimidate him; he read his paper, and the King figned it.

With this authority for his conduct, he prefented himfelf to the council, and, in a manner at once decifive and modeft, returned his thanks to all the members, efpecially to his uncle, for their exertions in behalf of a government, which, during the melancholy fituation of his father, devolved to him of right. At the fame time he notified that he had formed a new council, and had excluded Meffieurs Rofencrone, Gulberg, Stehman, and Moltke, whom he, however, affured of his protection, and promifed to recompenfe for the lofs of their places by penfions or fome equivalent provifion. Finally, he requefted Prince Ferdinand to affift him with his advice, and to honour the new board with his prefence.

From the aftonifhed members, who, though they knew a revolution to be intended, believed it to be very improbable or diftant, the Prince went to the castle guard, and addressed the officers of foot and horse, whom he found assembled according to his orders. They immediately bound themselves to him by an oath, and he passed on to the apartment of Queen Julia, to inform her of what had been done, and to assure her that his conduct should always be marked with that respect which her rank required, and which his attachment to her person so much inclined him to shew. He invited her to retain the same apartments which she then inhabited, but at the same time gave her the liberty of choosing any of the royal castles to retire to, and very delicately insinuated, that for the future all affairs would be transacted by himself and his council alone.

After this visit, he assembled together the governor of the city, Prince Bevern, the commander of the citadel, the chiefs of the different departments, the commanders of the fourteen battalions in garrison, the colonel of the *Bourgeoise* and the officer of the police, and informed them that his orders were alone to be obeyed.

The same day Mr. de Shack, high-steward of the court, and Mr. Jacobi, reader to the King, received their dismissions, and were succeeded by four chamberlains, to whose immediate care the King's safety, health, and amusements were committed. Mr. de Shack was appointed grand-master of the ceremonies, an office not affording any employment

employment at court, and which gave him no right of accefs to the King's perfon. Upon his retirement foon after, his place was given to Mr. de Numfen, director of the chamber of tolls at Elfeneur, and fon of the lady who had the care of the Prince Royal in his infancy. This gentleman, who has refided in many foreign courts, and is a patron of learning and the polite arts, is here held in very high eftimation, as a man of tafte, politenefs, and knowledge of the world. At the fame time Mr. Sporon was difmiffed from his place of fecretary to the cabinet, which he had hardly enjoyed long enough to receive the compliments of his friends upon his appointment.

An exprefs was fent to Count Bernftorf, who refided upon his eftates in the country, inviting him to accept the office of minifter of foreign affairs, vacant by the difmiffion of the Count de Rofencrone, and held in the mean time by Mr. Shack-Ratlau.

Count Rofencrone, within a few days afterwards, retired to Jutland, where he has fome very confiderable eftates, and was rewarded by a penfion of 2500 crowns. Defcended from a family but lately ennobled, he was at firft employed only in foreign embaffies; but his adminiftration here gained him the character of an honeft man; and the mildnefs of his deportment and manners makes his abfence regretted

regretted by all who knew him as a man, or had occasion to transact business with him as a minister.

Count Schimmelman, son of the famous Schimmelman, succeeded to the post of minister of the finances, in the room of Mr. Stehman, who was appointed to the balliage of Hadersleben. Mr. Stehman, a laborious and able calculator, owes his fortune entirely to his abilities, which yet seem not sufficiently extensive or powerful to qualify him for the post of minister in a country, where the resources are but ill-proportioned to the necessities of government, and the many improvements projected throughout the kingdom.

Mr. Gulberg, quitting the ministry and the council, remains in the service of Prince Frederic, as high-steward of his household, a post bestowed upon him a few months before the revolution, with a pension of 2,000 crowns, to which he now adds another of 2,500, in quality of a dismissed minister. He is of plebeian extraction, his father having been a priest in Norway, and himself having served a church at Rotschild, which he quitted to become preceptor to Prince Frederic. But his powers have gained him the admiration, and his amiable qualities the love of all the nation. He is inquisitive, laborious, and seems to have little taste for what is generally called pleasure, as I have never seen him at any ball, fête, or public spectacle during my residence at Copenhagen.

The

The labours of study employ his mind, while domestic pleasures engage his heart. He has married successively the two daughters of a miller at Friedensburg. Prince Frederic and Queen Julia honour him with their entire confidence.

General Eichstadt, the late governor of the Prince Royal, who commanded the dragoons in the revolution of 1772, having quitted the council, and been dismissed from his post of colonel of the horse-guards, now lives in retirement upon his estates with the appointment of grand chamberlain of the realm.

The report of the Prince Royal's conduct was soon circulated through the city, and the people, who had always expected to see revived in him the virtues of his grand-father, Frederic the Fifth, began to assemble in great numbers before the castle, testifying their impatience to see the new regent. He appeared in his uniform as a general, and was saluted on all sides by the most joyful acclamations. Afterwards, accompanied by his Marshal, the Baron de Bulau, and followed only by one footman, he walked through the principal streets of Copenhagen, and from the immense crowds with which they were filled, continued to receive expressions of attachment and esteem.

His conduct was certainly equally distinguished by the firmness with which he executed his plan, and his moderation in enjoying the success of it.

Even

Even thofe whom he thought proper to difmifs from their employments, his humanity would not permit him to deprive of fupport. They were all recompenfed, in a greater or lefs degree by penfions, balliages, or other employments; and, although removed from all intereft in the affairs of the capital, were left to the quiet enjoyment of their own principles and poffeffions. Indeed, the late miniftry is admitted to have governed with moderation and gentlenefs, affording conftant encouragement to the arts and fciences, and endeavouring to promote the general welfare, by preferving the peace of the nation, and the domeftic tranquillity of the people. But the remembrance of the bloody cataftrophe by which they firft obtained their power; and of the fubfequent fufferings of an unfortunate Queen, excited a fpirit of difcontent, which the perfonal qualities of her children, and the endeavours of the Englifh party, confiderably tended to promote.

The actual council, to which, under the prefidency of the Prince Royal, all matters are reported, after paffing through the different departments, confifts, befides Prince Frederic, of the following minifters.

The Count de Bernftorf, minifter for foreign affairs, and prefident of the German Chancery; the Baron de Rofencrantz, prefident of the College of Admiralty; the Baron de Schack-Ratlau, patron

tron of the University of Copenhagen; Monsieur de Huth, commander in chief of the Artillery, and president of the College of War; and Monsieur de Stampe, president of the Danish Chancery.

The Count de Bernstorf is the nephew of the celebrated Count of the same name, known to posterity for his services under the glorious reign of Frederic the Fifth. By a personal intercourse with the different courts of Europe, he has obtained a profound knowledge of their interests; and with a state of health which seems at best to be precarious, he is laborious, active, and indefatigable. His present office is now held by him for the second time. Involved in 1771, under the administration of Struenzee, in the disgrace of his uncle, he was recalled in 1773 under that of Prince Frederic. In 1780 he was obliged to retire, a short time after having signed, conjointly with the ministers of Russia and Sweden, the famous treaty of armed neutrality. The Empress suspecting, from his known attachment to England, some delay in the preparation of the stipulated armaments, solicited and obtained his dismission. The Danish court had at that time strong reasons for conciliating the favour of that of Russia, and the regret which accompanied Bernstorf, upon his departure for his estates, together with the satisfaction of the nation upon his re-appointment by the Prince Royal,

Royal, prove that he was then made a sacrifice to its interests.

The Baron de Rosencrantz, during the absence of the King upon his travels, and before the administration of Struenzee, had the direction of the war department. He is a man of very superior powers, has great knowledge of the world, a polite and easy manner, with every qualification requisite for shining in a court.

The Baron de Shack-Ratlau is esteemed for his abilities, and acquirements in literature and the polite arts, and has acquired the general esteem of the nation for his noble and generous conduct at the beginning of the administration of Struenzee*.

Monsieur de Huth, who, at the age of seventy-five, appears to have all the vigour of a man of forty, owes his present elevation entirely to his own exertions. He was born in Hesse, and, after serving in several wars, came into the service of Denmark, as a lieutenant-colonel, under the administration of the Count de St. Germain. His manners are very plain, and, besides his reputation as a professional man, he has the character of great integrity, and moral propriety of conduct.

Monsieur de Stampe is also much esteemed.

The four first ministers are knights of the order of the Elephant; Monsieur de Stampe of that of

---

* The two last noblemen quitted the council in the end of the year 1783.

Danne-

Dannebrog. The Count de Schimmelman, a knight the order of Dannebrog, and minister of finances and commerce, has not yet taken his seat at the council*. His application and activity afford hopes that he will one day equal the reputation of his father, whose memory will for ever be respected in Denmark, especially by the merchants, who are now about to erect a statue of him before their exchange. A model of it, executed by an Italian, named Rosci, was shewn to me. He is represented in the dress of a knight, and surrounded by the different attributes of commerce.

The Prince Royal, not content with the presidency and the advice of this council, pays daily visits to the ministers and chiefs of the different departments, in order to acquire a knowledge of every public transaction, and enable himself one day to govern alone.

Having thus taken a view of the government of Denmark, permit me to conclude by assuring you how much

I am, &c. &c. &c.

* He took his seat in the beginning of the year 1789.

LETTER XVIII.

Copenhagen, Feb. ... 1786.

MY DEAR FRIEND,

To your enquiries respecting those circumstances in which the inhabitants of Sweden and Denmark differ from, or resemble each other, I am glad that my researches enable me to afford you an answer.

The Strait, called the Sound, separates the two nations, which, with the same origin and language, and, almost, with the same climate, have yet some considerable points of difference, which appear both between the countries and their inhabitants. In Denmark there are no rivers, and the whole country consists of rising hills and open valleys, with a rich but stony soil, and some small lakes. In Sweden, on the contrary, the lakes and rivers are very large, and one perceives only mountains, rocks, valleys, and forests. The Swedes are lively, laborious, and susceptible of sudden attachments. The Danes, with an inclination to repose, and a serious, phlegmatic disposition, are slower in forming friendships, but very constant in preserving them. The Swedes are of a slight, but strong make, which they shew by a short blue dress; while the

heavier

heavier figure of the Danes is covered by a long red garment. It is the opinion of some learned men, that the Swedes, in the eleventh and twelfth centuries, were of much greater size than at present; and upon this subject, the memoirs of their academy relate the following circumstances:

"On the 22d of July, 1764, in digging up the
" cemetery of the ancient monastery of Wreta,
" several stone chests were found at the depth of
" two ells under the earth, containing human
" bones of an immense size. At the depth of
" four ells, in a very fine white sand, a skeleton
" was found perfectly preserved, and about eight
" feet long.—And in laying the foundation of the
" tower at Lindkiöping, two skeletons of equal
" size were dug up, one of which still retained the
" mark of a deep wound in the skull.

" The bones of King Inge Halstansons, which
" repose in a stone coffin, in the church of Wreta,
" are nearly of the same dimensions, and history
" tells us that the Kings Stenkilson and his nephew
" Ragwald Knaphöfding, who lived in the begin-
" ning of the 14th century, were of still greater
" size.

" Such skeletons are also frequently dug up in
" ancient cemeteries.*"

* Memoires de l'Acad. des Sciences de Suede, tom. 27, pag. 334. tom. 28, p. 274.

The Swedish and Danish languages have one origin, and are, indeed, only different dialects of the same language varied by the manners and characters of the people. They are both pronounced in a singing, or chanting tone, but the Swedes chaunt more quickly, and, after lowering the voice upon the penultimate, raise it again upon the last syllable. The Danish words end chiefly in consonants, as book, hest, baker; and the Swedish in vowels, of which *a* is the most common, as boka, hesta, baka. The words in each language mean *a book*, *a horse*, *a mountain*. The Swedish manner in speaking would inspire even an unintelligent listener with gaiety, while the mournful accent, and, almost guttural pronunciation of the Danes, impresses only sensations of melancholy.

The women of both countries are handsome, amiable, and well educated, having delicate, and, for the most part fair complexions, blue eyes and fine hair. The Swedish women are well made, have an animated air, expressive countenances, and light figures: those of Denmark are duller, and inclined to become corpulent. The first seem more susceptible of the desires, the latter of the tenderness of love. In Denmark the women of the middle and lower classes are very fond of shew,

The famous Cajanus, who was publicly exhibited, and died in Holland, was a Swede, of the province of Ostrobothnia. He is said to have been above eight feet, and might have given one a very good idea of an ancient Goth.

and their drefs, which is prepared with great care, and obtained at any rate, is compofed of materials of many colours, amongft which red is the moft prevalent. The Swedifh women of the fame condition always wear veils, and thofe employed in the labours of the field have their's of black crape; an ufeful cuftom in a country where the eyes are liable to be weakened by the glare of the fnow in winter, and the reflection of the fun from the rocks during the long days of fummer.

The Danes readily permit ftrangers to fettle amongft them, and there are many foreign noblemen and perfons in political, military, and private employments, eftablifhed in all parts of the kingdom. But the Swedes preferve their diftinction as an original people, having mingled with very few families of foreign extraction. By the tenth article of the new conftitution it is enacted, in conformity to the old one, " That no ftranger, of whatever " condition, or rank, not even a prince, fhall be " employed in the political, military, or civil de-
" partments, or fhall be capable of holding any " poft not immediately belonging to the court."

Both nations are attached to the Sciences and Belles Lettres, and have cultivated them fuccefsfully. The Swedes boaft many learned men, not only known and efteemed at home, but admired throughout all Europe. Among thefe are Linnæus, Bergmann, Celfius, Menanderhielm, Wargentin,

Wargentin, de Geer, and that able hiſtoriographer Lagerbring*.—Tycho Brahe, Roëmer, Gaſpard Bartholin, Simon Pauli, Wormius, and Holberg, may be ſelected from the liſt of Daniſh men of ſcience; and to theſe permit me to add Mr. de Kratzenſtein, Rector of the Univerſity, and Profeſſor of Experimental Philoſophy; the Chamberlain de Suhm†, and Meſſrs. de Treſhaw, and Kaliſchen, Profeſſors of Divinity and Chirurgery.

The greateſt part of the nobility of both nations, after an excellent preliminary education at home,

* He died in 1788.

† Extract of a letter from the worthy and learned Profeſſor de Treſcouw, dated Copenhagen, Feb. 17th, 1789.

"To Mr. de Suhm we owe all that is exactly known concerning the Hiſtory of Denmark. This learned man, by a perfect knowledge of the ancient languages, and an incredible aſſiduity in hiſtorical reſearches, has been enabled to give the public fourteen quarto volumes, the titles of which are as follows: 1. Upon the origin of Nations in general, Copenhagen, 1769. 2. Upon the origin of the Northern Nations, 1770. 3. Concerning Odin and the Mythology of the Northern Nations, 1771. 4.---5. Upon the Emigration of the Northern Nations, 1772, 1773. 6---9. Critical Hiſtory of Denmark, 1774---81. 10---13. Hiſtory of Denmark. 14. Collection of Hiſtorical Pieces concerning Denmark.

"It is to be lamented that theſe works have not yet been tranſlated. The Hiſtory of Norway was publiſhed in 1771, in three volumes, 4to. by another reſpectable hiſtorian, named Schionning. The want of tranſlations of theſe performances is in ſome degree recompenſed by ſome publications upon the Hiſtory of Denmark, Norway, and the Dutchies of Sleſwig and Holſtein, in which Meſſrs. Gebhardi and Chriſtiani have availed themſelves of the labours of de Suhm and Schionning."

acquire

acquire a knowledge of the laws and manners of foreign nations by travel, and local inveſtigation. They are equally diſtinguiſhed for an eaſy and engaging politeneſs, to which thoſe of Sweden add the primitive virtue of hoſpitality.

In the military and naval departments of Sweden, thoſe only can obtain promotion, who have ſerved under ſome foreign power; a qualification neceſſary in Denmark only to naval officers, who often acquire experience in the ſervices of England or Ruſſia, and ſometimes on board merchant ſhips.

The King of Sweden ſends from time to time ſeveral young men to Rome and Paris, to ſtudy the chef-d'œuvres of ancient and modern art. But, notwithſtanding the natural aptitude and dexterity of the Swedes, their artiſts by no means equal thoſe of Denmark, where the encouragement is much more general and liberal. Amongſt the latter is an hiſtorical painter, whoſe compoſitions will bear a compariſon with thoſe of Pierre or Weſt*. For an annual penſion of a thouſand crowns granted him by the court, he is obliged to furniſh each year, upon the King's birth-day, a painting upon ſome ſubject taken from the Hiſtory of Denmark. Twenty-two of theſe are to be finiſhed, and they are to be placed in the ſuperb hall of the knights, the deſign and execution of

* The Profeſſor Abalgaard.

which is by a French architect, named Desjardins. By the King's permission, an eminent portrait painter† has the use of a large hall in the castle, in which a copy of each portrait painted by him is preserved, so as to form an interesting collection of likenesses, from which a disciple of Lavater might form an opinion of the different members of society in Copenhagen. A young painter ‡, who has studied in the environs of Rome, and amongst the mountains of Switzerland, has been sent by the Prince Royal to take a series of views of the most picturesque parts of Norway, Denmark, and Jutland. Another hall of the castle will be ornamented by these paintings. Professor Hoyer, Secretary to the Academy of Painting, Sculpture, and Architecture, is a miniature painter of the first rate, excelling both in the elegance of his composition, and the delicacy of his pencil. The engraver Priesler is well known for the expression of his burine; and the two sculptors and statuaries, Professors Wiedfelt and Stanley, are distinguished, the one for the accuracy of his contours, the other for the richness and fire of his compositions. They are both constantly employed by the court.

Sweden, under many disadvantages, has a great number of able manufacturers, workmen, and tradesmen, who excel as much in their leather,

† Juel.   ‡ Paulissen.

gloves,

gloves, inlaid work and stoves, as those of Denmark in the manufactures of cloths, silks, hats, and painted linen. The Swedish peasant, after the payment of tithes and quit-rents, enjoys the profits of his own labour, and has a voice in the legislature of his country, as a member of the fourth estate; he is, therefore, vigorous, active, and laborious; and, although oppressed by the exaction of certain services, of which that of furnishing horses to the post is one, has an energy of character unknown to those of Denmark, who are attached to the soil in a state little better than slavery, humbled at once by their own indolence, and by the oppression of their lords.

No person has yet imitated the example of the late Count de Bernstorf, who, some years ago, liberated all his peasants, and thus, by rendering them rich and happy, advanced his estates to four times their original value. In memory of this good action, these peasants have lately erected a magnificent monument of Norway marble, upon which there is an inscription in letters of gold, intended to convey the name of Bernstorf to the latest posterity. It was executed by Weidefelt, the Professor of Sculpture, and stands upon one of the Count's estates, at the distance of a league from Copenhagen, and by the side of the great royal road, which leads from thence to Elsineur.

Notwithstanding

Notwithstanding the animosity and jealousy, which prevails between the two nations, the Swedish workmen are most esteemed in Denmark, and are employed in the manufactures, trade, and agricultural labours. Their superiority to the Danes I have myself witnessed at Droningaard, where a small colony of forty or fifty Scanians cleared as much land as treble the number of the former employed in the same work, and were at the same time chosen by the inspector, who was a native of Holstein, to execute all the most difficult parts of the undertaking. The same preference is given to them by the Holstein farmer in his harvest work: but what chiefly marks the difference between the Swedish and Danish labourers, is that, immediately after their work, the first repair to their huts of turf and earth, and there dance to the sound of a violin, or to the singing of their wives and daughters, while the latter, overcome with fatigue, retire to their brandy bottles and beds. At a fête-champetre given by my friend C...., these Scanians refused to mix with the other work-people, and, retiring to a corner of the field, opposed their own lively tunes and brisk attitudes, to the heavy music and solemn step of the Danish dance. A great number of Swedes, attracted by the difference in the price of labour, visit Zealand annually in spring, and return at the approach of winter; large parties also, consisting of more women than men, are

seen

seen to arrive, whenever the report of any great undertaking has been circulated on the oppofite fhore.

The bravery and activity of the Swedes in war has been fufficiently proved in the reigns of Charles the Ninth, Guftavus Adolphus, Charles the Eleventh, and Charles the Twelfth; fovereigns, who, inftead of directing the fpirit and abilities of their fubjects to the ufeful purfuits of agriculture, commerce, and manufactures, impoverifhed the ftate, and depopulated the kingdom from the vain ambition of making conquefts. An able writer, upon the fubject of population, mentions, as an inftance of the injurious effects of war in Sweden, that, " during the late war, a company of foot, confift- " ing of 128 men, raifed from the parifh of Skel- " leftra in Weftrogothia, was twice entirely re- " newed in the courfe of one year."

With refpect to the military character of the Danes, one of their own hiftorians writes thus: " The Danes, though no longer that fanguinary " and ferocious people, who thought it a difgrace " to die in their beds, are ftill a brave nation, and " have fignalized their courage in fome unhappy " wars, in which their want of fuccefs by land has " been recompenfed by their victories at fea."

The Swedifh, Danifh, and Norwegian languages are all derived from the ancient Scandinavian, and contain many Englifh, Frieze, and Low-German words.

words. In the days of paganism, the Swedes used a sort of characters in writing, which they called *runor* or *runer*, and engraved upon the *runic* stones placed round the tombs of their heroes, as well as upon the staffs which then served as calenders, and are still applied to the same use in some of the northern provinces. Many learned men suppose Odin to have introduced these characters in the north; and it is generally believed that they were taken from coins, and monuments of the Anglo-Saxons and Franks. The greatest part of those which I saw consist of shapeless strokes, placed obliquely, perpendicularly, and horizontally; the monuments, of which I met with several in my tour, being only circular collections of stones, with one in the middle that exceeds the rest in height.

The lower classes of the Swedish nation are very superstitious, and have a thousand trifling fantastical customs, the remains of the catholic, or, perhaps of the pagan religion. From their belief in sorcery, they are induced to attempt the cure of fevers, and other disorders by incantations, or the repetition of certain magical words. The success of their harvest they have no doubt depends upon the performance or omission of some ceremony; and, when their cattle are diseased, they bury a limb of one of the dead beasts in some neighbour's land, in order to transplant the disorder, and remove it from their own herds. Their marriages,

riages, births, baptisms, and burials are accompanied with a thousand mysterious practices; and, in the mountains, they believe in the existence of a subterranean genius, who, according to circumstances, is their friend or enemy, and whom they endeavour to propitiate by the performance of certain ceremonies to his honour.

 The Swedes, except at Stockholm and in Scania, build their houses entirely of wood, and those of the peasants are made by laying the trunks of fir-trees, hewn or unhewn, horizontally upon each other, joining them at the ends with wooden pegs, and filling up the interstices with moss. Some holes are left for windows, and the roof, which is very slight, is covered with strata of birch-bark and turf. The stove is built circularly of bricks, to the height of four feet, but has a flat roof, which is used as a sleeping-place. On one side of this is the chimney, the tunnel of which is closed on the top by a square board, that may be opened or shut at pleasure, and in the chimney they stick, upon a piece of iron, a long slip of lighted fir, which serves instead of a candle. The entrance is by a door four feet high, and the house consists generally of a sort of porch, and one common chamber, in which the beds of the whole family are placed one above the other, almost in the same manner as in Westphalia. The barns and stables are separate buildings, and in the houses of the post-masters there is always a second chamber destined to travellers, containing a bed, or, rather, crib, a table and some chairs; this they call the *strangers* room, and it is used for no other purpose. In summer, the floors in these, and in some better houses, are constantly spread with branches of fir cut into small pieces, which freshen the air, and exhale a very agreeable odour. The ceiling, stove, windows, and other parts are also hung with branches of birch, to attract the flies, which abound to a most offensive degree.

In Smoland, and the mountains of Dalecarlia, the houses of the peasants are yet more simple, having only one hole in the roof, exposed to the south, which answers the double purpose of a window, and a clock; the time of breakfast and dinner being regulated by the appearance of the sun's rays upon a chest placed beneath this hole, on one side, or upon the stove, which stands on the other. In these houses there is seldom more than one bed, appropriated to the master of the family and his wife; the other persons sleep upon benches placed along the partitions, and covered with straw or sheep-skins.

The houses of the better sort, both in town and country, are built with beams, and planks, and raised to the height of two, three, and, sometimes of four stories. Their appearance is often very noble, and in the towns they are chiefly painted of a red a red brown colour, with roofs of turf, tiles, or of pieces of wood shaped like slates. At Gottenburg, Carlscrona, and Fahlun, there are some very neatly painted in the manner of those at Sardam, and others, which have much the appearance of free-stone. In the country, the houses of the nobility and gentry, some of whom reside all the year upon their estates, have the outward grandeur and the internal magnificence of castles. Yet I have seen some of these, which in a few hours could be taken to pieces and transported to any other place.

I frequently amused myself at Copenhagen by walking in a large square, where houses of any size and price, according to the convenience of the purchasers, are constructed for exportation to Norway and Iceland. The height, length, and breath of the apartments, with other particulars, should be communicated to the undertakers, who immediately shape the pieces from wood already prepared, join them together, erect the house, inspect the condition of the whole, take it down, and, after marking and numbering the different parts, place it on board ship for exportation. I have seen such houses of considerable size constructed entirely without iron.

In Scania, where there are as few wooden-houses as in Denmark, the Dutch bricks are preferred to those of the country, on account of their being better baked, and less porous.

Having

Having thus endeavoured to satisfy your enquiries, I remain &c. &c. &c.

LETTER XIX.

Copenhagen, Jan. .... 1786.

MY DEAR FRIEND,

IT may give you a general idea of the difference between the state of agriculture in Sweden and Denmark, to say that the former kingdom, without the importation of foreign corn, would be liable to frequent famines; and the latter has always enough remaining from the internal confumption to form an article of commerce with other nations. Yet in no country is agriculture more encouraged than in Sweden, where the government confiders it as an important object of attention, and rewards by money, privileges, and an exemption from taxes, thofe who firft clear land for cultivation, or amend that which has been already cultivated by others. In this defign, alfo, the patriotic fociety co-operates, and the government, confidering a knowledge of the ftate of population as a neceffary preliminary to all improvements of this fort, has eftablifhed a college for the purpofe of digefting the reports, which the governors of

the

the provinces are obliged to fend annually, after the parochial and municipal regifters have been made out.

Befides this college, there is another compofed of a director, an infpector, five engineers, a fecretary, and an hundred and fixteen furveyors, who are difperfed through the different provinces, and are alfo directors. Their bufinefs is to take an exact furvey of the whole furface of the kingdom, examine into the nature of its different earths, and form geometrical and topographical charts. Formerly only a limited number of perfons were permitted to cultivate each *hemman* or farm, and, when this number was completed, the farmer was obliged to difmifs his eldeft fons, whom the government hoped thus to force upon the cultivation of new lands. But government, at length, perceived the mifchievous tendency of this meafure, which occafioned fuch frequent emigrations, efpecially from the maritime provinces, that at one time 12,000 Swedes were known to be employed as failors by England alone. In 1755, therefore, upon the eftablifhment of the college of furveyors, it was decreed that each father of a family, under the direction of the furveyor of the diftrict, might divide his hemman into as many portions as he pleafed, each portion being chargeable with its fhare of the impofts.

The late Mr. Fagot, a member of the Academy of Sciences, and Director of the College of Surveyors, calculated that Sweden and Finland, Lapland being unnoticed, contained, within an area of 9,000* miles, about half a million of inhabitants. According to a table drawn up in 1773 by Mr. Wargentin, secretary to the academy, founded upon an actual survey of the several provinces, and upon the reports of the provincial governors, there are in Sweden and Finland 5,000 square miles capable of culture, and 2,571,800 inhabitants. In 1781, the number of inhabitants appears from the same authority to have increased to 2,700,000; a degree of population which falls far short of that of France or England, the first of which, in a square of 10,000 leagues †, contains 24,000,000 of persons, and the latter, in 2,900 ‡ square geographical miles, about five millions. In the 104 cities of Sweden and Finland, they reckon 180,000 souls, allowing 70,000 for Stockholm alone; a number not equal to a thirteenth part of the whole, and, therefore, differing much from the calculations of those who reckon, that in all well peopled countries, the numbers of citizens should be to the inhabitants of the country as 1 to 4.

* It is difficult to say what sort of miles are here meant. Sweden Proper contains 47,900; Gothland 25,975; Schonen 2,960; Lapland and W. Bothnia 76,000; Swedish Finland, and East Bothnia 73,000; Gothland Isle, 1,000; and Oeland 560 square miles.
† France contains 138,687 square miles.
‡ England contains 49,540 square English miles, 69 and a half of which are equal to 60 geographical miles.---*Guthrie.*

Among the two millions and a half of inhabitants, they reckoned in 1760, 10,645 noble perſons, including 3597 children under the age of fifteen years. The number of noble families was then 2054, but in 1775 they amounted to 2176, of which 85 were thoſe of Counts, 231 of Barons, and 1754 of untitled nobility. That of Count de Brahe is the moſt ancient. From a ſeries of obſervations continued for thirteen years, Mr. Wargentin informs us, that the number of births in Sweden is always greater in the month of September, and leſs in that of June than in any of the other months; and that the number of deaths is greateſt in April. He remarks alſo, that for nine ſucceeding years, 100 men have died annually in the country out of every 3340, and 100 women out of every 3540; while in Stockholm the deaths of males were in the proportion of 100 to 1722, and of females in the proportion of 100 to 2128. That in theſe nine years there died 2,046 men, and 3,540 women above the age of 90; 20 above the age of 100; 3 above the age of 120; and one aged 127 years.

The government, having for a long time been aware of the great advantages to be obtained from an increaſed population, gives encouragement and ſupport to all eſtabliſhments likely to promote it, of which the college of medicine, and ſeveral others that have been already mentioned, are inſtances. With the ſame view, the King, in 1773, iſſued

issued an ordinance, exempting from the payment of certain capitations all peasants, workmen, artisans, fishermen, not enjoying the rights of burgesses, soldiers, sailors, and their wives, having four or more children. By these and some other regulations, emigration has been in a great degree prevented, and the number of inhabitants is said to have received an addition of 500,000, between the years 1751 and 1781. But no endeavours towards encreasing the population of Sweden can be so effectual, as the improvement of agriculture, the melioration of those articles which form the basis of their manufactures, and the holding out suitable encouragement to strangers, who shall settle in the country.

A learned Swede*, in a memoir presented to the academy, in 1750, thus estimates the proportion between the productions of the soil, and the number of inhabitants.

" Sweden, including Finland and the isles, con-
" tains 9,000 square miles, and something less
" than three millions of inhabitants; of this space
" only 4,000 miles are susceptible of cultivation,
" the rest consisting of mountains, rocks, lakes,
" rivers, marshes, and high roads; and there are
" only 1,000 of arable land, 2,500 miles being
" allowed to be occupied by meadows, gardens,
" orchards, &c. &c. Supposing two-thirds of

* Erick Solander.

" this

"this land to be annually fown, the quantity of
" feed, at the rate of 24,000 tons *per* mile, will
" amount to 24 millions of tons, and the produce,
" if eftimated in the proportion of 5 to 1, will be
" equal to 120 millions. If one-fifth part of this
" be re-fown, and one-fifth confumed by cattle,
" there remains 72 millions of tons of grain, a
" quantity, which, in France, has been found fuf-
" ficient for the fupport of 20 millions of perfons.
" Even if this eftimate be lowered by one-half,
" on account of any fuppofed exaggeration, or
" miftake, there muft ftill be much more than
" enough for five millions of inhabitants; yet
" fuch is the ftate of agriculture in Sweden, that,
" without the importation of foreign grain, the
" inhabitants, who do not much exceed half that
" number, have never been fupported."

Another learned inquirer*, in a memoir prefented to the academy, ufes the fame mode of calculation, but makes the number of fquare miles
amount only to 7,000. Either account, however,
fhews the quantity of land to be fuch as might
yield corn fufficient for three times the number of
inhabitants; and, therefore, almoft proves that the
produce muft be leffened by fome natural obftacles,
fuch as cultivation cannot overcome. Thefe, probably, are the great length and rigour of the winters, the fhort fpace between the feed-time and

* Menander.

harveſt, the exceſſive heat of their ſummers, which, by forcing a ſudden growth, renders all vegetables liable to be affected by the leaſt change of weather, and the ſhortneſs of the nights at that ſeaſon, when the plants have neither the moiſture nor coolneſs neceſſary to ſupport them under the parching heat of day. Add to this, that the ſnow, by which the earth is covered for ſeven months of the year, increaſes the difficulty of cultivating a ſoil by nature hard, compact, and ſtony; that the inhabitants are ſo thinly diſperſed over the country, as to have no opportunities of mutual aſſiſtance, and are at the ſame time ſo poorly provided with markets, that the ſale of their commodities is by no means ready or certain.

All theſe obſtacles have a permanent influence upon the ſtate of agriculture, and muſt conſiderably counteract both the endeavours of the huſbandman, and the generoſity of the ſtate. A Swede[*], who has very attentively ſtudied the effects of the climate, the nature of the ſoil, and the induſtry of the inhabitants, aſſures us that almoſt any other country will yield three times as much as can be obtained in Sweden by equal exertions. Of the dreadful effects produced by a dry ſummer ſucceeding to a hard winter, I was myſelf a witneſs laſt year; when the failure of the crops in Sweden and Finland produced a famine, and large bodies

---

[*] Lillecrantz.

of Swedes were seen arriving in Denmark, in search of employment, at the very time when it is usual for their countrymen to conclude their labours for the season. These emigrations, though casual and temporary, must tend to the decrease of population, there being always some natives who remain abroad, and are for ever lost to their country.

To diminish the effect of the many natural impediments to the success of agriculture in Sweden, care should be taken to leave no hands unemployed, and to prevent the peasant from being disturbed in the labours of cultivation. The establishment of bostelles, and the abolition of a great number of holydays, contribute, no doubt, to this end; but the oppressive services of the post are still exacted, and thus, according to the calculations of the able and zealous Secretary of the Patriotic Society *, the labours of 216,000 men, and of double the number of horses for one day are *(annually)* lost to Sweden. The calculation is in every respect very moderate, the stages being reckoned at only three hundred, which is much below the real number.

To all these disadvantages, arising from the nature of the climate, and the scarcity of inhabitants, should be added those produced by the ignorance and prejudices of the peasants, of which

* Mr. Modeer.

the influence is very visible in a great variety of pernicious customs, and in none more conspicuously than in that called Swediandet. This is the custom of burning all the trees and shrubs upon lands cleared for cultivation; thus forcing a sudden fertility, that lasts only for two or three harvests, when the soil is entirely exhausted, being unsupplied by the oils, salts, and other matters necessary to vegetation, which its too great compactness prevents it from receiving. Notwithstanding the dreadful consequences produced by the application of fire to such enormous forests, and the unprofitable tendency of the practice in other respects, the peasants remain attached to the custom of their forefathers, and are not to be dissuaded from it by any efforts; a sort of intellectual slavery, which I have myself witnessed in Holland and Denmark, and which, no doubt, exists in a greater or less degree in all countries.

Some Swedish politicians, having objected to the distillation of brandy, as consuming the corn which might be more usefully employed in the support of the inhabitants, the quantity allowed to be used in the distilleries was, by an ordinance of the King, dated 1776, limited to 300,000 tuns. From four to five hundred thousand tuns of foreign grain are annually brought into Sweden from other countries, yet it is the opinion of some, that the savings to be made, even by a total prohibition

tion of distilling, would by no means recompense the loss which the importation of foreign brandies would occasion.

The population and agriculture of Denmark have so often been treated of by very able writers, that I shall content myself with giving you a general idea of its superiority to Sweden in these respects. Denmark, then, which consists properly of Zealand, Fionia, and Jutland, contains, within the space of 850 square geographical miles, 168 cities, and one million of inhabitants; the corn produced in it exceeds the quantity requisite for internal consumption, and, therefore, forms an article of foreign commerce.

Many causes concur to produce these happy effects. The country, which is almost entirely surrounded with water, is by no means elevated, the highest point being only 308 feet above the level of the sea. The climate is much milder than in Sweden, the polar elevation less, the winters shorter, and the summers more temperate. Add to this, that the government gives great encouragement to population, and has succeeded so far as to attract a great number of strangers, who have settled, and become naturalized inhabitants of the country. Whole colonies of foreigners have sometimes arrived to the cultivation of lands abandoned as barren and worthless. In the year 1516, two hundred families from Waterland in North Holland,

land, settled in the isle of Amack, under Christian the Fourth; and, in 1760, about three hundred families established themselves in Jutland, upon lands never before cultivated. The first of these colonies now contains 800 families, and the island, which was before only one continued marsh, is now covered with gardens and meadows, from whence the 60,000 inhabitants of Copenhagen are supplied with all the roots, and the greatest part of the milk requisite for their consumption. The Amackese have also been able to build a considerable town, the residence of fishermen, who supply the markets of the capital with all sorts of sea-fish.

The greatest part of the farmers are foreigners, and those chiefly natives of Holstein, whose skill in the art of clearing and cultivating land much exceeds that of the Danes. But the idleness of the peasants, the slavish state in which they live, and the King's right of chase, considerably impede the endeavours of the husbandman; and the land is rendered difficult of cultivation by an immense quantity of stones scattered over it, of which some are so large as to require to be blown in pieces by gunpowder before they can be collected, and carried away in waggons. The land thus covered is often abandoned by the peasants, who do not think it worth their while to remove the stones. How much is lost by this sort of negligence, it would

require

require a very accurate knowledge of the country to eftimate.

The wild animals that run in troops over the country, and often ravage lands covered with the fineft corn, difappoint the hopes, and efcape the attacks of the hufbandman, who would be condemned to flavery for the flaughter of a ftag, an hind, or a roe-buck. But it cannot be doubted that the young Prince now at the head of government will direct his attention to thefe evils, and, by fome regulations more favourable to agriculture, prevent the complaints of the poor labourer, who now fometimes lofes in an hour the fruits of his toil for many months. The magnificent royal park, of four Danifh miles in circumference, would afford fhelter and food for a fufficient number of ftags, and the meadows, freed from their ravages, might be left open to the fupport of horfes for the fervice of the nation, to which purpofe alfo the lands now covered by the royal woods might be more ufefully applied. He will perceive that one of the fureft methods of increafing the induftry of the inhabitants, and the value of his eftates is the liberation of the peafants, who, thus invited to labour for themfelves and their pofterity, would acquire a degree of energy of which they are at prefent incapable, and mingle their wealth with that of the nation *.

* Towards the clofe of the year 1788, the peafants upon the crown lands were declared free by the Prince Royal.

Having

Having thus given you some account of the state of agriculture and population in these two kingdoms, permit me to conclude, by assuring you how much

I am, &c. &c.

LETTER XX.

Copenhagen, Feb. .... 1786.

MY DEAR FRIEND,

IF the surface of the soil in Sweden seems to yield but little to the efforts of art, the inexhaustible stores of nature afford the inhabitants some recompense. The timber, tar, and pitch of her immense forests are circulated throughout Europe; and iron, that original and necessary commodity, is to be found in many parts, in great abundance, and even in its pure state, at a very small depth in the earth. Dalecarlia, Warmeland, Westmannia, Ostrogothia, Lapponia, and, above all, Upland, contain it in the greatest quantities. Alum, vitriol, salt-petre, copper, lead, silver, and even gold itself are the productions which the Swedes also extract from the bowels of their uncultivated mountains.

Iron, which is the most considerable article of their commerce, is exported in lumps, bars, and in a manufactured state to the amount of 300,000 schisp *per annum*, for which, at the rate of five crowns and ¼ *per* schisp, they receive about 1,934,750 bank crowns. Of this sum 1,700,000 silver dollars are paid to the crown.

The copper mines, which after those of iron, are of the greatest value, yield annually about 308,000 bank crowns, being the amount of the copper exported, either in its plain or refined state, or after being converted into brass. The crown receives about 900 schisp, as a tithe of the produce.

The silver mines, of which those of Sahla alone yield more than the other six, pay, as a tithe to the crown 300 marks *per* annum.

The gold mine affords annually about 1000 ducats, which, with 8,000 silver dollars, allowed by the crown, are scarcely sufficient to pay the expences of working it.

All the lead obtained from the mines is consumed in precipitating the other metals, together with 960 schisp annually imported from England.

The alum works increase in value every day. The quantity at present exported yields about 30,000 bank crowns.

Timber, and other forest productions, are annually exported to the value of 387,580 bank crowns.

Besides these articles of commerce, which the Swedes, by the peculiar bounty of nature, are enabled

abled to extract from their mountains, rocks, and forests, the herring-fishery upon the western shores supplies them with another source of wealth, 160,000 tons being exported every year, at the price of 16 silver dollars *per* ton.

Sweden, which, by its situation between the North sea and the Baltic, is admirably adapted for foreign traffic, has also the advantage of a ready internal circulation, being interfected by a great number of rivers, and extensive lakes. The canals and sluices, projected for the improvement and extension of these natural communications, are already so far perfected, that goods unshipped from the vessels of the East India Company at Gothenburg, are transported across the kingdom to Stockholm, by which means the toll duties* of the Sound, and the dangerous rocks of the Baltic are avoided. Sweden has not long been known as a commercial power, having profited but little by the natural advantages of its situation, the industry

---

* These duties, to enforce the payment of which the castle of Cronenburg was built by Eric VII. in 1427, yield the annual sum of 400,000 rix-dollars to Denmark. The English, French, Dutch, Swedes, Spaniards, Portuguese, Neapolitans, and Hamburghers pay one *per* cent. upon all goods not mentioned in the tariff. Other powers pay one and a quarter.

Besides this tax, each vessel four rix-dollars, if laden, and two, if empty, as a contribution to the support of the lights, buoys, and maritime signals, necessary about the Cattegat and Sound. Four thousand vessels are reckoned to pass and repass annually.

of

of the inhabitants, or the value of its productions, before the middle of the laſt century. In 1626, a body of traders inſtituted a Southern Company; and in 1641 a treaty of commerce was concluded with Portugal, and an aſſociation formed for carrying on a trade with Africa. Another Company undertook the exportation of tar in 1647; in the following year, Helmſtadt, with the patronage and interference of ſeveral of the nobility, fitted out ſeveral fiſhing-veſſels, and in 1667 a permanent herring-fiſhery was inſtituted by the city of Gothenburg.

During the long wars of Charles the Twelfth, the progreſs of theſe good endeavours was checked, and many companies were diſſolved. Under Frederic the Firſt, commerce began to revive, and, in the reign of Adolphus Frederic, government, ſeriouſly adopting the intereſts of trade and navigation, paſſed ſeveral decrees, encouraging the exportation of indigenous productions, and the importation of ſome foreign commodities. The year 1731 was diſtinguiſhed by the inſtitution of the India Company; 1740 by the revival of the herring-fiſhery; and 1771 by the formation of a Levant Company. In 1774, ſome privileges were granted to an aſſociation eſtabliſhed for the purpoſe of carrying on the whale fiſhery*; and in the

* This company has not been able to ſupport a competition with that of Denmark.

year 1775 the port of Marstrand was declared free, to the great benefit of the merchants of Gothenburg, who here receive all sorts of foreign commodities, which they enter for exportation, but find means to circulate in contraband traffic, in Sweden, Denmark, Norway, England, and Scotland.

About the middle of the 14th century Sweden possessed only five or six ships, and its commerce was transacted by the Hanseatic towns. The city of Lubec afterwards absorbed the greatest part, but at length, towards the 17th century, the English and Dutch divided the whole between them. In 1724 appeared the celebrated *Placart, concerning productions,* by which foreigners were prohibited from importing commodities not the growth of their country, and from carrying any merchandize from one Swedish port to another. From this time the encouragement and the progress of navigation has been such, that the number of trading vessels, which then amounted only to 300, was in 1764 about 8,000, and at present they are not only sufficient for the commerce of the country, but are able to transact some part of the business of other nations, chiefly of the Spaniards, who permit them to work as coasting vessels.

As a further encouragement to navigation, an office was established in 1704 for executing insurances upon ships. The stock is divided into a thousand shares of 3,000 silver dollars each.

The

The company of divers, the only inftitution of the fort in Europe, deferves to be particularly mentioned. Its privileges were granted in 1734, by letters patent from the King and the ftates. Along all the coafts of Sweden, perfons in the employ of this company are ftationed, who, upon the firft news of a fhipwreck, fly to give their affiftance in faving all that is poffible of the fhip and cargo. Of this the company immediately give notice to the proprietors, and, after receiving their orders, proceed to the fale of the effects, deducting from the produce the amount of their dues. Thefe dues vary exceedingly, and depend upon the circumftances of the fhipwreck: When a veffel, for inftance, has been on fhore, and, by the exertions of the country people, has been floated and brought into port, the company, for putting it in complete repair, receives a premium of 10 *per* cent; but if the cargo has been damaged, fo as to make it neceffary to unload it, and difpofe of it at the next city, or upon the fpot, the company, by contributing a fourth of the expence, becomes entitled to a fourth fhare of the produce; and when goods are fifhed out of the fea, by means of the diving-bell, or any other machines, the company contributes the fame fhare of the expences, and receives a third part of the produce.

Of the hundred and twenty-four cities, which Sweden contains, only thirty-eight have any foreign

reign commerce, and of this they enjoy the exclusive right, with the title of staple cities, (stapel städer.) The greatest part is divided between Stockholm and Gothenburg, the former having $\frac{1}{2}$ and the latter $\frac{1}{4}$ of the whole. The importation of foreign goods is in different proportions; of these Stockholm receives half, Gothenburg one quarter, and the remaining thirty-six cities the other.

The interior commerce is open to all the cities, and to every individual, it being lawful for any person to purchase commodities in gross in the staple cities, and retail them through the other parts of the kingdom. If the Swedes have been active in obtaining a considerable export trade, which must continue to encrease, unless prevented by a competition with Russia, in the article of iron, they have been not less so in the establishment of manufactories in the different provinces. But the climate, which obstructs their progress in agriculture, prevents their arriving at excellence in manufactures. Either the articles to be manufactured are wanting, or are of inferior value, and can only be obtained from foreign countries at great expence. The rewards given by government have very litte effect against these obstacles, and the laws enacted for the protection of the manufactures are insufficient for the purpose, great quantities of contraband goods being in circulation.

It

It is computed, that within the fpace of thirty-feven years the nation has furnifhed to the wants of the manufacturers the fum of 117 tons of gold *. A merchant, named Jonas Aelftroemer, has diftinguifhed himfelf by eftablifhing manufactories of all forts of articles at Allingeos in Weftrogothia. From England, Spain, and Germany he imported fheep and rams, in order to obtain a fine fort of wool for the manufacture of cloths, and for a fhort time he had the fatisfaction to fee his project fucceed. But the animals foon degenerated in a climate fo unfavourable to them, and the expences attending a frequent renewal of the breed, rendered him unable to ftand a competition with foreign markets, favoured by the opportunities of contraband traffic. His cloths were worfe or higher priced than thofe of England, which, with other foreign ftuffs, are now worn conftantly by all people of condition, and find their way into the kingdom, in fpite of prohibitions and fearches.

Of 18,600 manufactories eftablifhed in Sweden fince the year 1738, and which coft the nation 10,273,917 filver dollars, only nine thoufand remained in 1774; and of 1,260 filk looms, which were worked in Stockholm, in 1762, only 400 remained in 1776. It appears from a report made to the College of Trade by Mr. Faxe, Commif-

---

* About 487,500l. T.

fary of that board, that in 1762, Stockholm contained 2,157 looms of all forts, and 8,007 workmen; and in 1767 the number amounted only to 1,062 looms, and 4,290 workmen. This fudden difference was occafioned by the return of a great number of foreigners, who, attracted by rewards and privileges, had come to Stockholm in the expectation of making fortunes, and had left the country the moment they perceived the vanity of their hopes. The number of manufacturers is faid to be greater now than in 1776, but it is to be feared that this is only a temporary increafe, which muft foon yield to the difadvantages of the climate, and the inferiority of the productions neceffary to be manufactured.

The Swedes, however, fhew their induftry by feveral articles made of copper and wrought iron, and excel in the preparation of furs and fkins of all forts, particularly in thofe of elks and reindeer, in the northern provinces, and of fheep in the fouthern.

I entered Sweden with the expectation of finding only copper and paper in circulation, and was furprized to find a fufficient quantity of filver money, which is much more abundant there than in Denmark. In the latter country, indeed, the adminiftration, in 1773, are faid not only to have prevented the realization of paper money, then in circulation,

circulation, to the amount of four millions of rix-dollars, but to have confiderably increafed the quantity fince that period *.

The corrupt adminiftration of the finances in Sweden, and efpecially the abufes in borrowing money at the bank, had fo much increafed the quantity of paper in circulation, that in 1769 it was eftimated at 500 tons of gold †. New plans were adopted by every diet for reftoring the finances and credit of the country, but with very little effect, till in 1769, it was refolved to realize, by degrees, the immenfe quantity of paper with which the kingdom was overwhelmed, and to bring fpecie into circulation. One of the parts of this plan was a loan of three millions of current Dutch dollars, at an intereft of 5 and $\frac{5}{9}$ *per cent.* Since the revolution in 1772, the King and the miniftry have continued their endeavours for the reftoration of the finances, and, befides the above loan, which was authorized by the ftates, have negociated in Holland a new one for the fum of two millions of Dutch florins.

---

* Upon the eftablifhment of the bank in 1736, Chriftian VI. for himfelf and his fucceffors, folemnly undertook, that the government fhould never, upon any emergency, interfere, directly or indirectly, with the affairs of the bank, but fhould leave to the directors the entire management of the funds and effects, intrufted to them by the proprietors.

† A ton of gold, in Swedifh reckoning, is equal to 100,000 *daalders filver munt*, which are worth about ten-pence each. T.

The following are the heads of the plan adopted by the King for promoting the circulation of specie:

1. From the year 1777, it was resolved to pay the salaries of all officers, as well civil as military, partly in money.

2. To call in all bank-notes under the value of 100 dollars.

3. To take up all notes brought to the bank, paying for the large ones *plotes*, or plates of copper, and for the small ones copper money.

4. To make copper-*plotes* liable upon exportation to no greater duties than common copper. And,

5. To issue the new notes, not for copper-money, but for rix-dollars or bank crowns, and at sums not less than ten rix-dollars each *. The bank was instituted in 1668, under the reign of Charles the Ninth, and the direction of it committed to the deputies of the states; it is at present governed by a commissary, and three deputies chosen from each order, making in the whole ten directors. All the revenues of the state pass through this bank, and there the rough copper belonging to the crown is deposited. One office is appropriated to the business of exchange, and the other to that of taking up money. The diet in 1778, con-

* This plan is attributed to Mr. de Liljencrantz, secretary of state.

sidering

sidering the great length of time, which, under the new form of government, elapses between their meetings, appointed commissioners to receive every third year, in the month of October, the reports of the directors, and to co-operate with them in such measures as may tend to confirm the credit of the bank. Their number is twenty-four, of which twelve are chosen from the three classes of the nobility, six from the clergy, and six from the burgesses.

In 1783, a little time after the departure of the King for Italy, the bank issued notes of 150 rix-dollars each, alleging, in justification, the failure of some foreign houses, and the high price of the exchange, on account of the want of paper currency, which, without this precaution, would occasion the exportation of the specie. By this measure the price of exchange was for a short time lowered; but the excessive importation of grain, and the decrease in the exportation of iron, soon restored it to its former price.

The revenues of the crown arise from the different imposts and taxes, both permanent and temporary, upon the persons, estates, and possessions of the inhabitants, as well as upon the produce of the customs, mines, and stamp-duties. But they are much less now than formerly, the value of money having fallen considerably since the time of Charles the Ninth, when they were finally settled.

To supply the deficiencies recourse is constantly had to the states, and each diet finds itself obliged to provide for the support of the kingdom by extraordinary contributions, loans, &c. &c. These contributions are levied upon the estates and mines, upon the houses in which brandy is retailed, and upon the trade, labour and personal resources of the inhabitants.

Upon the accession of the present King to the throne in 1771, the revenues of the crown, ordinary and extraordinary, were found to be as stated in the following table:

	Silver dollars.
Ordinary rents	2,133,997
Tithes of corn	295,037
Farms	70,837
Personal rents	730,000
Deniers received for the support of the seneschals courts	140,328
Deniers received for exemptions from the support of the military	2,546
Dues from the lime-kilns in Gothland	381
Convocation deniers	3,628
For the support of sailors	5,428
For giving employ to workmen	5,793
Share of judicial rights	23,620
Duties upon the sale of wood	225
Stamp-duties, and recognition fees	231,090

Rents

	Silver dollars.
Rents levied for the regiment of Varmie and Nerike	3,000
Extraordinary contributions	2,400,000
Tenths and taxes payable by the iron forges, tenths of alum, rents of copper, and the grand maritime duty	2,066,074
Tenths payable by the fulphur-works	1,705
Tolls and general excife-duties	800,239
Tenths of the copper of Ryddarhyte and Linfneburg	1,800
Duty upon the Aveftadt copper	20,000
Tenths from the mines, and from the coinage of filver	3,000
Control of gold, filver and wool	3,087
Duties upon cattle at Stockholm	390
Pofts	317,270
Deniers received for the fupport of light-houfes	29,016
Deniers received from pilots	1,368
Excife	300,000
Contributions of the chamber of revifion	5,232
Duties upon the cargoes of Eaft-India fhips	3,500
Funds for the fupport of the medicinal charity	5,400
Savings from vacancies	300,000

Contributions

		Silver dollars.
Contributions for supporting, and repairing the castle at Stockholm	—	163,776
Mortmain fund	—	5,057
Contribution granted since 1772, under the title of *Begrafenis och Kroeningsshielp*	—	2,000,000
A contribution of 4 *oere sent* from each person	—	2,000,000

     Silver dollars — 12,104,624

To these should be added the contributions granted under the name of a free-gift, which differ according to the exigencies of the state.

The diet of 1778 granted an addition of 100,000 crowns *per annum* to the private revenues of the King. During the three years 1696—1768, and 1773, the expences of the crown were as follow.

	Anno 1696.	Anno 1768.	Anno 1773.
	Silver dollars.	silver dollars.	silver dollars.
The court	576,096	1,658,446	2,804,735
Senate and administration	552,357	1,635,034	1,828,614
Civil list	320,903	482,808	514,063
Army	2,299,111	3,204,465	3,757,619
Navy	681,498	1,456,656	1,812,151
Extraordinaries	63,941	7,873,154	1,569,496
	4,489,906	16,310,623	11,586,678

From

From thefe ftatements it appears how much the monarchs of Sweden ought to give their attention to the prefervation of peace, and the promotion of manufactures, and that, if ever the power granted to Guftavus III. fhould fall into the hands of an ambitious fovereign, the kingdom would very foon be reduced to the fame miferable ftate, in which it was found by the fucceffors of Charles XII.

I am, &c. &c.

LETTER XXI.

Copenhagen, Feb. ... 1786.

MY DEAR FRIEND,

IN the following fketch of the Swedifh hiftory, I by no means intend to give a detailed narrative of events, or to delineate the private lives of the fovereigns; it will be fufficient for me to exhibit a view of the forms of government adopted at different times, and of the frequent revolutions produced by the ambition of the fovereigns, the turbulence of the nobility, and the people's natural defire of freedom.

Defcended from the hofts who deftroyed the Roman Empire, and overwhelmed the furface of Europe, the Swedes have preferved, in fome degree, the energy of character which diftinguifhed
their

their anceftors. Their hard climate and barren mountains, fcarcely invite or reward the labours of the hufbandman, while the forefts and lakes offer an independent fubfiftence, which removes the neceffity, and prevents the habits of fubordination. The Dalecarlians, efpecially, in the moft northern and defolate of the provinces, appear to retain this original hardihood; jealous of their rights, and refentful of the flighteft oppreffion, they have been always ready for rebellion, and have feveral times changed the conftitution of the kingdom.

The feudal form of government is unknown in Sweden, though a mode fomething refembling it has been partially introduced. In the year 814, King Anun, having cleared a great quantity of foreft land, divided it amongft his fubjects, upon the condition of their serving him in war, or purchafing their exemption by a fettled tribute. This was the origin of the eftates called *kronohemmans*, and of the fervitude of the crown-peafants; the nobles having no vaffals but thofe obtained upon the alienation of thefe fiefs. The only fort of flavery ever permitted in Sweden was that of prifoners taken in war, of perfons convicted of certain crimes, and of thofe who fold their freedom and fervices. This latter practice was prohibited by Birgis Jart, in the year 1335, and flavery was entirely

tirely abolished, about two years afterwards, by Magnus Ladiflos.

In the remoteft ages, the Kings never poffeffed abfolute power, but by ufurpation. The fovereignty always belonged of right to the states-general, to which citizens of every clafs were elegible, the pooreft peafant having a vote in the choice of reprefentatives. In the intervals between the fittings of thefe affemblies, the kingdom was governed by a fenate. The King, or rather the chief magiftrate, was elected by the nation affembled, and endued with limited power. He was unable to make peace or war, to raife money, or levy troops, without the confent of the ftates-general; "and could neither build new forts, em-
"ploy foreign troops in the kingdom, nor beftow
"the government of caftles upon any perfons,
"not of Swedish origin*."

A government, fuch as this, though highly gratifying to individuals, was liable to very great difforders, of which the hiftory of the country affords fufficient proof. The kingdom, being elective, was expofed to frequent and dreadful civil wars, during which the contending nobles invited the affiftance of foreign powers, and thus gave them an opportunity of an eafy conqueft.

The Chriftian religion being eftablished in Sweden towards the clofe of the ninth century, the

* Vertot.

ecclefiaftics

ecclefiaftics by degrees acquired fuch an afcendancy in wealth and power, as to be able to difturb the peace of the kingdom, and ultimately to beftow the crown upon Chriftian II. a monfter thirfting for human blood *.

Margaret Waldemar, the celebrated Semiramis of the North, under the fpecious pretext of maintaining the liberty of the Swedes, obtained poffeffion of the kingdom, which fhe held with thofe of Denmark and Norway, and, almoft converted into a Danifh province. Her fucceffor Eric VIII. was dethroned in a rebellion inftigated by the Dalecarlians, but, in a fhort time after, Chriftian I. by the authority of the treaty of Calmar, feized upon the throne, and governed Sweden with a rod of iron. He was twice depofed, and as often re-inftated in his authority.

Upon his death Chriftian II. furnamed 1513. the Tyrant, mounted the throne. He is known in hiftory by the famous maffacre of Stockholm, in which the moft illuftrious of the Swedifh nobility perifhed publicly upon a fcaffold. When dethroned by Guftavus Vafa, and immured for life in an obfcure prifon, his fate formed a fignal inftance of divine vengeance, and held out a leffon to Kings, which may make the proudeft fhudder. Upon this occafion the Dalecarlians had again the glory of delivering their country,

* Archenholtz.---Cantzler.

and

and Guftavus, thus raifed to power, reftored the ancient liberty of Sweden, and detached it for ever from the union of Calmar.

Guftavus was declared adminiftrator in 1521, and King in 1523. The Swedes, confidering him as their father and deliverer, in teftimony of his fervices, declared the kingdom hereditary in his pofterity. At this period the fovereignty returned to the ftates-general, compofed of the fenate, and four orders of the ftate; but the influence, which Guftavus had acquired, concentered their whole authority in his perfon, and he governed as abfolutely, as if born to the throne. His fubjects, happy under his government, gave him the diftinguifhing title of father of his country, and comparing the prefent times with thofe in which the diffenfion of the nobles, the avarice of the clergy, and the ambition of the Kings continually oppreffed them, they rejoiced in the happinefs of their fituation, and fcarcely perceived, that an anthority, founded, at firft, upon affection and gratitude, might at laft become defpotic, and be the means of their mifery.

The Lutheran religion, perhaps, owes its eftablifhment as much to the policy as to the piety of Guftavus. The afpiring fpirit, and exceffive power of the Romifh clergy juftly excited his fears and refentment, and their poffeffions, if confifcated,

would

would increase the revenues, and confirm the security of the state.

But the Dalecarlians, who placed him on the throne, bore the extension of his authority with less patience than the inhabitants of the other provinces. Six times the suspicion of some encroachment upon their privileges induced them to revolt, and they remained in arms, till convinced that their fears were groundless. In 1518, the introduction of the new religion roused them again; but they were abandoned by their chiefs, and obliged to sacrifice their opinions, rather to treachery than to force. Another revolt was occasioned by the apprehension of some change in the national dress, which they resolved to retain themselves, and demanded that Gustavus and his court should continue to wear.

In his conduct to them, Gustavus always appeared mindful of their former services, and was unwilling to take up arms, before the failure of milder measures made a recourse to them necessary. At length he won them to such a degree of attachment, that at the conclusion of his long reign they were amongst the most faithful of his subjects, and, at his death, they joined with the other Swedes, in receiving his son Eric as the Sovereign of an united and happy people. This Prince found his subjects equally sensible of the horrors of war, and the blessings of peace; a treasury able, for the first time,

time, to support the expences of the kingdom; and a nobility humbled, and weakened by the power and the crimes of his predecessors, the most powerful and enterprising having been removed in the massacre of Stockholm, or the frequent civil wars which preceded it. The Reformation had suppressed the pride and turbulence of the Catholic Prelates; the act, which declared the kingdom hereditary, rescued it from the effects of the treaty of Calmar, and from its dependence upon the crown of Denmark; and the monastic possessions, seized during the change of religion, contributed to the support and increase of the royal dignity. The people, knowing themselves to be happy, believed that they were free; and the bonds of arbitrary authority, so artfully formed by Gustavus, would never have been broken, had his successors, in exercising their power, preserved those appearances of moderation by which he obtained it.

Eric XIV. 1560. But the prosperity of the kingdom, and the power of the crown were useless to Eric, who, driven from the throne, and declared incapable of reigning, on account of his cruelties and perfidy, was at length poisoned by order of his brother John in the castle of Gripsholm. By him the dignities of count and baron were created.

John. 1569. The reign of John was disturbed only by some religious disputes, occasioned

casioned by the endeavours of his wife Catherine Jaquellon, daughter of the King of Poland, to restore the Catholic religion, and bring Sweden again within the pale of the church. The reformed mode of worship was by no means fully established, and the Queen's influence over her husband, gave her an opportunity of assisting the discontented party. Her endeavours were interrupted by the death of the King A. D. 1592.

SIGISMUND. 1592.
Sigismund, son of John, although a Catholic, succeeded to the throne, after having engaged to give no opposition to the Lutheran form of worship, which, at a diet, held at Upsal, in 1593, was ordered to be universally followed in Sweden. At the happy termination of some disturbances he went into Poland, and refusing either to return, or to permit his son to be educated in the Lutheran religion, the states annulled his claims to the crown, and declared his posterity incapable of succeeding to it.

CHARLES IX. 1600.
Charles, Duke of Sudermania, his brother, and administrator of the kingdom during his absence, succeeded to the throne. In this reign, which was spent in continual wars with the dethroned King, the right of succession was extended, in default of males, to unmarried females.

Charles

Charles IV. of Denmark, who obtained the crown by force in 1610, died in 1611, after having sacrificed 80,000 Swedes to his ambition, of whom 144 suffered by the hands of the common executioner.

GUSTAVUS ADOLPHUS. 1611.
Gustavus Adolphus, his son, began his reign by the institution of a new order in the diet, which, for the future, was prohibited from deliberating upon any subjects, not originally proposed by the King. Upon the death of the Dukes of Sudermania, and Ostrogothia, their revenues were annexed to the crown, which thus received a further accession of strength. During these political arrangements, Gustavus became involved in the celebrated thirty years war, carried on under pretence of religion, but undertaken from very different motives. In the conduct of it, however, his abilities soon became conspicuous. The celebrated Generals, Tilly and Wallenstein were severally defeated by him in the battles of Leipsic and Lutzen, but the latter victory cost him his life, at the moment when he seemed almost able to take possession of the empire. During the whole war, the desire of humbling the house of Austria, induced the King of France to send an annual subsidy of 400,000 crowns to Sweden.

The unanimous praises of all the historians, who have described the character of this great man,

excite

excite one's regret that his abilities were not more usefully employed, and rather directed to the preservation of his people's happiness, than to the acquisition of military glory. An author of reputation *, after an eulogium upon Gustavus, expresses his surprize that the protector of the liberties of Germany should wish to become absolute in his own country. His despotic disposition at home, is, indeed, fully proved by the restriction imposed upon the deliberations of the diet; but was it the love of liberty, or the desire of glory, which actuated him in the expedition to Germany?

Christina, his only daughter, succeeded him in the throne, having promised to reign according to a form of government composed by Chancellor Oxenstiern, under the direction of Gustavus, and confirmed by the diet in 1634.

Mean while the war in Germany continued with various success. The Swedish troops, after the unfortunate day at Norllingue, obtained some considerable advantages, under General Baner, against the Saxons, and under General Tortenson against the Imperialists; successes which tended to produce the celebrated peace of Westphalia, concluded in 1648. Another not less glorious, was ratified in 1645, between Sweden and Denmark.

Christina, after reserving a considerable revenue, abdicated the crown at the age of twenty-seven,

* Sheridan.

and,

and, quitting Sweden, made her profession of the Catholic religion at Infpruck. She died at Rome in 1689, admired abroad, and very little regretted by her own fubjects, who accufed her as well as Guftavus, of wafting the property of the crown, by gifts, fales, and mortgages of the lands.

CHARLES X.
1654.
Charles Guftavus, fon of John Cafimir, Duke of Deux Ponts, and of Catherine, eldeft daughter of Charles IX. was appointed by Chriftina as her fucceffor; and the ftates, who claimed their ancient right of election, on account of the extinction of the iffue of Guftavus Adolphus, confirmed her choice. His reign was paffed in continual wars, which feem to have been chiefly provoked by the ambition of his neighbours. John Cafimir, King of Poland, youngeft fon of Sigifmond, reviving his father's claim to the crown, was oppofed by Charles in feveral battles, particularly in that of Warfaw*, which lafted three days, and almoft afforded the latter a complete conqueft of Poland. After this, Frederic III. of Denmark, declared war † againft Sweden, and Charles, though at that time contending with Ruffia, Poland, Brandenburgh, and the Empire, paffed the Belt upon the ice, and obliged him to yield up for ever Scania, Halland, Blekin, and Bohus-leen ‡. In a fubfequent war with Denmark, he laid fiege

* 1656.   † 1659.   ‡ 1657.

to Copenhagen, but was repulsed with great loss, and died at Gothenburg in 1660, whither he had summoned the diet to meet him.

CHARLES XI.
1660.
   Charles XI. succeeded to the crown at the age of nine years, under the tutorage of the Queen Dowager*, his uncle, Adolphus John, Generalissimo of the army, and of four great officers of the crown appointed by his father, Charles X. This arrangement was, however, altered by the states, who excluded Adolphus, and supplied his place by a fifth great officer; enacting at the same time, that all affairs of state should be settled in concert with the senate, of which the Queen Mother should have the presidency, with the right of two votes.

Under this new administration, peace was restored with the neighbouring nations; the Emperor, the Elector of Brandenburgh, and the King of Poland, desisting from their pretensions upon Sweden, the war with Denmark being concluded by the exchange of the island of Bornholm, for some hereditary estates of small importance; and that with Russia, by the reciprocal restoration of conquered places. But the debts of the crown, which, at the death of the late King, amounted only to 16,030,000 silver dollars, were increased to 20,376,000; the fortifications were

* A Princess of Denmark.

badly

badly supported; and an unjust partiality was shewn to the nobles, to the prejudice of the inferior orders. On these accounts, the King, who, upon his first coming of age, had discharged his guardians from all responsibility, afterwards ordered a review of their administration.

Charles entered into an alliance at the Hague, with England and Holland, in order to oppose the enterprizes of Louis XIV. and was also included in the peace of Aix-la-Chapelle, after which he drew himself into a war with the Emperor, Brandenburgh, several German Princes, Holland and Denmark. The Swedes lost the battle of Fehrbellen, and their fleet was very severely handled by the Dutch and Danes, but, on the other hand, they beat the latter by land near Halmstadt, Lund, and Carlscrona. At length the calamities of war produced a peace, and the Swedes, renouncing the close alliance which had till then subsisted between them and France, concluded a treaty of commerce and reciprocal defence with Holland, for the maintenance of the treaties of peace of Westphalia and Nimeguen.

Upon his first accession to the powers of government, Charles XI. bound himself by an oath to respect the laws of Sweden, not only as they relate to the states, but to the rights, privileges, and properties of the lowest order of subjects; and in case of any alterations held necessary for the safety or exigencies of the kingdom, to act only with the advice of the senate, sanctioned by the knowledge and concurrence of the states. Yet within two years after this public assurance was given to his subjects, Charles became the most despotic of all the Princes who have worn the crown of Sweden, and was confirmed in his authority by the consent of the people.

The great privileges enjoyed by the nobles, their exemption from taxes, and the possession of the crown domains, had so much excited the jealousy of the three lower orders, that, to humble their oppressors, they were even willing to disfranchise themselves. Accordingly they declared, " That " the King was bound simply to the maintenance " of the laws, without adherence to any par- " ticular form of government; that the senate, " when required by the King, might give advice, " but that his Majesty had the full power of decid- " ing, and was responsible only to God for his " actions."

Although this declaration in fact conferred the *sovereignty* upon Charles, the word was never used before the *recess* in 1693. From this time the senators were distinguished only by the title of Royal Counsellors, and the restoration of the crown being now no longer opposed, the King issued a decree, by which all lands, dismembered from the crown since the year 1609, were declared re-united to it. By

this

this measure a great number of the nobility were reduced to poverty, the compensations being by no means proportioned, either to the value of the estates, or the prices actually paid for them. The lands were distributed into allotments for the support of the army *(Indelnings werket)* and into *boftelles* annexed to several civil and ecclesiastical offices.

Charles XI. died in 1697, at the age of forty-two years. Under his reign, rendered absolute, even to despotism, trade and manufactures flourished, agriculture was encouraged, the arts and sciences made considerable progress, and the finances were re-established. He employed 90 tons of gold in paying the public debt, and left a treasure of 1,849,000 silver dollars, besides a large sum in the private coffers. The kingdom, under his government, acquired some advantages; but the means employed were shocking to humanity, and such as no success, or convenience could justify. The payment of a large part of the public debt, and the enrichment of the treasury, were dearly purchased at the expence of the honour of the Sovereign, and the property of half the inhabitants.

CHARLES XII.
1697.

The Archbishop of Upsal, in right of his office, would have crowned the new king, but Charles, fiercely taking the crown from the

the prelate, placed it himself upon his own head; thus giving an early intimation of his character, which alarmed those who were already aware of the obstinacy which prevailed in it.

This Prince, to use an expression of one of his historians, appears to have estimated the strength of his kingdom by it's figure upon the map. With the qualities of a brave soldier, and an able general, posterity will never allow him the character of a great Monarch, or a good King. If he deserves the title of a hero, it can only be in the field of Mars; if he was a perfect master of the art of war, he knew not how to render his subjects happy. All his victories gained nothing but glory for himself and his armies, without producing any advantage to his kingdom or subjects.

Instead of profiting by the authority bestowed by the nation upon his father, in order to increase the riches, and promote the welfare of his subjects, he depopulated the country, ruined the commerce, destroyed the armies and fleets, and deranged the finances to such a degree, that it was necessary to make an assessment for the paltry sum of 398,000 silver dollars, wanted for a new levy of troops, with which Count Stenbock passed into Pomerania; and at his death the quantity of the famous *money of distress*, *myn lecken*, found in circulation, amounted to the sum of 37 millions of silver dollars.

At

At this æra, when the aristocratic party, under the pretence of delivering the nation from slavery, established itself upon the ruins of the former despotism, permit me to conclude my letter, by assuring you how much

I am, &c. &c. &c.

LETTER XXII.

MY DEAR FRIEND,

THE Princess Ulrica Eleonora, youngest sister of Charles XII. and wife of Frederic, hereditary Prince of Hesse Cassel, was received as Queen, upon condition of her renouncing for herself and descendants the claim to absolute authority, and signing an act by which she recognised the right of election to be in the nation assembled. The senators resumed their ancient title of senators of the realm; the senate became more powerful than ever, acknowleging only the superiority of the states; and the nobility regained all their rights.

Peace was successively concluded with England, Denmark, the Elector of Brandenburg and Russia; and in 1720 the Queen yielded the crown to her husband, interfering no farther with the affairs of government.

government. She died in 1741, loved and respected by the whole nation.

FREDERIC I.
1720.
Frederic I. having embraced the Lutheran religion, and signed the royal assurance, by which he bound himself to govern under the restrictions accepted by his wife, was elected, and proclaimed King of Sweden. The states, not contented with the abolition of the sovereign power in the diet of 1720, added several articles relating to the new form of government, and granted new privileges to the nobility and clergy in the diet of 1723. Of the articles enacted in 1720, the following were the most essential:

" The supreme power ought to reside for ever
" in the assembly of states, composed of the re-
" presentatives of the four orders of citizens, the
" nobility, clergy, burgesses, and the immediate
" peasants of the crown.

" The states, whether convoked or not, shall
" assemble every third year, to review the conduct
" of the senate, colleges, and other departments
" in the execution of the laws entrusted to them;
" and to adopt such measures as may be necessary
" for the welfare and glory of the realm.

" The crown of Sweden shall not be held by
" any Prince under the age of twenty-one years;
" and the states shall have the right of appointing
" tutors for the education of the Royal Family.

" The

" The legiflative power shall be wholly in the
" states, whose consent shall be necessary to give
" validity to the decrees passed by the King and
" senate, in the intervals between the meetings of
" the diets.

" The states reserve to themselves the right of
" making war, but, in case of invasion or domestic
" commotions, the King in concert with the se-
" nate, may take measures for repelling force by
" force, without waiting for the meeting of the
" states, which shall, however, be convoked with-
" out delay.

" The King may coin money, but the standard
shall be regulated by the states.

" The King shall not upon any occasion leave
" the kingdom, without the consent of the states.

" In case of a vacancy in the senate, three can-
" didates, natives of Sweden, shall be nominated
" by the states, of whom his Majesty shall accept
" one.

" During the illness, or absence of the King,
the senate shall sign all public acts.

" All the superior military officers, from field-
" marshals to colonels inclusively, shall be ap-
" pointed by the King.

" The states, assembled in diet, shall give re-
" dress to all persons prejudiced by the regulations,
" or decisions of the states.

" The

" The ancient privileges of the senate shall be
" for ever inviolable, but no new privilege, relat-
" ing to any separate order, can be valid without
" the consent of the whole.

" To these in 1723, were added the following:

" The King, in concert with the senate, may
" convoke the states, before the expiration of the
" three years.

" Upon the death, absence or illness of the
" King, the senate in a body, may convoke the
" states; which they may also do, when the wel-
" fare of the country, or the liberty of the states
" are in danger.

" If, in the above cases, neither the King nor
" the senate shall convoke the states, within the
" time prescribed, the states shall declare every
" thing done in the interval, both at home and
" broad, null; of which they shall order notice
" to be given, by the governor of Stockholm, and
" the governors of the different provinces, that
" the states may assemble of their own accord at
" the proper time and place.

" When the throne is vacant, the states, whe-
" ther convoked or not, shall assemble at Stock-
" holm, thirty days after the death of the King,
" and shall proceed to a new election.

" The individuals, who compose the states, shall
" bind themselves by an oath not to propose,
" agree to, or execute any thing that has a ten-
" dency

"dency to change the form of government: and whatever shall be decreed by the states to the prejudice of the liberty and independence of the nation, shall be null and invalid.

"The senate and the King, shall be responsible for their conduct in the intervals between the meetings of the diet.

"There shall be a secret committee for affairs not proper to be fully discussed; and this shall be composed of the three first orders, to the exclusion of the peasants; all matters referred from the whole body shall be settled here, and the members shall be absolutely prohibited from conferring with foreign ministers.

"The states shall make the laws, but they shall be signed by the King, and executed in his name. In default of the King, the senate shall sign, and cause them to be executed.

"Each order shall have a vote in the regulation of affairs relating to the nation in general, and the plurality of the four votes shall decide the question; but where the just privileges of any single order are concerned, the matter must be decided by an unanimous vote of all the orders."

By the regulations of this diet, the royal power was reduced to a mere name; the King being disabled from levying troops, disposing of the effects of the crown, or appointing the officers, who compose his court. The orders of the burgesses and peasants were equally oppressed by the nobility, who usurped the whole power, and converted the government into an arbitrary aristocracy. The two votes possessed by the King in the senate, and the right of deciding when the voices were equal, formed the royal share of the executive power, which, upon the separation of the diet, was said to be divided between the crown and the senate. But the authority thus transferred to the nobles soon gave rise to two parties, which have subsisted un-interruptedly ever since, under different forms.

The policy of the cabinet of Versailles, for a long time directed to the corruption of the members of those courts, whose assistance was necessary to the completion of its projects, exerted itself in Sweden, upon every change of the ministry, with a view of obtaining the controul of the national powers. The defects of the new mode of government increased the opportunities, and the advantages of corruption, and a considerable party was soon formed, devoted to the interests of France, and distinguished from the rest of the nation by the appellation of HATS. This party, pretending to aim only at the recovery of some domains formerly belonging to Sweden, endeavoured to produce a breach with the court of Russia, and a strict alliance with that of France.

Opposed

Oppofed to it, under the denomination of CAPS, was the party who had contributed to the eftablifhment of the new form of government. Their object was the promotion of the peace and happinefs of the nation, and the meafure propofed by them was a ftrict alliance with Ruffia, without any connection with France.

By a gradual extenfion of its influence, the court of Verfailles obtained a decided majority, and in the diet of 1783, which fat for the unufual time of eleven months, the pacific meafures of the CAPS were entirely overcome, and a rupture with Ruffia refolved upon. The lofs of Finland, and of a fine army was the confequence of the war, and the Count de Lewenhaupt became the unhappy victim of a rafh and ill-contrived project. From the year 1726, when the influence of France firft began to appear in the diet, it continued to extend itfelf over all the powers of government. At length the cabinet of Verfailles fhewed its enmity to the court, and its power over the ftates, by adding to the reftrictions of royal authority, the controul of the perfonal property of the King.

Frederic I. died the 25th of March, 1751, at the age of feventy-fix years, and was fucceeded by Adolphus Frederic.

To this Prince the eftates prefented, in 1756, a very extraordinary addrefs. It ftated that, by the 13th article of the ordinance of 1723, the ftates

R were

were impowered to infpect the jewels, and moveables belonging to the crown, as well as thofe of the royal treafury; that, as an exercife of this right, they defired to examine the diamonds prefented to the Queen upon her marriage; and, therefore, wifhed to know when it would be convenient to their Majefties, that a deputation fhould be appointed to compare them with the inventory.

The jewels in queftion were delivered to the Queen, by Count Teffin, the Swedifh embaffador, before his departure from Berlin, as a perfonal prefent. She, therefore, refufed to permit an infpection of them, but declared that as foon as they could be feparated from her own, they fhould be furrendered to the ftates, fince, " after fuch an in-
" dignity, it was beneath her to keep them." A fevere reprimand followed this anfwer. The ftates complained to the King, that the Queen had fhewn contempt not only for them, but for the fenate and great officers of the crown; and, from her capricious conduct, appeared to have no confideration of the dignity of their characters. " It
" fhould be remembered," faid they, " that the
" Queen came into this kingdom, as a companion
" to your Majefty, not to increafe the royal au-
" thority." They then ftated feveral caufes of complaint, and concluded by faying, " that the
" ftates defired not any change of fentiments in
" the King concerning the Queen, but wifhed the
" Queen

" Queen might change her difpofition towards the
" kingdom."

The King made a long apology for the conduct of the Queen, and imputed the offenfive expreffions to her ignorance of the national language; but as no infpection of thefe jewels had been before demanded during the ten years that they had been in her poffeffion, fhe thought the meafure implied a diftruft very injurious to her honour; the more fo as the diamonds had been given to her, and were, therefore, to be confidered as her own.

But, notwithftanding all the proteftations of his Majefty, the ftates perfifted, and the infpection was made. A fecond remonftrance, very *humbly* prefented to his Majefty, has the ironical expreffions, " The ftates befeech your Majefty to remain " Mafter in the court, and King in the king- " dom, and *humbly* pray that all further corref- " pondence upon the fubject may ceafe."

But the humiliation of their Majefties did not end here. The King, believing that he had at leaft the right of appointing thofe immediately about the perfons of himfelf and his children, had chofen a fub-governor for the Prince Royal; this privilege the ftates would not permit him to ufe; they, therefore, declared the place ufelefs, and difmiffed the fub-governor, accompanying their refolution with an injurious and ironical letter to the King.

Not contented with this, they sent an order, in the form of a *most humble request*, for the discharge of Mr. Dalin, Governor to the Prince Royal, and the appointment of the Senator Count de Scheffer in his place. To this order the King objected, alleging, that by the third article of the form of government, the right of choosing a governor for the Prince belonged to him; but his arguments and wishes were equally useless; the Count de Scheffer took possession of his new post, and, soon after, several other officers were named by the states to be immediately about the person of the Prince.

To complete this series of insult, a sort of seal was made, by order of the senate, having upon it an engraving of the royal signature, instead of which it was intended to serve, in order to give validity to resolutions made without the knowledge, or against the consent of the King. Thus did the HATS, at the instigation of France, deprive the crown of its rights and constitutional privileges, under the specious assurance of giving liberty to a nation, which, by those very means, they reduced to slavery.

The lapse, however, of a few years, and an alteration of interest, that fountain of political principle, detached from the cause of France her warmest partisans, and arranged them on the side of the King. But the royal authority could only be restored

stored by vigorous measures and combined efforts, such as an injured King, and an oppressed people were entitled to oppose to a nobility, fortified at once by power and precaution.

A plan of a revolution in favour of the King was communicated to Count Brahe and Baron Horn; and endeavours were used to gain the garrison and seamen of Stockholm, who, as well as the people, were known to be well disposed. But the conspiracy was discovered at the moment when it would have taken effect; Count Brahe and Baron Horn, with several other persons, were seized; and the most cruel tortures were used to wring from them a discovery of their accomplices. Brahe and Horn were beheaded.

The policy of the court of Versailles, in opposing the aggrandisement of Russia, engaged Sweden to conclude a treaty with the Turks, in the year 1740. Denmark was solicited to become a party in this alliance, but was restrained by the fear of a rupture with Russia, and by a knowledge of the advantages to be obtained from its assistance. England, for political and commercial reasons, being desirous of humbling the power of France in Sweden, made secret remittances of money to the King, who, under his own hand, had solicited such assistance. But the French party having prevented the reception of an English minister at Stockholm, during the war with Russia, on pretence of the alliance between England and Pruffia, all correspondence between the two courts had ceased, and the negociation was carried on by means of the English Embaffador at Copenhagen.

Since the turbulent diet of 1756, the HATS, by the violence of their proceedings, loft the confidence of the nation, and the credit of the CAPS was proportionably increased. The failure of the war with Pruffia, in which Sweden was involved by the intrigues of the HATS, the want of money, occafioned by the heavy and ufelefs expences of the army, and the withholding of the fubfidies promifed by France, at length, roufed the nation to a fenfe of its true interefts; and the fum difperfed among the CAPS by Sir John Goodricke, was not without its ufe in the diet of 1762.

At this period the arrears of fubfidies due from France, amounted to eleven millions of livres, and the court of Verfailles, inftead of paying the debt, propofed the conclufion of a new treaty for ten years, by which Sweden fhould engage to furnifh a fquadron of ten fhips of the line and frigates, receiving as a recompenfe from France the annual fum of one million and a half of livres.

England, alarmed by a propofal which would have thrown the greateft part of the maritime power of Sweden into the hands of France, ufed fuch exertions as occafioned it to be rejected. No anfwer was returned to the demands made of the arrears

arrears due from France; and, during the difcontents occafioned by this conduct, Sir John Goodricke was received at Stockholm as Envoy Extraordinary from the court of England. He arrived in April, 1764. The fubverfion of a form of government, firmly eftablifhed for more than twenty-eight years, feemed by no means an eafy object of endeavour, and its fuccefs can be attributed only to the failure of the fubfidies, the diforder of the finances, and the divifions of the ftates, which gave England an opportunity of overcoming entirely the projects of France.

The critical ftate of the kingdom at this time obliged the fenate to convoke an extraordinary diet at the beginning of the year 1765. The minifters of England and Ruffia laboured fo ftrenuoufly for the interefts of their courts, that, notwithftanding the intrigues, of France, and the money which fhe again expended, the CAPS were found at the diet to compofe the greater part of the ftates. After fome debate it was decided; That the alliance with France had been highly detrimental to Sweden, having burthened it with heavy expences, to the amount of three times the money agreed upon as a recompenfe, of which money the payment was denied, and the fum total reduced by chicanery from 11 to 7 millions.

While this, and fome other refolutions were paffed in the ftates, the Embaffador of France engaged

gaged the Queen in a treaty, by which the fovereignty was guaranteed to the King upon the condition of a renewed alliance between the nations. Of this fecret information was given to the minifters of England, Ruffia, and Pruffia, who, thus abandoned by the court, were obliged to change their ground, and endeavour to obtain an influence in the fenate. On the other fide, France, to fupprefs the complaints of the nation on the fubject of arrears, propofed to pay twelve millions in eight years; and the fenate thought it prudent to accept the offer. The HATS, by uniting with the court, gained a confiderable majority in the order of nobles, which the minifters of England and Ruffia endeavoured to counteract, by attaching to their intereft the three other orders of the ftate, and the fecret committee, in which the CAPS had the fuperiority. By the power of this committee, feveral fenators under the influence of France were difmiffed for abufing the confidence of the ftates, and the appointment of a minifter to the court of Verfailles was prevented. Soon after the ftates abolifhed the fecret committee, and re-eftablifhed the fenators; a meafure which was the next day declared void by the clergy and two inferior orders.

During thefe fluctuations of oppofite interefts, the CAPS prevailed fo far that a treaty with England was figned in February, 1766, by which the fubjects of each power were admitted to all the advantages

vantages of the moft favoured nation in the kingdoms, ports and havens of the other. But, after the difmiffion of the fenators, the court no longer concealed its enmity to this party, on its connection with France; and the HATS, having enumerated at length, the diforders occafioned by the new adminiftration, declared that nothing but the eftablifhment, and interpofition of the Royal Authority could fave Sweden from becoming a province to Ruffia.

The effect of thefe endeavours was a confpiracy in favour of the court, which was foon difcovered, and defeated by the precipitate conduct of the party. On this occafion the CAPS adopted the form of trial followed in 1756; but they ufed it with more moderation. Hofman, the chief, with two of his accomplices, were beheaded; and the HATS, forgetting their own conduct fome years before, called the court, by which he was condemned, a *tribunal of inquifition*.

The CAPS, whofe intention it was, at the beginning of the diet, to extend the Royal Authority, now perceived that the fuppreffion of it was the only meafure by which they could refcue Sweden from the machinations of France. Hitherto, upon a vacancy in the fenate, the King had been allowed to felect one from three candidates nominated by the ftates; but by a law paffed at the in-

ftigation

ſtigation of the Caps, this right was abolifhed, and the ſtates were allowed to preſent one candidate three ſeveral times, whom, after as many rejections, they might conſtitute a ſenator of their own authority. The Baron Debel, being thus preſented, and rejected, was placed in the ſenate by the ſtates; but the King refuſed to ſign the patent of appointment, and the Queen would not permit the uſual ceremony of kiſſing her hand. This reſolute meaſure was ſucceeded by another, which ſhewed the King to be confident of proper ſupport. He rejected three perſons preſented to him for the office of ſecretary of ſtate, and, of his own authority, appointed a fourth, in direct oppoſition to the exiſting form of government.

The influence of France would at this time have yielded eaſily to the offer of a ſubſidy from England or Ruſſia; but the miniſters of thoſe courts relied upon their majority in the ſenate, and upon the exertions of the ſecret committee. The marriage of the Prince Royal with the Princeſs of Denmark, a meaſure accompliſhed under the auſpices of the Caps, marked the concluſion of the diet, which was ſcarcely diſſolved before the ſenate and adminiſtration were ſtrenuouſly preſſed to convoke another. At this juncture France offered to pay four millions and a half for a renewal of the treaty of 1738, and, by her emiſſaries, endeavoured

voured to make it understood, that the acceptance of this subsidy would render the taxes lately imposed unnecessary.

In the mean time the treaty with England proceeded slowly. The minister refused to listen to any proposals for money, and the CAPS, desirous of offering the nation some recompense for the subsidies tendered by France, demanded the sum of 50,000 l.

At length the court party, perceiving the failure of all their schemes for the convocation of an extraordinary diet, engaged the King to feign an intention of abdicating the throne. The Prince Royal, in a journey through the provinces, gained the affection of the people, and induced the governors, merchants, &c. to present addresses, complaining of the disorders in the interior government, commerce, &c. by which the convocation of the states was rendered necessary. The death of Count Lowenhielm, the sworn enemy of France, and the breaking out of the war between Russia and the Porte, favoured the views of the HATS; while the King was encouraged by frequent promises to enter upon the scheme of feigned abdication. After refusing, therefore, to sign an act presented to him by the senate, he wrote a letter*, demanding the convocation of an extraordinary diet, as the only means of remedying the disorders

* Twelfth of December, 1768.

complained

complained of by his subjects. The following words expressed his intention of abdicating.

" If, contrary to all expectation, the senate should reject this proposal, I shall be obliged to renounce the burden of a government, rendered insupportable by the wretched state of the kingdom, and the groans of an unhappy people taxed beyond their power. When my faithful counsellors shall have assembled the States, the reasons which induce me to resign shall be communicated to them; in the mean time I absolutely forbid the use of my name in any resolutions of the senate.

Signed, " Adolphus Frederic."

The answer to this letter, which was required in eight-and-forty hours, was not returned in five days. At length the King went in person to the senate, and was requested to allow them further time; they were desirous of examining all the reasons for and against the convocation of a diet, but, with respect to the abdication, they expressed their hopes that his Majesty would desist from a resolution so contrary to the laws and to his own promises. To this the King replied that, the answer was only to be considered as a refusal, and he should, therefore, interfere no farther with the government.

Immediately afterwards, the Prince Royal went in great state to the chancery, to demand, in the King's

King's name, the stamp of his signature. From the chancery, where his request was refused, he went to the other colleges, declaring at each that his father had abdicated, and delivering to all the members a printed copy of the reasons for his Majesty's conduct.

Four deputies, who arrived from the senate, found the king to all appearance inflexible; a mode of conduct which he preserved, till a second deputation, consenting to his measures, induced him to resume the powers of government.

The diet was convoked for the 28th of April, and all the measures of England and Russia were deranged, the senate not daring to negotiate the treaty, without the participation of the States. Thus the intrigues and the bribes of France again began to acquire the ascendancy, and the King, returning to the senate, testified his approbation of their conduct, protested the innocence of his views, and declared the welfare of the nation to be his only object.

The daring conduct of the HATS upon this occasion proved their reliance upon the support and influence of France in the ensuing diet. The Embassador of this power at Constantinople, had promised the Porte to assist them by making a diversion in their favour, and every endeavour was therefore used to provoke a war between Sweden and Russia, and to detach Denmark from Russia

and

and England. Amongst other measures, a report was circulated that the ministry of France would soon have at their disposal the sum of twelve millions, of which ten were already deposited in four different houses at Amsterdam, to be employed in presents, subsidies, &c. A considerable subscription was also raised amongst some Swedish merchants in favour of the French party.

By these active measures, and the large sums of money distributed by the French minister, the HATS obtained a considerable advantage over their competitors in the election intrigues, notwithstanding the endeavours of Russia, England, and Denmark. General Ferfen, elected marshal of the diet, and all the members of the secret committee, were devoted to this power. Happily, however, for the CAPS, their antagonists were divided into two parties. Of these one, called the Court or Royal party, aimed at rendering the King absolute, and the other, called the OLD HATS, had no other object than to supplant their antagonists, without effecting any change in the constitution.

The disposition of the secret committee soon appeared. Their first act was the dismission of all the senators, who had been appointed under the influence of Russia or England. Yet all that could be obtained from this diet by the French minister, who had expended so much money to obtain its appointment and favour, was a declaration, " That
" the

"the English aimed only at the empire of the
"sea and the extension of their commerce, which
"they were desirous of acquiring at the expence
"of other nations; that Sweden, therefore, could
"not consider them as her friends; that, though
"it was the interest of Sweden to be upon good
"terms with the neighbouring powers, she could
"by no means enter into an alliance with either of
"them; but that she recognized France and the
"Porte as her natural allies, together with Spain
"and Austria, as the friends of France." The
plan of giving to the King and the senate the
power of contracting alliances, and declaring war
between the diets, was succefsfully resisted by
Colonel Pecklin, a man of great ability and integrity, at the head of the party called the OLD
HATS. If it had succeeded, all the military forces of
Sweden would have fallen into the hands of France,
who would have immediately employed them in a
war with Russia.

Thus failed a scheme, by which France hoped
to overturn the constitution of Sweden, and excite
a war in the north. The expensive method of
employing the States themselves to effect this purpose was proved to be useless, yet no more probable means of success remained. The hardy and
courageous character of the people, which rendered a revolution by surprise not impossible, was
contrasted and counteracted by the soft and pacific
dis-

disposition of the King, who could never be brought into any measure, by which the safety or interest of his family might be endangered. With all the virtues that fit a man for society, and constitute the happiness of private life, Adolphus Frederic was destitute of the ambition necessary to the formation and accomplishment of great enterprises. Even the scheme of a feigned abdication excited his fears; and nothing less than the most positive assurances of success could have induced him to undertake it. His love of tranquillity increased with his years, and France abandoned the hope of accomplishing a revolution by force during the life of the King. In the mean while a journey undertaken by the Prince Royal into France, at the express request of the Duke de Choiseul, revived the hopes of the Court party, who doubted not that it would produce some efficacious measures for the establishment of the Royal authority.

GUSTAVUS III.
1771.

Such was the situation of Sweden, when the death of the King entirely changed the face of affairs. The Prince Royal, who was at Paris, thus adding the title of King to the energy of his talents for negotiation, obtained a subsidy of a million and a half of livres *per annum*, besides the promise of money for the support of his party in the approaching diet.

The

The States, which, according to the laſt form of government, ſhould have aſſembled within thirty days after the death of the King, on account of the abſence of his ſucceſſor, were not convoked by the ſenate till the following June. The new King wrote a very gracious letter to the ſenate, and arrived at Stockholm in May.

Having thus given you a ſketch of the hiſtory of Sweden to the commencement of the preſent reign, permit me to conclude this letter, and to aſſure you how much

I am, &c. &c.

LETTER XXIII.

MY DEAR FRIEND,

GUSTAVUS III. was proclaimed King of Sweden at the age of 25 years. His character, as drawn by Sheridan, who had opportunities of examining it, forms a happy union of talents and virtues, matured by education, and directed to the difficult purpoſe of acquiring the arts and the powers of government. Thoſe who ſaw him only in public were captivated by the force of his eloquence and the charms of his addreſs, while the ſtrength of his judgment and the extent of his knowledge confirmed the affections, and raised the admiration of his intimates. The ready congratulations of the people at Stockholm gave him an opportunity of extending his popularity, by the affability of his manner and the ardour of his professions. To extirpate corruption, to create unanimity, and to reign in obedience to the diet, without being of any other party than that of the nation, he declared were the constant objects of his hope.

Thus recommended by his own qualities, and assisted by the influence of an embassador, now first appointed by the court of France*, Gustavus III. met the diet, and found the three inferior orders attached to the Hats, who were also masters of the secret committee. The small party of his personal friends urged him to follow the secret dictates of his own ambition, and promised to risk their lives in whatever he should undertake. The murmurs of the people excited his hopes; but their indignation was scarcely sufficient to ensure any active exertions in his favour. His uncertain knowledge of the disposition either of the nation or the army, and the incomplete state even of his plans, shewed the danger of hasty measures, while delay was rendered almost equally hazardous, by the excessive power of England and of Russia.

* Mr. de Vergennes. France had hitherto employed only a minister of the second order.

The

The King saw the delicacy of his situation; and the conduct, which he adopted, proved his prudence and penetration to be at least equal to his difficulties.

A series of obstacles, by which he very dexterously interrupted the resolutions of the States, reduced the diet to a state of inactivity, or of useless exertion; while his friends increased the disagreement between the nobility and three orders of the state. The two principal subjects of debate in the diet were the regulation of the royal assurance, and the dismission of the senate. With respect to the first, the nobility aimed at preserving that signed by the late King, in 1751, and the three inferior orders wished to include the mention of the new laws passed since that period.

According to the constitution, every measure adopted by three orders out of the four, obtained the validity of law; but the nobility eluded this ordinance, by proving that several articles, now proposed to be added to the royal assurance, related to their privileges, and, therefore, required an unanimous consent. The King, in refusing to sign any assurance without the concurrence of the nobles, protracted the regulation of affairs, and gained time for the completion of his plans. These and some other difficulties suspended all the operations of the diet for eight months, at the end of which, the affair of the royal assurance was settled by the moderation

deration of some chiefs of the HATS, and the King signed it, professing his desire of uniting all parties, and promoting the welfare of the kingdom. In the mean time, the delay had been sufficient to expose the defects of the government, and the influence of foreign powers; while the wisdom, disinterestedness, and patriotism of the King, seemed exerted in continual offers of mediation, and endeavours to terminate all the disputes in the diet. His Majesty, had also made use of this delay to take some secret measures preparatory to the blow that was meditated, and his party had employed themselves in different parts of the kingdom in fermenting the discontents of the people, exciting their dislike to the constitution, and engaging them to revolt.

The affair of the royal assurance being concluded, another month was spent in deliberating upon the dismission of the senate. A charge brought by the secret committee, accusing the senators of having abused the confidence of the states, induced the three inferior orders to resolve upon the deposition of the whole body; and means were found to gain the consent of the nobles. A measure thus violent was accomplished entirely by the intrigues of the CAPS, who very unwisely drove the HATS to despair, at a time when it was known that some change in the constitution was meditated. This absurd conduct of a party, elevated by success, inflamed

by

by animosity, and instigated by the desire of making themselves masters of the honours and emoluments of the state, contributed to the overthrow of the constitution, and to the ruin of those by whom it was adopted.

Soon after this, a great number of the HATS secretly devoted themselves to the King, and those, who in public gave the greatest opposition to the re-establishment of the royal authority, withdrew to their estates in the country. Amongst the latter, was General Count de Ferfen, one of the ablest of his party, who, though a zealous partizan of France, had always shewn himself attached to the present constitution. He held the office of colonel of the Guards, and his absence was one of the most favourable circumstances for the King.

After the deposition of the senate, it was proposed to establish another; and the King employed the powers given him by the law to protract the nomination to a great length; thus prolonging the sitting of the diet, and suspending its operations. A corps of 150 officers, commanded by Lieutenant Colonel Sprengporten, and assembled under the pretence of being exercised, were gained by the endeavours of the King, and testified the most zealous attachment to his cause.

In the mean time a scarcity of corn was lamented throughout the kingdom, and the court party endeavoured to impute it to the prohibition enacted by the States against the importation of foreign corn, and the little care taken to supply the people. The accusation, though ill-founded, was rendered plaufible by the artifices of the provincial governors, who were induced by the Court party to withhold the corn sent to them for distribution.

By these means, the nation, which was before prepared for a change, was at length led to defire one. The emissaries of the Count, perceiving and encouraging the difpofition of the people, invited them to repair to Stockholm, and explain their grievances at the foot of the throne. The intentions of the royal party, which had hitherto operated only in fecret, now began to appear without difguife. The CAPS, alarmed by the libels difperfed through all the public places of the capital, wifhed for the affiftance of the fecret committee; but the Marfhal of the diet, entirely devoted to the King, refufed to convoke it, and very much retarded a meafure neceffary to be executed with the greateft difpatch. At length the committee affembled, and iffued orders to the regiments of Upland and Sudermania, to hold themfelves in readinefs for marching. Colonel Sprengporten, of whom the CAPS had fufpicions, was immediately fent into Finland, under pretence of preventing a rebellion, and General Rudbeck, a man a man implicitly entrusted by the new senate, was dispatched to Scania, Gothenburg, and Carlscroon. The safety of the capital, during the absence of the governor, was committed to the care of General Pecklin.

These precautions, which alarmed the royal party, had little effect upon the King, who relied upon the garrison of Stockholm, and believed that he had nothing to fear for his own person. In order, however, to obtain the favour of the provincial regiments, the King's brothers made several journeys into Scania, and Ostrogothia, where they gained a large part of the troops. A pretence for assembling them, and for justifying the officers in their obedience to the royal dukes was still wanting. On this account the following scheme was adopted. Upon a day appointed, the Commandant of Christianstadt, named Hellicius, published a manifesto against the States, in which he set forth the miseries of the people, the dearness of all the necessaries of life, the increase of taxes, &c. attributing the whole to foreign influence, and the corruption which prevailed in the diet. When the manifesto appeared to have taken effect, he excited the garrison to revolt, shut the gates of the castle, and put it in a state of defence. Of this he immediately gave secret advice to Prince Charles, who, under pretence of quelling the revolt, engaged the officers in the neighbourhood to assemble their troops, and put themselves under his orders; thus obtaining the command of five regiments.

The troops being entirely ignorant of what was passing at Stockholm, it was not difficult to persuade them that endeavours were used to subvert the constitution, abolish the monarchy, and establish an aristocratical government under the protection of Russia, to which country the Swedes have an hereditary aversion.

At this time General Rudbeck, in the course of his tour, arrived at Christianstadt, and, finding the gates shut, immediately flew with the intelligence to the States, who sent orders to the regiments of Upland and Sudermania to march towards the capital. Two regiments of cavalry were sent to invest Christianstadt, the streets of Stockholm were patroled by the cavalry of the burgesses, and the senate requested his Majesty to remain in the city, and to send orders to his brothers to return without delay. The King, with much affected surprise at the news of the revolt, appeared to approve the measures taken by the senate for the suppression of the rebellion and the defence of the States; of which dissimulation, as it was understood only by the five or six persons who were in the secret, the whole kingdom was very easily rendered the dupe. He accompanied the cavalry of the burgesses in their patrols, professing that he

was

was himself defirous of watching over the fafety of the capital, but having really no other view than that of gaining the burgeffes, in which he fucceeded fo well, that at the decifive moment they declared for him.

Two days afterwards, a letter from Prince Charles informed the King of the revolt, and of the methods ufed to fupprefs it. He immediately fent this letter to the fenate, with the affurance, that the troops raifed fhould be employed only in the reduction of Chriftianftadt, and feconding the requeft of his brother to be continued in the command by their authority. Without any attention to this requeft, the fenate appointed one of their members to the command, thus marking a decifive moment at which the affairs of the King would admit of no delay.

Whilft his emiffaries were employed on all fides in gaining the foldiers in the garrifon, the King affembled the officers, whom he knew to be devoted to him, and proceeded with them through the public ftreets, fpeaking indifcriminately to all the citizens. The fenate, when informed of the difturbance, which began to appear on all fides, either relied upon the precautions already taken, and difbelieved that any attempt would be made againft them; or were intimidated by the popularity of the King, and thought any proceedings that could be ufed to oppofe him, would rather accelerate

than

than prevent a revolution. It was refolved, therefore, to wait the arrival of the regiments, which were now within one day's march of the capital; and the fame reafon, which induced the fenate to delay their operations, preffed the King to the execution of his plan.

On the morning of the 19th of Auguft, 1772. three days after the arrival of General Rudbeck, the King refolved to perifh, or to regain the power fo long abufed by the ftates. At ten o'clock he was on horfeback, and, furrounded by a great number of officers perfonally devoted to him, began by vifiting the park of artillery. There he called for Lieutenant-General Count de Heffenftein, and demanded that he fhould take an oath; to which the General replied, that, having already taken one oath to his Majefty, it was unneceffary for him to take a fecond. He then laid his fword at the feet of the King, and, furrendering himfelf a prifoner, was confined in the library of the caftle.

His Majefty redoubled his politenefs and familiarity to all thofe whom he met in the ftreets, and, upon his return to the caftle, finding the guards drawn out to be relieved, he addreffed them, with all the eloquence fo natural to him, informing them that his life was in danger, and lamenting the wretched ftate of the kingdom, the flavery in which the nation was held by the influence of

foreign

foreign gold, the diffenfion in the ftates, the prolongation of the diet for fourteen months and the mifery of the people. He affured them that he had no other wifh than to remedy thefe evils, to banifh corruption, re-eftablifh the liberties of Sweden, and revive the luftre of the Swedifh name. After renouncing in the moft pofitive terms all claims to abfolute power, he concluded with thefe words: "I am obliged to defend my own liberty, "and that of my kingdom againft an ariftocracy, "which reigns defpotically. Will you be faith- "ful to me, as your anceftors were to Guftavus "Vafa, and to Guftavus Adolphus? If you will, "I am ready to rifk my life for your welfare, and "that of my country." The officers, who were chiefly young men, and already attached to the King, readily took the oath of fidelity, and promifed to follow him wherever he fhould lead. Three only refufed. One, named Cederftroom, a captain of the guards, alleged, that having already taken the oath of fidelity to the ftates, he could not take that now tendered to him by his Majefty. The King, looking ftedfaftly upon him, faid, "Confider what "you are doing." To which Cederftroom replied, "I have well thought of it, and my opinion to- "morrow will be the fame as to-day. If I could "break the oath already taken to the ftates, I "might alfo break that which I fhould take to "your Majefty." The King then demanded his

fword,

sword, and dreading the impreffion which such resolute conduct might have upon the reft of the officers, he told him in a more gentle manner that, as an inftance of confidence and good opinion, he would return his sword upon no other condition than that of being accompanied by him. But Cederftroom, ftill preferving his firmnefs, anfwered, " that as his Majefty could not truft him on that " day, he begged to be excufed from all further " fervice."

The King, followed by all the officers, was defirous of addreffing the foldiers, who appeared irrefolute and unquiet. He was furprized, ftopped, and appeared to hefitate. This moment was critical. A fergeant decided it in his favour, by exclaiming, " All fhall be well—Long live Gufta-" vus !" The King immediately anfwered, " In " this cafe I will run the rifque;" and, afterwards, advancing, he fpoke to them nearly in the fame manner as to the officers, and with the fame fuccefs. The foldiers anfwered with acclamations. One voice only cried, " No;" it was heard, but not attended to.

The officers immediately affembled, by order of his Majefty, the regiments of guards and artillery. In the mean time the royal party circulated a report of his being arrefted, and the populace run in crowds to the caftle, teftifying their joy at feeing him free, by frequent acclamations.

The

The senators, assembled in the council-chamber, hearing the noise and seeing from the windows what was passing, descended to discover the cause. Thirty-six grenadiers, with bayonets fixed, drove them back into the hall from which they came, and locked them in it. From thence they were conducted into different apartments, and confined for three days, to prevent their appearance at the new assembly of the States. During this time they were allowed to provide themselves with all necessaries, and the King sent to their families, promising that they should receive no injury, and be dismissed after a detention of a few days.

He then re-mounted, and followed by all the officers, sword in hand, with a detachment of soldiers, and a great number of people, went to the different quarters at which parties of the garrison were stationed, and administered the oath of fidelity. At each place he repeated his declaration, that he had no other view than to save and defend his country; and that, if they had not confidence in him, he would desist from his enterprize, and relinquish the crown.

In the space of an hour, the King became master of all the military in Stockholm. He distributed cartridges to the soldiers; placed cannon at all the avenues, bridges, &c. and forbad the departure of any person from the city without a passport signed by his hand. In the mean time
he

he diftributed a manifefto, exhorting the burgeffes and the inhabitants to continue in peace, and difpatched an officer to the regiments of Upland and Sudermania, then at a fmall diftance from Stockholm, with orders for the regiments to return to their quarters, and for the commandant to repair to the capital. The orders were obeyed without the leaft difficulty, being figned in the ufual form, and with the counter-fignature of the fecretary of ftate; but, though thefe regiments, upon which the States relied fo much, were at that time ignorant of what had been done in the city, no perfon having been fuffered to leave it, they were no fooner informed of the revolution than they defired to take the oath of fidelity to the King.

The King continued vifiting the different quarters of the city, his fuite increafing every moment, and the white handkerchief, the mark of diftinction appointed by the King for his friends, appearing upon every arm. He received the oaths of the magiftrates and colleges, and paffed the night in patroling the ftreets of the city, while the garrifon remained under arms. Being, afterwards, defirous of adminiftering the oath to all people in a body, a meafure by no means ufelefs, when we confider the religious character of the nation, many thoufands of perfons were affembled two days after the revolution in a large fquare. The King appeared on horfeback, with his fword in his hand.

hand. He addressed them in a very pathetic speech, and with a pronunciation so clear and distinct, that not a syllable was lost. After declaring that it was his intention to restore the tranquillity and liberty of his country, by abolishing an aristocratical government, and to revive the ancient laws, such as they were before the year 1680, " I renounce," said he, " all claims to absolute " power or sovereignty, considering it as my prin- " cipal glory to be the first citizen of a people " really free." At these words he was interrupted by loud acclamations. His artful adoption of the title of CITIZEN; the fine word LIBERTY, so flattering to an oppressed people, and his renunciation of the sovereignty, pronounced in the language of the country, which no King of Sweden had spoke since Charles XII. drew tears of joy from the assembled multitude.

In the mean time the heralds, by proclamation in the several quarters of the city, summoned an assembly of the States for the ensuing morning, and declared all members traitors to their country, who should not appear.

Thither his Majesty repaired in all the pomp of royalty, surrounded by his guards, and holding in his hand the silver scepter of Gustavus Adolphus. In a very forcible speech, he lamented the unhappy state to which the country was reduced by the conduct of a party ready to sacrifice every thing to

its

its ambition, and reproached the States with adapting their actions to the views of foreign courts, from which they received the wages of perfidy. " If any one dare contradict this, let him rife and " fpeak."—Conviction, or fear, kept the affembly filent, and the fecretary read the new form of government, which the King fubmitted to the approbation of the States. It confifted of fifty-feven articles, of which the following five were the chief.

1. The King has the entire power of convoking and diffolving the affembly of the States, as often as he thinks proper.

2. His Majefty alone has the command of the army, fleet, and finances, and the difpofal of all offices, civil and military.

3. In cafe of an invafion, or of any preffing neceffity, the King may impofe taxes, without waiting for the affembly of the States.

4. The diet can deliberate upon no other fubjects than thofe propofed by the King.

5. The King fhall not carry on an offenfive war without the confent of the States.

When all the articles were gone through, the King demanded if the States approved of them, and was anfwered by a general acclamation. The CAPS, who, but a few days before, had given law to the kingdom, and even talked of arrefting the King, upon this occafion behaved with a fubmiffion as bafe as their former haughtinefs. The marfhal of the diet, and the speakers of the four orders signed the new form of government, after which the States took an oath dictated by his Majesty. He then dismissed all the senators from their employments, adding, that in a few days he would appoint others; and concluded this extraordinary scene by drawing out of his pocket a small book of psalms, from which, after taking off the crown, he gave out Te Deum. All the members very devoutly added their voices to his, and the hall resounded with thanksgivings, which it is to be feared never rose to heaven, if sincerity was necessary to their passport.

The next day, all those who had been arrested, General Pecklin alone excepted, took the oath of fidelity, and were dismissed. He was released in the month of February of the following year, and, soon after, desired to resign the command of his regiment. . The revolution, which brought reward to many, occasioned punishment to none. Several of the CAPS were admitted to offices of profit and confidence, and the members of the new senate were selected by the King from all parties.

Captain Hellicius, who produced the concerted revolt at Christianstadt, received, with the rank of Colonel, the surname of *Gustaffs Schildt*, or Shield of Gustavus, and was ennobled, with permission to

carry

carry a fhield in his coat of arms, having, in the center, the letter G.

Colonel de Sprengporten was created commander of the order of the Sword, at the head of three regiments of infantry, and one of dragoons, with which he arrived from Finland a few days after the revolution, having been detained at fea by contrary winds. When the King heard of his arrival, he went to meet him, and prefenting him with the enfign of the order, " Receive, Sir," faid he, " a " teftimony of that gratitude which you have fo " well deferved."—A few days afterwards the King appointed him Lieutenant General, and Chief of the guards.

In a proclamation, publifhed for the purpofe of abolifhing the names by which the feveral parties had been hitherto diftinguifhed, the King expreffed his wifhes, that for the future there fhould be no other party than that of true patriotifm, every member of which fhould contribute, by his efforts, to the welfare of his country.

On Sunday, the 23d of Auguft, the whole Royal family affifted at the finging of Te Deum in the Cathedral. For the firft time, the prayer for the States and fenate was omitted, no perfons being mentioned, but the King and Royal Family.

Prince Charles, Prince Frederic, and feveral general officers, received the oath of fidelity from the

the troops, and colleges of the provinces, in the King's name, and in a few days the new conftitution was univerfally acknowledged throughout the kingdom.

The States, foon after their ratification of the new form of government, affembled to vote an addrefs of thanks to his Majefty, expreffing their gratitude to him, for having delivered the kingdom, at the rifk of his life, from the ftate of anarchy and confufion, in which he found it, in memory of which event, the order of nobles refolved to have a medal ftruck, and the three other orders defired to contribute to the expence of it.

On the ninth of September, the King announced the feparation of the diet, and appointed the year 1778 for the meeting of the new one. The fuccefs of this revolution, now completely accomplifhed, was notified by the King to the feveral courts. Upon the diffolution of the diet, he applied himfelf to the eftablifhment of an adminiftration, and to the feparation of the different departments, fo as to render each refponfible directly to himfelf. The diftribution of juftice particularly occupied his attention; and, amongft other feafonable matters of reform, was the entire abolition of the ufe of torture. Liljenftrate, the Chancellor of Juftice, was directed to enquire into, and correct the frequent abufes in the provincial courts,

courts, and all prevarication and delay was feverely punished, without exception of perfons.

A commiffion was appointed to regulate the public income and expenditure, and meafures were taken for the realization of the enormous quantity of paper money. In remedy of the diftreffes occafioned by the prefent famine, corn was diftributed in all the provinces, the free importation of it was permitted, and the diftillation of brandy prohibited.

Engineers were fent to examine the fortreffes, and frontier towns in Sweden and Finland, the King making his greateft exertions in the military department, in order to protect himfelf againft the anti-royalift party, which ftill exifted, and againft the power of the court of Ruffia, which had guaranteed the ancient conftitution in 1721. In the beginning of November, his Majefty, according to the cuftom of the ancient kings, went to receive the homage of the provinces, after having entrufted the capital to the care of the Duke de Sudermania. He was accompanied by the Duke d'Oftrogothia, and in the journey vifited Carlfcroon, the fluices of Trolhetta, the frontier places, and the magazines. Throughout the whole tour, he converfed familiarly with all perfons who offered themfelves, expreffed his fatisfaction in finding himfelf at the head of a free people, and was received with unfeigned teftimonies of joy. In him his fubjects believed they faw a fecond Guftavus Vafa, and they compared the ariftocracy from which he delivered them, to the tyranny of Chriftian.

On his return to Stockholm, he was received by the Queen Dowager, his mother, who was in Germany at the time of the revolution; and the public rejoicings, by which the inhabitants of the capital would have celebrated this event, were prevented only by his benevolent requeft, that the money, thus intended to be expended, might be employed in relieving the diftreffes of the poor. His own efforts were an example to his fubjects. A large quantity of corn was taken from the magazines of the crown, and, with fome fupplies in money, was diftributed by his order in the capital, and the provinces.

During the interval of fix years between the meetings of the diet, the King applied himfelf, with inconceivable activity, to the eftablifhment of the new conftitution, the encouragement of commerce, agriculture, and manufactures, and to the prevention of the cruel famines, by which Sweden is fo often liable to fuffer. At Stockholm, as well as at Gothenburg, he eftablifhed public workfhops in which the poor might earn a fubfiftence. Thefe he furnifhed with the materials ufed in feveral manufactures, and, at the end of the year 1773, his Majefty jesty had the satisfaction to see 12,000 persons employed in his own residence. He facilitated the importation of corn, prohibited individuals from depositing it in magazines, and prevented every sort of monopoly in that article. But, notwithstanding all the methods used to supply the nation with abundance of necessaries, he could not prevent the discontents, and even outrages occasioned by the prohibition of distilling. For the three first years, the King adhered to his determination, which he was several times obliged to enforce by the assistance of the troops; but in 1775, he recalled the prohibition, declaring all distilleries royal, and permitting the partial use of them by lease from the crown. The want of a sufficient number of farmers induced him afterwards to distil brandy upon his own account; he bought all the utensils formerly used in the private distilleries, prohibited the importation of foreign brandies, and imposed very rigorous punishments upon all who should offend against his privilege. The peasants, on all sides, sent deputations to the King, reclaiming their ancient right of distilling for their own consumption; and, these being disregarded, the discontent rose to such a height, that, at Stockholm, guards were obliged to be stationed round the royal distilleries, to protect them from the violence of the populace.

The

The King gave particular attention and encouragement to commerce, to promote which he instituted a college for the regulation of all affairs relating to trade, and the finances. The counsellor of commerce, *Westerman*, was ennobled and appointed president, with the name of *Liliencrantz*, and the title of Commercial Secretary of State. An office of discount was also established at Stockholm, and the small city of Marstrand was declared a free port.

In the naval and military departments, the King exerted himself with great activity and success. The fleet, which he found decayed and feeble, he in a few years restored to a respectable footing, and, besides changing the regulations of the navy, he raised a new corps of sailors, and formed them by continual exercise under the direction of Admiral Wrangel, who had the care of the fleet and all its dependencies, while that of the dock-yards was entrusted to Admiral *Ter Smeden*. Hitherto the two departments had been united under the college of Admiralty, but for the future the King decreed that the chiefs should make their report only to him, and that the college, in order to execute his orders with the greater readiness, should be removed from Carlscroon to Stockholm. At the same time the dock-yards throughout the kingdom were restricted from building any vessels for the use of foreigners.

The army, which, as well as the navy, had been neglected during the aristocracy, was next to be reformed. The King began by giving cloaks, tents, and new arms to all the regiments. Afterwards, under the direction of Field Marshal Count de Hessenstein, a new exercise was introduced, and several camps were formed, in which the soldiery were manœuvred by the King himself. The sale of military offices, which had been permitted for many years, was entirely suppressed; and the King provided not only for the re-establishment of discipline and good order in the army, but for the future welfare of the individuals which composed it. He increased the pay of the officers, and made such regulations as ensured the support of the soldiers in their old age. The old *council of war* was abolished, and a new one created under the title of the *college of war*, the members of which were obliged to reside at Stockholm. The fortifications of Christianstadt, Malmoe, and Landscroon, with the fortresses in Finland, and upon the frontiers of Norway, were put into a state of defence, and furnished with artillery, which had for a long time been kept in the magazines.

The King made frequent journeys through the different provinces, receiving reports of the state of manufactures, and the interior police, punishing every act of injustice, and supporting all persons in the enjoyment of their rights and privileges.

leges. In one of thefe tours, a charge of malverfation, brought againſt Baron de H..... governor of Nericia, was heard, by the King's order, before Mr. de Liliencrantz; and the Baron, notwithſtanding the favour formerly ſhewn him by the King, and his intimacy with Mr. de Liliencrantz, was difmiffed from his office. The ſame puniſhment was inflicted upon the fenefchal and treafurer of Dalecarlia, convicted of prevarication, although they were connected with the firſt families in the kingdom. But the example, which had the greateſt effect in rendering the judges circumfpect and impartial, was the fentence paffed upon one of the firſt courts of juſtice, that of Oſtrogothia, refident at Jenkoping. A charge of injuſtice, brought againſt this court, after having been enquired into by a commiſſion, confiſting of Mr. de Liliencrantz, and two fenators, was brought before the fenate at Stockholm, where the accufed members were obliged to appear, and permitted to make their own defence. The caufe was pleaded publicly in the prefence of the King, who opened the firſt feffion by a brilliant fpeech, concluding with thefe words: " I have delivered you from an oppreſſion " which rendered all juſtice venal. I have made " laws for fecuring the rights of my meaneſt ſub- " jects, and thefe laws have been infringed. I " owe to pofterity an example of juſtice." The charge being proved, four members were difmiffed

from

from their offices, and some others were suspended for several months.

These acts of justice, together with the King's popularity in other respects, made his arrival in the provinces matter of joy to the inhabitants. The peasants, also, were now released from the oppressive services of the posts, the King paying for the horses used by himself and family.

In the midst of these endeavours for the improvement of the several branches of government, the King was not unmindful of the interests of agriculture and population. He directed the ministers of Sweden, in the different courts of Europe, to inform themselves exactly of the number of Swedes resident abroad, and of the motives which induced them to quit their country. Invitations were given to these persons to return home; and, although these were not always effectual, the research had its use, in ascertaining what were the principal causes of emigration. The small town Eckelstuna, not far from Stockholm, was assigned by the King to a colony of persons, who have been induced by promises of benefit to quit Solingen, in the duchy of Berg, and settle in Sweden. There they have established a manufactory of swords, sabres, and bayonets, and thus prevented the loss of the large sums of money before sent out of the country for the purchase of these articles.

Several

Several citizens, zealous for the public welfare, and encouraged by the special protection of his Majesty, have united under the title of the Patriotic Society, for the laudable purposes of promoting population and agriculture, relieving the necessitous, and giving their assistance in every thing relating to the interior œconomy of the kingdom.

His Majesty, in his assiduous concern for the welfare of the kingdom, is not less eager for the advancement of the sciences, arts, and polite literature. He began by procuring a fine version of the bible, and employing several men of learning in improving and forming elementary books used in the education of youth. At the Academy of Sciences he very often assists in person, and sends questions in a fictitious name, proposed with a view of leading to some new discovery, or some measure for the benefit of his people.

His respect for the memory of his ancestors the King has made conduce to the progress of the arts. A statue of Gustavus Erickson, or Vasa, and another of Gustavus Adolphus, are worthy of the heroes they represent, and of the artist who executed them. They are both by Archeveque, and the expence of the latter alone amounted to 300,000 silver dollars. The design of a medal, struck to the memory of Linnæus, was furnished by the King himself. One side has a bust of Linnæus, the other the figure of the goddess Cybele in a mourning attitude, furrounded by the different attributes of the mineral, vegetable and animal kingdom, with thefe words; ' *Deam luctus angit* ' *amiſſi*;' and in the exergue, ' *Poſt obitum d. x.* '. *January*, 1778. *Rege Jubente.*' The Exchange, palaces of the Duke de Sudermania, and of the Princefs Albertina, the houfe appropriated to balls and public concerts, a magnificent ftone bridge, the fine fquare of Guftavus Adolphus, and the Opera Houfe, the laft of which coft 400,000 filver dollars, at the fame time that they contribute to the ornament of the capital, have afforded to artifts of all forts opportunities of exerting their talents, and difplaying their tafte.

As a relief from the labours of the cabinet, the King feeks the pleafures of fociety, and frequents the affemblies of the nobility and burgeffes, where his amiable manner conciliates the affection of the company, and his condefcenfion removes thofe reftraints which the prefence of a King ufually impofes. His lively imagination, and inventive genius, appear continually in the magnificent fêtes, fpectacles, ballets, caroufals, and tournaments, which he gives to his court, and in the fplendid performances of national operas, of which the fable, and even the words are fometimes furnifhed by himfelf. In 1776, a tournament and caroufal were exhibited at Eckholmfund, with very extraordinary pomp, in the firft of which the King, as a foreign knight, supported this position, "That love is both more lively, and more permanent in the hearts of those who latest become subject to its influence." His Majesty was victorious at the tournament, and his Esquire, Major Monck, gained the prize in the carousal. This spectacle, which cost 400,000 copper dollars, was repeated in the following year in the square before the castle at Stockholm, and in almost all the succeeding years carousals, more or less magnificent, have been given, differing only in the habits of the knights who compose the troops, and in the subjects represented.

But though the King takes these methods to produce a circulation of money, and to give encouragement to artists, he has endeavoured very strenuously to suppress the taste for luxury and expence, which prevails over the whole kingdom, and especially in the capital. Having for a long time meditated the adoption of a national dress, in order to prevent the continual introduction of foreign fashions, he, at length, in the year 1774, sent a gold medal, of the value of thirty ducats, to the Patriotic Society, as a reward for the person who should give the best answer to the following question. " Whether, to restrain the absurdities " of fashion, and prevent the importation of pro- " hibited goods, it would not be useful to esta- " blish in Sweden a national dress, suitable to the
" climate,

"climate, and differing from that of foreign na-
"tions?"

In the beginning of the year 1778, the plan was submitted to, and approved by, the senate, and a few days afterwards there appeared a circular letter to the governors of the provinces, signed by the King, and written in a stile of moderation, such as no monarch ever before used to his subjects. After enumerating his own endeavours for the suppression of luxury, and lamenting the loss occasioned by the introduction of foreign commodities, he concludes by saying that, not thinking himself authorised to constrain his subjects, or to influence them in such a matter any otherwise than by his example, he only gave notice that on the 8th of the following April, he should appear with his whole court and senate in a new dress, which he should also cause to be adopted by the army. The dress was soon received by all the men, from the first senator to the lowest peasant, but has never been generally used by the other sex.

At length the time appointed for the meeting of the diet approached, and the King enjoyed the satisfaction of observing the increased prosperity of the kingdom. The administration was well regulated, the army and navy were placed upon a respectable footing, tranquillity was established within and without, commerce flourished, and, to increase his happiness, the Queen found herself pregnant

for

for the firſt time, after having been married for ſeven years. To all theſe advantages was to be added, that of being upon very good terms with the neighbouring powers. In the preceding year, the King had paid a viſit to the Empreſs of Ruſſia, by whom he was received with great diſtinction, and entertained in the capital with very brilliant fêtes. He returned to Stockholm in the month of Auguſt, in a ſuperb *jagt*, given him by her Imperial Majeſty, and with preſents for himſelf and ſuite to the amount of 400,000 roubles.

The King preſſed the convocation of the diet, being willing that the Queen ſhould be delivered during its ſitting, that thus the ſtates might become the ſponſors of a child born under their own eyes. The ordinance iſſued by Guſtavus Adolphus in 1617, was adopted as the model of all the regulations; in conſequence of which, the King named Major-general Baron de Saltze marſhal of the diet, and appointed the ſpeakers or preſidents of the three other orders.

On the 30th of October, the King opened the diet with a ſpeech, in which he declared that, notwithſtanding the neceſſities and the expences of the three preceding years, he had been enabled, by prudence and œconomy, to put the kingdom in a ſtate of defence, and reſtore it to its ancient ſplendor, without exhauſting the national finances; that he, therefore, had not called them together to demand

mand fuccours or fubfidies, but merely to rejoice with him in the happy fituation of the country, to be witneffes of the delivery of his wife, and, finally, that he might perform his promife given at the diffolution of the laft diet. He intreated them to become the fponfors of the infant, which he expected would fhortly fee the light, and concluded by faying, " If heaven fhould grant me an heir to
" my crown, may he be worthy one day to af-
" cend the throne of Guftavus Erickfon (Vafa)
" and Guftavus Adolphus; may he remember that
" it is the firft duty of a Swedifh King to love
" and honour a free people, and may the crown
" be his no longer than he fhall act in conformity
" to this truth. It would make me wretched if
" I believed my pofterity likely to forget, that
" providence, in placing them at the head of a
" great nation, has entrufted to their care the hap-
" pinefs of a free and generous people."

Two days after the opening of the diet, the Queen was delivered of a Prince, the firft immediate heir to the crown born in Sweden fince Charles the Twelfth. He was baptized by the Archbifhop of Upfal in the chapel of the caftle, and in the prefence of a deputation from the four orders of the States, his fponfors, who gave him the name of Guftavus Adolphus.

The joy of the Swedes on this occafion difplayed itfelf in acts of beneficence, more honourable

nourable than the erection of marble monuments, which speak only to the imagination, and are entirely without use. Several persons obtained leave of the King to open a general subscription under his immediate protection, for establishing a new house of education. The corps of horse employed in escorting the Royal family sent a donation of 10,000 copper dollars to the Foundling Hospital, instituted by the Free Masons in the capital. The officers of the guards established a school for military education, and of the 300,000 crowns, given by the States to the young Prince, the King desired that one third might be employed in relieving the poorer part of his subjects in the assessment of duties.

The diet granted to the King a free gift of 600,000 crowns, payable in seven years, of which 300,000 were for increasing the private revenues of the King, 100,000 for the expence of the baptism of the Prince Royal, and of the Duke de Sudermania's marriage, 100,000 as a present to the Queen, and 100,000 for the dower of the Duchess of Sudermania.

On the 25th of January, 1779, the King closed the diet with a speech, in which he expressed, with his usual eloquence, his satisfaction at being the first King in this century, who could dissolve the free States, without having exercised or suffered oppression. He called himself, not only the founder, but the promoter and defender of their liberty and laws, and thanked them in the moſt lively manner for the affection and attachment they had expreſſed to himſelf, the Queen, and the young heir, whom he deſired to ſee worthy of the name of Guſtavus Adolphus.

One of the moſt laudable reſolutions of this diet was that which gave permiſſion to foreigners to exerciſe their religion in Sweden, under no other reſtrictions than thoſe uſual in other countries, diſtinguiſhed by the ſame toleration; a meaſure which induced the court of Rome to ſend a pre- late thither in the following year, charged to act in concert with the government in the arrange- ments neceſſary for the exerciſe of the Catholic religion. After much oppoſition, a reſolution moved by Count Axel Ferſen, who had retired from the ſenate in the year 1773, for giving new inſtructions to the commiſſioners of control over the bank, was paſſed, and unanimouſly approved.

A ſhort time after the ſeparation of the diet, the peaſant repreſentatives having returned to their conſtituents, with accounts of their unſucceſsful endeavours for the re-eſtabliſhment of private dif- tilleries, the murmurs of the people were heard on all ſides, and in Smoland and Dalecarlia broke out into violence. Theſe diſcontents were in- flamed and ſupported by a great number of libels, and, amongſt others, by one inſerted in the pub- lic papers, in which the perſon of the King was attacked

attacked in the moft indecent manner. Of this rhe author, named Haldin, was known, and, together with the Editor and Printer, was condemned by a court of juftice to an imprifonment of feveral weeks, which the fenate, taking cognizance of the affair, changed into a fentence of death. Both fentences were remitted by the King, who alfo, upon a fimilar occafion, faved the life of an officer, condemning him, at the fame time, to bread and water, for having fpoken difrefpectfully of the King his father. This magnanimity gained the hearts of his fubjects, who perceived him always inclined to mercy, except in the punifhment of flagrant inftances of injuftice, or fome invafion of the rights of the citizens.

A war having broke out between France, 1780. America, and England, the King of Sweden, at the requeft of the merchants, refolved to fend convoys with their veffels; a meafure which was rendered more neceffary, by the conduct of one of the belligerent parties, who feized upon neutral veffels, under the pretence of the cargoes being deftined for the enemy. The court of Stockholm had already complained of thefe proceedings to that of England, confidering it as an infringement of the treaties of 1661, and 1666; and the latter court had juftified their conduct under an article, taken from one of thefe treaties, but not admitted to be authentic in Sweden. The King,

King, therefore, applied to Denmark and Ruffia, to join their forces with his; and thefe powers acceded as far as related to the Baltic, and that part of the North Sea near the fhores of their kingdoms, leaving Sweden the only power which protected its commerce in all parts of the world*. A fquadron of eight men of war, and four frigates, equipped at Carlfcroon with great celerity, failed under the orders of Vice Admiral de Gerten towards the North Sea. The expence of this fquadron, and of another deftined for the Mediterranean, was defrayed by an additional duty of 5 *per cent.* impofed upon foreign commodities imported.

In the mean time, England continuing to feize all veffels without diftinction, the Emprefs of Ruffia joined herfelf to Sweden, in order to engage the neutral powers in an alliance for the protection of commerce not only in the Baltic, but in all the feas of Europe, and in the two Indies. The celebrated armed neutrality, of which the motives were very laudable, and the effect trifling, was thus formed. It was confirmed by a treaty figned between Ruffia, Sweden, and Denmark, on the 9th of June in the fame year, by which the two latter powers agreed to furnifh each fixteen fhips of the line, and frigates, and Ruffia twenty fhips and frigates. To this league Holland, Pruffia, the Emperor, and the King of Naples, afterwards became parties.

* During the courfe of this war Sweden exported a great quantity of cannon, anchors, and fails to America and Holland.

1781.
1782.

The King paſſed a great part of the following ſummer at Aix-la-Chapelle and Spa, for the re-eſtabliſhment of his health, and returned to Stockholm, through Holland, at the end October. Soon afterwards the care of the Prince Royal's education was entruſted to the Senator Baron de Sparre, and, in a ſhort time, the Queen again declared herſelf pregnant. She was delivered of a Prince in the month of Auguſt, 1782, within a few weeks after the death of the Queen Dowager, a Princeſs diſtinguiſhed by her great elevation of mind, and fondneſs for the ſciences and fine arts. The joy occaſioned by the birth of the young Prince afforded only a ſhort conſolation for this loſs: he received the name and title of Charles Guſtavus Duke of Smoland, and died at the age of ſeven months.

1783.

The beginning of this year was diſtinguiſhed by a revolt amongſt the Dalecarlians, who bore with leſs patience than the inhabitants of the other provinces the prohibition of private diſtilleries. A body of troops reſtored order, and ſeized the principal ring-leaders; but it was impoſſible to ſuppreſs the diſcontent, which the King's perſeverance in maintaining the ſole right of diſtilling cauſed throughout the kingdom. In this year the King had an interview with the Empreſs of Ruſſia at Frederickſham, a ſmall city and port of the Baltic, upon the confines of Ruſſia and Swediſh

dish Finland. The designs of the Emprefs upon the Crimea, and the navigation of the Black Sea, required that she should be well assured of the friendship of a monarch, whose respectable forces by land and sea might enable him to put in execution any plans dictated by his own ambition, or by the influence of the court of Versailles, against a province which he could hardly be unwilling to re-conquer.

The King set out for Finland in the beginning of June, for the purpose of reviewing the troops in the dutchy. There a volley from a party commanded by himself startled his horse, and he had the misfortune to break his arm by a fall. The interview with the Emprefs, though retarded by this accident, was effected on the 29th of June, and celebrated, during the three days which their majesties remained together, by continual fêtes. The Emprefs had caused a very elegant wooden palace to be erected at Frederickham, richly ornamented and furnished, in which was an elegant theatre, appropriated to the performances of a troop of French comedians provided for the occasion. The King gave the Emprefs very positive assurances of an exact neutrality, and returned to Stockholm on the 4th of July, entirely recovered of the fracture. The burgesses of Stockholm, in memory of the happy return and recovery of their Monarch, set apart the sum of 4,000 rix-dollars, for the perpetual support of some beds in the Royal
Hospital,

Hospital, at which fractures of arms and legs are to be cured *gratis*. These are called beds of *Loulais*, from the name of the camp at which the accident happened to the King.

In the several journeys, which the King made into Finland, he perceived that the province was unequally divided into four districts, and that the court of justice at Abo was not alone sufficient for the number of inhabitants. Another court was, therefore, established at *Vasa*, and the ceremony of installing the members was performed at Stockholm, with great pomp, in the presence of the Royal Family and a brilliant court. The King, in an eloquent and energetic harangue, exhorted the members to protect the persecuted and the orphan, and to give particular attention to the lower class of citizens, by whom the state was defended and supported.

About the latter end of August, the King notified to the senate, that, in obedience to the advice of his physicians, he should pass the winter in Italy. Before his departure he pressed the equipment of a small squadron of observation at Carlscroon. It was ready in September, and, in the month of October, the King began his journey, to defray the expence of which he borrowed a considerable sum upon the revenues of the royal distilleries.

His Majesty, after passing the winter and spring in Italy, first at Pisa, where he used the baths, afterwards at Rome, Naples, Florence, Genoa, and Venice,

Venice, arrived at Paris in the beginning of June, 1784, where he remained till the end of July, and was received by the court and city as the ancient ally of France. Amidst a succession of pleasures, he was not unmindful of his interests. From the year 1779, the court of Versailles, under pretence of the expences of the war, had neglected the payment of the usual subsidies; but the King now managed so well, as to obtain the sum of 1,200,000 livres in discharge of a great part of the arrears, and to conclude a treaty by which France ceded to him for ever the island of St. Barthelemi*, near Guadaloupe, on condition of being allowed to establish a staple for its northern commerce in the city of Gothenburg.

On the third of August his Majesty returned to the capital, after an absence of ten months, and the burgesses, upon this occasion, built at their own expence a stone bridge over the canal of Ritterholm, with the following inscription:

1784.

<blockquote>
Gustavo III. O. R. salvo et sospite.
Ex itinere Italico patriæ reddito.
Hunc pontem sexto lapide constructum,
Lignei loco jam vetustate collabentis. Fortunæ reduci et lætitiæ publicæ, dedicarunt
Cives Holmenses--- D. iii. Aug. M,DCC,LXXXIV.
</blockquote>

---

* This island, which contains seven or eight hundred inhabitants, and produces a great quantity of cotton, is very well situated for contraband traffic.

In the beginning of the year 1786, the King judged it neceffary, after an interval of eight years, to convoke the diet. For the three laſt years the kingdom had been ravaged by a famine, of which the effects were fo very powerful and diſtreſſing, that in the high-roads and woods, but efpecially in Dalecarlia, many perfons were found ſtarved to death. The defire of affording fome relief to the poor under this calamity, and of introducing the Prince Royal to the States, his fponfors, were the reafons alledged for the convocation of the diet, which began to fit on the 7th of May. The King, in his opening fpeech, defcribed the flouriſhing ſtate of the kingdom with refpect to its commerce, navy, army, and fortifications, and enumerated the many advantages enjoyed by the nation fince his acceffion to the throne, of which the chief were the independence of the people, and the prefervation of peace.

"But from the viciſſitude," faid he, "to which
" all human fituations are liable, ours has not been
" exempted. The productions of the earth, the
" firſt of all riches, have been denied us for the
" laſt three years; and this calamity has not a little
" increafed the weight of my cares, who feel for
" my fubjects as for myfelf. What endeavours
" I have ufed to prevent the difaſtrous effects of this
" failure, and what fuccours I have given for the
" relief of my fubjects, you already know by the
" effects.

"effects. May they animate you to concur with me in such measures as may protect our country from similar misfortunes in future." He then spoke of the Prince Royal, of his education, and of the efforts used to render him worthy of being the head of a free people. "I rejoice," said he, "that the first object which occurs to his innocent view, is the union of a people essentially free, submitting to the laws, conjointly with the King, who, at the same time that he is invested with authority, is himself, bound by the same laws." He concluded his speech by presenting the four following propositions to the diet:

1. That the punishment for *infanticide* be changed from death to perpetual imprisonment, with a public whipping once every year, on the day upon which the crime was committed.

2. That estates shall no longer be divided, but shall descend from the father to the eldest son, charged with the portions of the other children.

3. That the King be authorised to draw from the bank a fund sufficient for the establishment of a magazine of corn, in any place which he shall judge convenient, in order to prevent the excessive dearness of that article.

4. That the King be impowered to draw from the bank a fund for defraying the expences of the mines; and particularly for the purpose of securing that of *Fahlun* from inundation; upon the condition,

dition, however, of his depoſiting in the bank a quantity of copper, equal in value to the ſpecie taken from it.

In this diet, which was by no means ſo tranquil as the preceding one, the King met with conſiderable oppoſition, and only thoſe of his propoſitions were adopted, which related to the eſtabliſhment of magazines. The clergy oppoſed the change of puniſhment for *infanticide*, and the equeſtrian order would not conſent to the article which forbad the diviſion of eſtates. The ſum demanded by the King for the improvement of the mines of Fahlun was refuſed by the ſtates, who alleged that the impoveriſhment of the mines was to be attributed only to the miſconduct of thoſe concerned in working them, and appointed a committee of inſpection, with orders to make a report of their interior management*. The diet of 1778 granted the uſual entries, and for an unlimited time, but by the preſent diet they were limited to the term of four years; and, as a further proof of the influence of the antiroyaliſt party, the States refuſed to acknowlege as debts of the ſtate, thoſe which were contracted by the crown without their conſent. The order of peaſants having propoſed to redeem the right of diſtilling, his Majeſty declared, that, for the ſatisfaction of his faithful ſubjects, he was willing to receive in exchange a duty upon coffee, and the

* To this committee the proprietors refuſed to render an account.

annual

annual sum of eighteen tons of gold. These terms were rejected, and the right remained Royal.

The diet was dissolved on the 24th of June, and the King expressed his disapprobation of its decrees in the speech which concluded it. He lamented "that an unquiet distrust, ill-founded and unde-" "served, seemed likely to interrupt the union and" "concord, which, for fourteen years, he had en-" "deavoured to maintain, even to the detriment of" "his own private interests." He appealed to pos-" "terity to do justice to his conduct, and finished an eloquent and sentimental speech, with remitting the sums granted him for the fourth year of the subsidy, which he desired might be appropriated to the relief of his subjects.

Towards the end of the year, the King conducted the Prince Royal to the university of Upsal, and assisted constantly at all the public and the greatest part of the private exercises performed by the young Prince during a stay of six weeks. The ardour and success with which, at the age of only eight years, he applied to his studies, was highly gratifying to the King, who, in order to familiarize him with the people, whom he was born to govern, and to give him an early knowledge of the kingdom, had already led him over several of the provinces.

During the fourteen years, which had passed since the revolution, the King, by his indefatigable exertions for the welfare of the kingdom, had placed

placed the trade, navigation, fleet, army, courts of juftice, and magazines entirely upon an improved footing. But the fatisfaction due to his labours was interrupted by a cruel famine, which, for the fecond time in his reign, afflicted his kingdom, by the influence of the anti-royalift party in the laft diet, and by the continual murmurs which arofe upon the fubject of the diftilleries. In fome provinces thefe difcontents prompted the populace to rife in open revolts; the royal houfes were burnt to the ground, and the infpectors and officers of the diftilleries were murdered. By frequent outrages of this fort, and by the continual ufe of private diftilleries, the King's profits were fo much leffened, that he was induced to relinquifh his privilege, receiving in return an annual contribution of rye from each *hemman*, or farm. In the large cities, however, brandy is ftill diftilled upon his account.

In the courfe of the prefent year, the King has inftituted an academy for the melioration of the Swedifh language. The plan is the fame as that of the French Academy, founded in 1635, except that the number of members is here limited to eighteen. Poetry and eloquence are the objects of both academies, and, in the difcourfes of the Swedifh Academy, the characters of Guftavus Vafa, and Guftavus Adolphus, are deftined to receive thofe praifes, which, in thofe of the other,

are

are given to Louis the Fourteenth, and Cardinal Richelieu. On the same day, his Majesty revived the Academy of Inscriptions and Belles Lettres, founded by his mother, adopting the regulations of that established for the same purpose in Paris by Louis XIV. The Academy of Sciences, founded in 1779, makes the third institution of this sort in Stockholm, and does honour to the reign of a monarch, whose moderation, humanity, and sagacity, are equalled only by his activity, and his constant exertions for the welfare of the kingdom. Gustavus III. in the annual tours which he makes through the provinces, employs himself in listening to the complaints of individuals, in watching over the administration of justice, redressing abuses, establishing the discipline, and protecting the happiness of the army, and, in one word, in endeavouring to render his subjects happy, his forces respectable, and the Arts and Sciences flourishing*. During the fourteen years of his reign, the kingdom has enjoyed a constant peace, which it is to be feared the ambition of Russia, operating upon the suppressed, but not extirpated, policy of the aristrocratic party, will one day disturb.

And, indeed, a war, raised by the intrigues, or jealousy, of the neighbouring powers, can alone

* The King has composed several theatrical pieces in the language of the country, and designed the plans of two fine buildings, the one a catholic church at Stockholm, the other a country seat, called Haga.

interrupt

interrupt the prosperity of Sweden, under a monarch, who has hitherto used his arms only for the protection of commerce, and the honour of the Swedish flag, and whose pacific disposition is proved by the article, inserted upon his own motion in the new form of government, by which he restricted himself from carrying on an offensive war without the consent of the States.

I am, &c. &c.

LETTER XXIV.

Copenhagen, ... 1786.

MY DEAR FRIEND,

THE year 1772, celebrated in the History of Sweden, for the succefsful intrepidity of a young King, and the humiliation of a turbulent aristocracy, is rendered not lefs remarkable in the annals of Denmark, by the misfortunes of an amiable Queen, the victim of a party, who sacrified her peace, and the lives of two unfortunate men to their ambition.

The Counts Brandt and Struenzee, who thus suffered by her fall, were both undeserving of the punishment inflicted on them, though the latter certainly exceeded the limits of his authority, and aspired to the exercise of a power, which the following history will shew he was unable to retain.

Struenzee

Struenzee was born at Halle, in Saxony, in the year 1737. His father, then a Lutheran minister in that city, afterwards obtained a provoſtſhip at Altena, and was at length ſub-intendant-general of the churches in Sleſwig and Holſtein. His mother was the only daughter of I. S. Carl, firſt phyſician to the King. From theſe parents he imbibed an early taſte for knowledge; and this tendency, with his lively genius and promptneſs in judging, formed the beſt parts of a character, in which ambition, the love of pleaſure, and a contempt of religious and moral reſtriction, very ſoon began to appear. His diſpoſition and the advice of his friends led him to the ſtudy of phyſic, in which obſcure and intricate ſcience he ſoon acquired conſiderable reputation, and in the practice of which, as a profeſſion, he became acquainted with two men, whoſe deſtinies were afterwards intimately connected with his own. Theſe were the Count de Rantzau Achberg, and Brandt, the firſt the principal inſtrument of his fall, the latter the unfortunate companion of his ſufferings. There alſo he acquired the friendſhip of Madame de Berkentheim, the widow of the grand marſhal of Frederic V. by whom he was firſt recommended to the court, and through whoſe means he obtained the appointment of phyſician to the King; 1768. an office, which induced him to dedicate himſelf entirely to his royal maſter, whoſe favour

favour he obtained in a journey during which he was ordered to attend him.

Soon after the marriage of the King, a coolnefs was obferved between him and the young Queen, and this was wrought into an open difagreement, by which Queen Julia hoped to regain her loft influence, and tranfmit it to her pofterity. The mifunderftanding, which was thus raifed between the two Queens, increafed after the birth of the Prince Royal, and the journey of the King into foreign countries by no means diminifhed his indifference for a wife, who deferved a better fate.

Upon his return, the intrigues which afterwards operated fo forcibly, began to appear. The nation was then divided into parties, of which the moft numerous, and that which comprized the minifters and chief members of the ftate, was headed by the young Count de Holk, the favourite of the King. The adherents of the Queen Dowager partook with her the tranquillity of her retreat at Friedenfbourg, and only fome young perfons, without refources or influence, remained to Matilda, and relied upon her youth, beauty, and agreeable manners, to effect a future reconciliation with the King. But thefe were wholly inexperienced in the intrigues of a court; and the young Queen, unable to truft them, adopted another plan more likely to forward her views. She perceived that the only method of recovering

X the

the confideration due to her rank was to regain the confidence of the King; and as fhe was aware that this could never be effected during the influence of the Count de Holk, fhe refolved to attempt the deftruction of this favourite.

Many circumftances confpired to affift her endeavours. The Count de Holk, fearful of lofing his afcendancy over the King, laboured to increafe the difagreement between their Majefties, and believing that Struenzee was as offenfive to the Queen as himfelf, he perfuaded the King to carry him with him when he vifited his confort. This meafure contributed to the ruin of Holk, from whom the King's confidence was gradually transferred to Struenzee. The Queen perceived the change, and could not avoid comparing the fierce and arrogant conduct of the former with the refpectful manner of the latter, who even appeared to be fecretly hurt by the neceffity of offending her fo often by his prefence. This circumfpection was favourably interpreted by the Queen, who by degrees acccuftomed herfelf to his company, and whofe averfion infenfibly changed into admiration of his wit, knowledge, and penetration.

About this time the Prince Royal was inoculated, and the Queen, when fhe entrufted this operation to Struenzee, declared that his fuccefs fhould be rewarded with the care of the young Prince's education. The diforder was very favourably received,

and

and Struenzee was recompenſed with the place of Counſellor of Conference * and reader to their Majeſties, with an appointment of 1,500 crowns; an office, which, with that of tutor to the Prince Royal, obliged him to a conſtant attendance upon the court.

During the progreſs of the diſorder, Struenzee entirely conciliated the good will of the Queen, whoſe anxiety for her ſon induced her to take the care of nurſing him upon herſelf, and would ſcarcely permit Struenzee to be abſent for a moment. The hours that upon this occaſion ſhe was obliged to paſs in his company were ſpent in inſtructive and amuſing converſation, from which ſhe at firſt received conſolation, and afterwards pleaſure. Theſe converſations became more and more intimate and confidential, and the Queen at length believed that ſhe had found a man, to whom ſhe might entruſt the execution of her projects.

Struenzee, having thus the aſcendancy over the King, and the power of giving valuable advice to the Queen, reſolved to profit by the occaſion, and to open to himſelf the road to fortune. By his influence, the King was ſoon reconciled to his conſort, and beſtowed upon her a degree of confidence, of which the firſt effect that appeared was his indifference for Holk.

In the mean time the miniſters began to dread the influence of Struenzee, whom they endea-

* In Denmark this title is next to that of Privy Counſellor.

voured in vain to remove from the confidence of the King, or the intimacy of the Queen. The Court soon after set out for Slefwig, and the King was accompanied, as in his former journey, by Count Bernstorf, Holk, and Schimmelman. Warnstadt, an adherent of Holk, and Struenzee, were also in the suite; and the two parties, thus opposed to each other, would have been nearly equal, but for the presence of the young Queen. The Count de Rantzau Afchberg, who had been involved in the fall of the Count de St. Germain, was recommended to the Queen by Struenzee, as a man whose suppleness might render him useful in gaining the ministers; and Brandt, who had also been formerly a favourite with the King, was recalled at her solicitation, and destined to fill the place occupied by Holk.

The King descended frequently from the dignity of his character, and Count Bernstorf, who was alone able to restrain him within the bounds of propriety, every day lost his influence, while, on the other hand, the Queen was rendered fatally unsuspicious by the goodness of her heart, and the vivacity of her disposition prevented her foreseeing the consequences of a conduct not always so prudent as her situation required. Holk, however, by degrees lost the favour of the King, and his fall marked the approaching ruin of his party. His place was given to Brandt; soon after which,
the

the King retired to Hirfcholm, a feat within two miles of Copenhagen, accompanied only by the Queen and thofe in her intereft.

The Count de Bernftorf, though unable to conceal, even from himfelf, the lofs of his influence with the King, relied upon the favourable opinion of the public, and refolved rather to await in tranquillity the blow which menaced him, than to anticipate his fate by retiring. He was not long fuffered to remain in fufpenfe. While he was labouring for the welfare of his country, he received notice of his difmiffion from the King. The firft fenfation was painful, but, recovering himfelf, "I have received my difmiffion," faid he to the only one of his domeftics who was prefent; and then, raifing his eyes wet with tears to heaven, uttered this fhort prayer: " Great God, fave this country " and its King."

Thus Denmark loft an active, laborious, and zealous minifter, after whofe fall the other members of the adminiftration were foon difmiffed, and their places given to the friends of the Queen and Struenzee. The Count de Rantzau, General Göhler, and the Baron Schak Ratlau, were admitted into the council of State; but the latter, being difpleafed with fome innovations, foon retired to his own eftates. The Count de Schimmelman alone, having had the precaution to make no declaration of his party, and the prudence to retire to Hambourg, during the dangerous moment, avoided the common fate of miniſters. He was appointed miniſter for foreign affairs, and, in order to leave the court of Ruſſia no opportunity for intrigue, it was notified to all the embaſſadors that they muſt in future addreſs themſelves immediately to the King. This meaſure, of which the motive was very apparent, was highly reſented by the Ruſſian miniſter, who uttered public menaces on the part of his court, and immediately diſpatched a courier with the news. In the mean time, Mr. de Warenſtät, on behalf of the King, had informed the Empreſs of the change in the adminiſtration; and the court of Ruſſia, notwithſtanding the menaces of the miniſter, reſolved not to interfere with the affair.

The Queen Dowager, remaining in retirement at Friedenſbourg, a quiet ſpectator of theſe tranſactions, expreſſed her compaſſion and goodwill towards all thoſe who ſuffered by the ſucceſs of the new miniſtry.

At length the triumph of the young Queen was complete; the King treated her with all the affection ſhe deſerved, and beſtowed his confidence on Struenzee. During the public tranquillity which followed this revolution, no endeavours were ſpared to enſure its continuance. Struenzee, whoſe ambitious views extended to the poſſeſſion of the whole Royal authority, perceived that his

pur-

purpose could only be effected by concentrating the power in one point, which point should be the person of the King. He, therefore, endeavoured to remove him from all society; and Brandt was intrusted with the care of providing amusements for the continual occupation of his time. A mode of life so agreeable to the King confirmed the influence of Struenzee, and facilitated a measure more essential than any hitherto effected, the resolution of the King not to transact business personally with his ministers.

The year 1770 concluded with a remarkable event, which entirely changed the form of government, and rendered the power of the young Queen and her minister entirely absolute. On the 27th of November, an act signed by the King dissolved the council of state, and a commission of secret conference was adopted in its stead, composed of the chiefs of the different departments, and endued with a very limited share of authority. The members were forbid to assemble, except at stated times, and being without title, rank, emoluments, or influence, might be dismissed without trouble, whenever occasion should render it necessary. But the council now dissolved had always claimed the first rank in the state after the King, and in the celebrated revolution under Frederic the Third, had obtained the distinguishing privilege of exercising, during a minority, the powers of the regency conjointly

jointly with the guardians of the young King. Even the humiliating change of 1660 had left the powers of this body entire, which was regarded in some measure as representing the nation, and exercising the office of a mediator between the laws and the royal power.

The right of sitting at this council was in the Danish nobility, who, therefore, considered the dissolution of it as an infraction of their privileges, and from that moment resolved upon the destruction of Struenzee. The same sentiments animated the Count de Rantzau, who, with his seat at this board, lost all his influence and credit. Struenzee, in the mean time, took farther measures for the establishment of his authority, and persuaded the King to entrust the whole labour of the cabinet to him. Secretary Panning, who had been appointed by the influence of the court of Russia, was dismissed, as was Mr. de Warnstädt, who had betrayed himself by some impudent conversations. By degrees, all the old ministers were removed, and the whole form of the Danish government was changed, all business being transacted in the name of the King, by those immediately about his person. Thus, in the space of a few months, was a revolution completely effected by a youthful Queen, a man of obscure birth, and some young persons, who before were without respect or credit.

But the destiny of Denmark, thus entirely entrusted to Struenzee, did not long remain in his power. During his short and disturbed reign, his conduct was unequal; and that courage, which, at the commencement of an ambitious design, seemed to border even upon rashness, sunk into pusillanimity when his measures were opposed. The war in which Russia was engaged with the Turks, the luxury which prevailed at that court, and the interior troubles of the country, secured him, however, from the dread of the Empress's menaces, and his confidence was confirmed by the favour of the ministers of Sweden and Russia.

If his arrangements with foreign courts seem to have been dictated by sound policy, his plans for the interior administration were not less skilful, and prove him to have possessed a very remarkable talent at combination; but his ambition and his fears perverted and overpowered those abilities which might otherwise have contributed to the welfare of Denmark.

Struenzee meditated a reform in the management of the finances, which, if entrusted entirely to one office, would be more easily reviewed by the King. He projected the diminution of several imposts, the payment of rents in ready money, the suppression of those manufactures which were unsuitable to the climate and the soil, the retrenchment

ment of useless pensions, and the encouragement of agricultural labours. He wished also to regulate the administration of justice, diminish the number of proceedings, and of courts, reform the army, and improve, without increasing, the navy.

But his great object was to humble the nobility, by keeping them at a distance from the capital, and by taking from them their hereditary claim to offices. In the execution of his scheme he did not perceive that the nobles, finding their privileges every day attacked, had already entered into a league for his destruction.

His design of improving the state of the finances induced him to adopt a new plan of œconomy for the court and government. Courtiers were dismissed, pensions retrenched, and the number of servants, both in the royal palace and stables, considerably diminished. The grand Marshal Moltke, several ladies, and many pages received their discharge; the profits of the Chancery were brought into the royal coffers; the colleges of admiralty, excise, and commerce, were abolished; and commissions established in their stead.

An order of cabinet, signed on the 3d of April, 1771, dismissed them agistrates of Copenhagen*, and the assembly of thirty-two, appointing, in the room of the former, two, burgomasters. The privileges of the foreign ministers were considerably altered,

* They were restored in 1772.

the horse-guards were discharged, and their duty assigned to three hundred dragoons; measures by which a great number of persons were deprived of subsistence.

His scheme for abolishing the personal services of the peasants, and permitting them to hire their lands at certain rents, was strenuously opposed by the nobility, and was, therefore, relinquished by Struenzee, though proposed to be tried at first only upon the crown estates.

Schumacker, the secretary to the cabinet, a man of known probity and talents, was dismissed from his office by Struenzee, and the whole kingdom was shocked at an act so despotic and unseasonable, the secretary having always appeared contented with his situation, and by no means addicted to intrigue. Struenzee had, however, a reason for his conduct, with which very few were acquainted. All the orders for the changes effected by this minister were settled in the cabinet of the King, and sent from thence immediately to the several departments, it being thought necessary to keep them secret till the moment when they were to be put in execution. A clerk, implicitly trusted by Schumacker, and employed by him in official concerns, gave notice of these orders, which were found to be publicly known even before they were delivered from the cabinet. A long search discovered the offender, who was punished, and dismissed. The secretary,

secretary, also, lost his office, and was obliged to deliver up all his papers.

The recal of the Count de St. Germain, another measure of Struenzee, was attributed to an intention of placing him in the military department, as a counterpoize to the authority of the Count de Rantzau. But Struenzee had other views. The Count de St. Germain had enjoyed since his dismission a pension of 7,000 crowns, a part of which it was believed he would be willing to resign rather than appear again in Denmark. His return to Copenhagen was therefore unexpected, and, though he was rewarded with honours, he was not entrusted with employment. Struenzee had no other resource than to conciliate his friendship; and the Count was the only knight of the order of the Elephant created by the court during his administration.

In the same year, 1771, the order of Matilda was instituted upon the birth-day of the King, and was bestowed only upon persons in very particular favour. Upon this occasion, the Baron de Schimmelman gave a very superb fête in his palace, at which the young Queen was present with her usual suite.

Upon the first appearance of fine weather, the court set out for Hirscholm, accompanied by Brandt, the physician Berger, and some confidential

dential perfons, who were ordered to be continually about the King, and to alienate him from all thofe who were fufpected. The King became every day more indifferent not only to public affairs, but the concerns of the court; he paffed his time in perpetual amufements; and his intellectual faculties appeared to become weaker and weaker. Monfieur and Madame de Göhler, Madame de Schimmelman, the lady of honour Deuben, and Colonel Falkenfchiold, compofed the ufual fociety of the Queen. Struenzee divided his time between official bufinefs, and the care of the Prince Royal's education. Of his brothers, the elder, well known by an excellent treatife upon the fortifications, obtained a poft in the new college of finances, and the younger in the military department.

On the 7th of July, 1771, the Queen was delivered of a Princefs, who was baptized by the name of Louifa Augufta. Matilda was not ignorant of the injurious reports raifed by her enemies; and thefe were the more diftreffing, as they were faid to originate at *Friedenfbourg*. She fought confolation in the friendfhip of Mademoifelle Deuben, and from her received affurances of the good intentions of Queen Julia, of which her kindnefs in becoming the godmother of the Princefs feemed a fufficient proof. The Queen, though fomewhat foothed by thefe endeavours, could not conquer her fears of the ufe which might

be

be made of such reports, in wresting the authority from her hands; and Struenzee, to whom she imparted her uneasiness, regulated his conduct in consequence. By degrees the rumours ceased, tranquillity was once more restored to Hirscholm, and every thing went on as before.

At this period, Sir Robert Keith, the new minister from England, arrived at Copenhagen.

Struenzee, blinded by his fortune, but still more by his unlimited ambition, was desirous of adding to the real power which he exercised, the honour of inrolling his name amongst the first nobility of Denmark. He was ennobled with the rank of Count, a title unequal to his wishes, and from which he aspired to some distinction suitable to the consequence he enjoyed. There being then no title exactly expressive of his situation, the new one of *Privy Counsellor of the Cabinet* was invented and bestowed upon him, together with a degree of power, which, like the title, was without a precedent. He was authorised to express in writing, in what manner he should judge most convenient, the orders which he received personally from the mouth of the King, and to send them to the different departments, sanctioned by the seal of the cabinet, instead of the signature of his Majesty. An ordinance signed by the King with his own hand, enjoined all the departments to pay respect to these orders, of which an extract was

shewn

shewn to him every Saturday by Struenzee. The concurrence of the King, thus obtained to the orders issued in the course of the week, was considered as a sanction equal to his actual signature.

The situation of a young Monarch, betrayed into a conduct so unusual, raises our pity, while the abuse of his confidence excites our contempt of the favourite, whose measures tended to the destruction of an authority, which, by a more prudent use of circumstances, he might have enjoyed for several years. If he had continued the use of the King's signature, and shown more respect for the privileges of the nobility in particular, and of the nation in general, Struenzee might have reigned under the protection of the Queen, and have defied the efforts of a party, who sought and obtained the possession of his power. But his ambition, which rendered him discontented with all his acquirements, pressed him forward to an insupportable degree of exaltation; and the momentary glory of his reign was concluded by a cruel punishment, and by the fall of a young Queen, whose virtues deserved a better fate.

The unbounded liberty of the press, introduced by Struenzee, with a view of discovering the sentiments of the nation concerning the actual government, was a formidable weapon in the hands of his adversaries, who used it to exhibit an aggravated picture of his faults, to point out the ambitious

tious part of his character, his abuse of the King's confidence, and to revive the injurious reports before circulated against the Queen. The abuse of this privilege at length proceeded so far, that it became necessary entirely to retract it; rewards were promised for the discovery of the authors of these writings, and the most rigorous punishments were denounced against those who should in future write any thing against the King, the Queen, or the minister. This measure, by which the writers of the opposite party were intimidated, and silenced, was adopted too late for the reputation, or safety of Struenzee. The minds of the people, once incensed, continued to be agitated; his friends became cool; those who remained attached to him were rendered diffident, and the populace were accustomed to despise his authority and name. At this critical moment, the courage, which he had so much occasion to exert, appeared entirely to abandon him.

Towards the end of October, three hundred sailors arrived from Norway, to be employed in an expedition against Algiers, and, according to custom, their pay was withheld till the moment of embarkation. A stay of six weeks at Copenhagen, without employment, or pay, reduced these poor people to a state of beggary, from which the government refused to release them. Thus driven to desperation, a large party set out for Hirscholm, after

after having notified that they went to seek relief, or revenge. When the news of the revolt arrived at Hirscholm, the King and Queen were out on a hunting party, and an adjutant-general went to meet the sailors, who declared that they came " to " speak to their father, from whom they expected " relief." A party of dragoons was then ordered to advance, upon which the sailors produced arms, and shewed themselves prepared to repel force by force. The officer endeavoured to appease them; and their short, but fierce, statement of grievances procured a promise of redress, by which they were induced to return to the city. The law, however, was not repealed, but Vice Admiral Rühmor, the commander of the squadron, who had certainly done his duty, received his dismission.

By this conduct, which was equally imprudent and unjust, the sailors were induced to suppose their conduct was approved, and were encouraged to new violences. The labours of the dock-yard ceased; all sorts of disorders were committed, and an amendment of their condition was demanded with threats, by which the court was much alarmed. Struenzee, dreading the consequences of a disturbance, by which the whole nation might be inflamed, applied himself very assiduously to the suppression of it, and, as one of the most effectual methods of quelling the discontents, he gave a magnificent fête at Frederickshourg, a royal seat within half a quarter of a league of Copenhagen. The sailors, after being thus diverted and pleased, returned tranquilly to their homes, and were afterwards embarked. But the cloud was by no means dissipated; and the fear which Struenzee discovered upon this occasion encouraged his enemies to aim seriously at his destruction, and that of his protectress.

Their plans were, however, arranged with prudence, and, at present, operated only in gaining the confidence of the nation, by rendering Struenzee suspected, and in discovering those amongst the enemies of the reigning party, who were most proper to be employed against him. The old Count de Tott, Count Oaten, and the Count de Rantzau were selected for this purpose. The natural irresolution and inconstancy of the latter was well known, but his personal enmity to Struenzee, and his increasing dislike of the actual government, seemed to render him a suitable instrument of their vengeance. Of these arrangements, notwithstanding the secrecy which was observed, some notice transpired to Struenzee, whose fears were increased by a false report of a design against his life, by which he was induced to throw himself at the feet of the Queen, expressing all his gratitude, attachment and concern, and beseeching her instantly to permit him to retire from a country and a court, where he saw himself surrounded with enemies, and where

where the general difcontent appeared ready to difcharge itfelf upon him. He reprefented to the Queen her own danger in perfifting to protect him againft enemies, of whom the number increafed every inftant, and upon whofe fuccefs fhe could have no reafon to expect protection from the King. The Queen denied his requeft, and Struenzee tremblingly, was obliged to fwear never to make it again.

The contrary party carefully obferved every thing that paffed at Hirfcholm, and were ready to profit by the moft trifling circumftances which occurred. The three hundred dragoons, commanded by Mr. de Munfen, by whom the horfe-guards were replaced, were every where ftationed around the palace, to the furprize of the Danes, who had never yet feen their Kings guarded with fuch precaution in the country. The Norwegian failors were haftily fent home; thofe who were before defpifed were now treated with kindnefs, and every meafure was ufed to gain the populace of the capital.

In this dilemma Struenzee doubted not that his power and perfonal influence would be fufficient to protect him, as long as he could reftrain his enemies from all communication with the King, whom he knew too well to believe capable of loving any perfon, and whofe favour was only the effect of fear, or of undue fubjection. He, therefore, prolonged the ftay of the court at Hirfcholm, and appointed

pointed confidential persons, of whom the Count de Brandt was the chief, to be continually about the person of the King.

Having taken these measures for securing his influence at court, Struenzee applied himself to official business, the burden of which, now become too heavy for his oppressed spirits, he endeavoured in vain, to share with his brother, by placing him at head of the department of finances. The alterations made by Struenzee in the police of Copenhagen, which he endeavoured to render similar to that of Paris, furnished his enemies with another opportunity of rendering him odious to the burgesses and people of the capital. The plan, which was in some respects a good one, and which was suitable enough to the manners of a people addicted to pleasure, was disagreeable to the tranquil and phlegmatic inhabitants of Copenhagen, who looked with horror upon the laxity of the new regulations, as dangerous to the morals of the people.

At length, the season arrived when it became impossible to remain any longer in the country; but the Queen and Struenzee dreaded to enter the capital, where the court of Friedensbourg was already arrived. They, therefore, persuaded the King to pass a few days at Friedrikfberg, a small castle at the gates of Copenhagen, being desirous, before they entered a place where their enemies were assembled together, to know the success of an undertaking,

dertaking, which they hoped would contribute confiderably to their fafety. It was propofed to break the regiment of foot-guards, the foldiers of which they had fome reafon to diftruft. The refolution was taken on the 21ft of November, and executed two days afterwards.

The companies being affembled, an officer announced to them the intention of the King, according to which the regiment was to be broke, and the foldiers incorporated in other battalions. A general murmur, which ran from rank to rank, foon rofe into loud cries, and the foldiers demanded, either a formal difmiffion, or the eftablifhment of a new corps, in which all fhould be received without exception. Their officers in vain endeavoured to reprefent to them the neceffity of obeying the King's orders; neither perfuafion, nor menaces, could prevent their quitting their ranks and difbanding. They drew their fwords upon the guards who were brought forward to feize them; blood began to flow on all fides, and the alarm and terror became general. Other guards were brought from a diftance; a new conflict enfued, and a fmall number of the difcontented were obliged to furrender, while one company, which efcaped, flew to the North-gate, and, having forced the guard, proceeded directly to Friedrikfberg, and the others ran to the caftle, where they intrenched themfelves in the guard-houfe. Struenzee, to whom an exprefs was fent by the commandant, received the intelligence with confternation, but perceived that, at this critical moment, peace could only be reftored by very mild meafures; and, therefore, fent an officer with an order of the cabinet, which promifed all that was demanded by the revolters. The officer was received with tumultuous fhouts, and the foldiers, declaring their intention of fpeaking with the King, continued to advance, notwithftanding the appearance of a guard under arms, whom they fhewed themfelves very well prepared to refift. The commander of this guard, and the officer, who bore the order of the cabinet, at length perfuaded the revolters to return to Copenhagen, where they joined their comrades at the caftle.

Encouraged by the conceffions which had been made, but not fatisfied with the fimple promife of a difmiffion, the whole body took an oath of reciprocal engagement; and each man folemnly bound himfelf rather to die than abandon his companions. Three regiments of infantry, and two fquadrons of horfe, drawn up round the caftle, did not deter them from their defign. Their own officers alone were permitted to approach them, and, after a negociation, which lafted during the whole day and part of the following night, they obtained what they demanded, and gave up their arms about one in the morning. Each man received his difcharge, figned by the King's own hand, with a

present

present of three crowns, and of his full uniform. They then separated, and the rest of the night passed tranquilly. The next morning, at break of day, about four hundred of these, after traversing the city in good order, and bidding adieu in a tender manner to their fellow citizens, set out for their homes. Their departure made a great impression upon the people, who began to assemble on all sides, while the burgesses threw money to the soldiers and the Norwegian sailors, running about the city, began to talk of vengeance. The minds of the people were thus roused, and nothing was heard on all sides, but shouts, oaths, and menaces. General Gude, commandant of the city, who with several officers, endeavoured to disperse the populace, was thrown from his horse, and drawn through the mud; many officers and soldiers were ill-treated, and some were wounded. But the dismissed soldiers quietly left the city without taking any part in these riots, which continued during the whole day after their departure.

This terrible scene increased the fears and irresolution of Struenzee, whose situation now became more and more critical. The English minister, from whom nothing escaped, foresaw the approaching fall of the favourite, and his uneasiness for the young Queen induced him to press the dismission, of which Struenzee himself was desirous. Believing that the want of money alone prevented his departure,

departure, he offered him a sufficient sum; but the Queen opposed this step in the strongest manner, from an apprehension that his adversaries would immediately obtain possession of the King and of the royal authority.

Struenzee, in the mean time perceived the necessity of concealing his fears from his enemies, and of attending to all their measures. He, therefore, thought the King's return to his residence should be no longer delayed; and the Queen, though impressed with a *presentiment* of the dreadful fate, which awaited her, yielded to his reiterated intreaties, and resolved to return to Copenhagen. Aware, however, of the danger to be apprehended from a new revolt, Struenzee took all possible measures for his security. The guards at the castle and arsenal were doubled; cannon was placed in several parts; and 6,000 cartridges were distributed to each regiment; precautions, which had a bad effect, by warning the public that he who used them was conscious of having injured the people against whom they were used. The royal authority fell into contempt, and the great influence of Struenzee seemed a dream which was speedily about to vanish.

At length, every thing concurred to promote the success of the schemes projected against the young Queen. The party of her enemies was strengthened by the addition of a man, who had sworn an

eternal

eternal hatred to Struenzee, and refolved to revenge himfelf at any rate for the refufal of an office to one of his friends. This was Colonel K....., the commander of one of the regiments in garrifon at Copenhagen, a man, whofe approved courage, firm mind, and ambitious fpirit, qualified him for a great undertaking, and whofe enmity to Struenzee was fuch, that he voluntarily offered his fervices to the party. They alfo affured themfelves of the Count de Rantzau, and of Colonel Eichftadt, commander of the dragoons, whofe affiftance was the more neceffary, as they could not rely upon the chiefs of the other regiments, moft of whom had received their pofts from the kindnefs of Struenzee.

The moment now approached, which was to conclude the reign of the unfortunate wife of Chriftian VII. whofe power and influence had been envied from her firft arrival in the kingdom. That the attempt, however, might not be made before its fuccefs was enfured, every method was ufed to leffen the attachment of thofe nobles, who adhered to the Queen, and to increafe the hatred of the nation for Struenzee. At length, the 17th of January was fixed upon for a cataftrophe, which was to feparate the King for ever from his wife, and to give the death blow to the maternal heart of a young Queen, by taking from her every thing fhe held

moft

moſt dear in the world. This was thought *neceſſary for the honour of the nation and the welfare of the kingdom.*

A ball which was given at court facilitated the execution of the deſign. On the 17th, before day, the inhabitants of Copenhagen heard with terror and aſtoniſhment that Queen Matilda, Count Struenzee, his brother, the deputy of the finances, Count de Brandt, and all their friends had been arreſted during the night. A day had been choſen, on which the caſtle and its environs was guarded by the regiment of Colonel Köller. The young Queen having, with her uſual vivacity, partook of the pleaſures of the dance, of which ſhe was very fond, concluded the ball at one o'clock in the morning with Prince Frederic.

At three the ſound of the clock gave the appointed ſignal, and a dead ſilence reigned over the caſtle, when Köller, running to the different guardhouſes, conducted all the officers into the inmoſt part of the caſtle, and there declared to them that he had the King's orders to arreſt the Queen. He ordered them to follow him; and the importance of the order, the authoritative manner of their chief, his coolneſs, and the ſerene air, with which he ſpoke, ſo overcame theſe officers, that no one thought of deſiring to ſee the order, a requeſt which would have expoſed the whole plan. But Köller was equally ſucceſsful and enterpriſing. The officers

cers followed him to the rendezvous, and, in the mean time, Colonel Eichſtädt put his dragoons under arms, and drew them up round the caſtle.

From thence Rantzau went to the apartment of the King, and undrew the curtains with a noiſe which awaked and alarmed his Majeſty, who was not ſuffered to recover his ſenſes before he was told that his perſon, and his kingdom were in danger. "Whither ſhall we fly? What can be " done?" ſaid the King with agitation. " Aſſiſt " me. Adviſe me." " Sign this," ſaid Rantzau, " this will ſave my King, the Royal Family, and " the whole kingdom." The King took the pen, but threw it away when he perceived the name of Matilda. At length he yielded to perſuaſion, and Rantzau went to execute the fatal order.

Colonel Köller, who was charged to arreſt Struenzee, was already in his chamber, without waiting for the order ſigned by the King. He left the officers by whom he was accompanied in the antichamber, and went alone to the miniſter, who, terrified by the noiſe and by the appearance of Köller, demanded tremblingly what was the occaſion of a viſit at ſo unſuitable an hour? " Of that," ſaid Köller, " you will ſoon be informed. Riſe imme-
" diately." He then ſeized him by the throat, and ſhook him violently. Struenzee loſt all courage, and yielding himſelf eaſily to the efforts of this ſingle man, was conducted with his friends to the citadel,

citadel, and secured in a dungeon. If the unhappy minister, by resisting Köller, had obliged the officers to enter into his chamber, and in their presence had demanded a sight of the King's order, his enemy would, perhaps, have fallen a victim to the rashness of his own undertaking.

The elder brother of Struenzee, the Count de Brandt, General Göhler and his wife, Colonel Falkenschiold, General Gude commandant of the city, the Baron de Bolouw, Zoga, the Secretary of State, and some others, were separately committed to prison.

Count Rantzau and Colonel Eichstädt, went with some officers to the apartment of the Queen, who, alarmed by the noise in her anti-chamber, called her women, and in the paleness of their countenances read their fear. She enquired what had happened, and was at length told that Count Rantzau, in her anti-chamber, demanded to speak with her on the part of the King. She expressed in the most lamentable manner her grief, her apprehension that she was betrayed and ruined, and her resignation. Then, acquiring fortitude, she went, half dressed to Rantzau, who read the order of the King, which she heard with firmness and without interrupting him. Being still unable to give credit to it, she read it herself, without betraying any mark of fear, and Rantzau intreated her obedience to the order. " An order," said she,

" of

"of which, perhaps, the King himself knows no-
"thing, or which has been obtained from his weak-
"ness by the moſt horrid perfidy. No: to ſuch
"orders a Queen gives no obedience." Rantzau,
with a ſevere air, replied, that his commiſſion would
permit no delay. "No ſuch order," ſaid ſhe,
"ſhall be executed againſt my perſon before I
"have ſpoke to the King; let me go — I muſt,
"I will ſpeak to him." At theſe words ſhe advanced towards the door, but was withheld by Rantzau, who changed his intreaties into menaces. "Wretch," ſaid ſhe, "is this the manner
"of a ſubject to his Queen?" The fierce and irritated Rantzau gave a ſignificant look to his officers, of whom one, more daring than the reſt, advanced towards the Queen. She tore herſelf from his hands, and called loudly for help, but no perſon came. At length, being alone and defenceleſs, in the midſt of armed men, this unhappy princeſs, tranſported with rage, ran to a window, and would have precipated herſelf from it, but ſhe was withheld. They endeavoured to carry her away, and ſhe defended herſelf till her ſtrength and recollection failed. When ſhe recovered herſelf and perceived no means of eſcaping, ſhe yielded, and was allowed time for dreſſing, after which ſhe was conducted to the carriage which took her to the caſtle of Cronenburg.

The

The news of this revolution being spread abroad, the Queen Dowager, with her son Prince Frederic, appeared in a balcony, and the multitude assembled before the castle saluted them with cries of " Long live Queen Julia—Long live Prince " Frederic," while a deadly silence reigned over the rest of the city. At noon, the King, in a gala habit, accompanied by Prince Frederic, went in the state coach through the principal streets of Copenhagen. Some persons prepared to unharness the horses and draw the carriage, but Prince Frederic signified that the King did not wish it.

During this time Queen Julia gave audience, and expressed " how much she was hurt at " being obliged to use measures so violent and re- " pugnant to her disposition, but the welfare of " the kingdom, and the safety of the King's " person, rendered them necessary." At night the whole city was illuminated; on the Sunday following thanks were returned to heaven for the happy revolution which had saved the state and church, and, in the course of the week, the theatre resounded with the praises of those, who had changed the form of government.

All those who had been employed were re- warded. The Count de Rantzau was made a Knight of the order of the Elephant, and a Ge- neral of Infantry; Köller received the order of Dannebrog, and the rank of Lieutenant General, and

and was befides ennobled with the name of Banner, which had been formerly borne by an ancient family, now extinct. Eichftadt, promoted, at firft, to the rank of Lieutenat General, was, afterwards, made Governor to the Prince Royal, and each officer was advanced one ftep.

The council of ftate was re-eftablifhed, under the name of the fecret council of the cabinet, and appointed to receive the reports of all the affairs of the kingdom. The old Count de Tott, the Baron de Shack Ratlau, Count d'Often, Count Rantzau, and General Eichftädt obtained feats at this board.

Sir Robert Keith, upon this occafion conducted himfelf with the greateft dignity and prudence; and his conduct is ftill mentioned at Copenhagen with all the praife it deferves. His declaration to Count Often, who was appointed to the management of foreign affairs, was fhort but energetic. He threatened all the vengeance of his court, if the flighteft attempt fhould be made againft the perfon of Matilda, immediately difpatched a courier to England, and avoided, as much as poffible, appearing at court.

Struenzee behaved in the weakeft manner from the firft moment of his imprifonment, to that in which he expired under the moft cruel torments upon a fcaffold. Brandt, on the contrary, to his

lateft

lateſt breath, preſerved his preſence of mind, and exhibited an intrepidity of conduct, a portion of which would, perhaps, have ſaved his friend and the unhappy victims of his ambition.

Of thoſe who were impriſoned, many were releaſed, with the loſs of their employments, and an order to quit the capital. Madame Göhler was forbid to appear at court, and her huſband, General Göhler, was broke and baniſhed to the iſlands of Zealand and Fionia, but with permiſſion to retain his penſion of one thouſand crowns. Colonel Falkenſchiold, having been the intimate friend of Struenzee, was confined for life in the citadel of Munkholm, with an allowance of half a crown a day.

The brother of Struenzee was releaſed, but was forbid ever to ſpeak, or write, upon the ſubject of the revolution. The Vice Admiral Hanſen, Lieutenant Colonel Heſſelberg, Willebrandt, the counſellor of ſtate, and ſeveral others were baniſhed, but were allowed to preſerve ſome ſmall penſions.

Such is the hiſtory, and ſuch was the end of a man, who, born in obſcurity, raiſed himſelf to the higheſt degree of exaltation, and was from thence precipitated into an abyſs of miſery by his unlimited ambition, and by a conduct at once raſh and puſillanimous. His fall involved the welfare

of

of a young Queen, whofe virtues deferved a better fate, together with that of her moſt intimate friends *.

I am, &c. &c. &c.

* The information giving in the foregoing hiſtory is drawn partly from intelligence collected by the author upon the ſpot, and partly from the papers of a perſon, who was included in the difgrace of Struenzee, and died in 1782. His name was known in the republic of letters, the German Reviews having more than once taken notice of his productions.

The work has evident marks of partiality and paſſion, and, therefore, only thoſe facts are mentioned here which the preſent author has reaſon to think well ſtated. Its title is as follows:

Authentiſche und hofienerk wurdiſh auflarungen, &c. i. e. —Authentic and remarkable Elucidations, relating to the Hiſtory of the Counts Struenzee and Brandt, contained in a Manuſcript compoſed by an illuſtrious, but anonymous Author, firſt printed in Germany in 1788.

F I N I S.

BOOKS

LATELY PUBLISHED BY

G. KEARSLEY.

Continental Excurſions.
In a pocket volume, with a correct MAP of the ROUTES of the POSTS and PUBLIC CARRIAGES, correctly engraved from one juſt publiſhed by authority at Paris,
A New Edition of
THE GENTLEMAN's GUIDE in his TOUR through FRANCE.

Containing obſervations on every curious or intereſting object, the Expence of travelling in a Poſt Chaiſe, Stage Coach, or inland Water Carriage. The diſtances of the Towns, and the beſt Houſes of Accommodation. Alſo, an Account of the Products and Manufactories; with Mr. Neckar's Account of the Finances. The different Coins are here reduced to Engliſh Money,

Price 3s. 6d.

It may alſo be had at Dover, Margate, Weymouth, and Brighton.

A TOUR through HOLLAND, DUTCH BRABANT, the AUSTRIAN NETHERLANDS, and part of FRANCE.
In which is included a deſcription of Paris, and its environs.
With an accurate Map of the Low Countries.
By the late HARRY PECKHAM, Eſq;
One of his Majeſty's Counſel, and Recorder of the City of Chicheſter.
The 4th edition, price 3s. 6d. half bound.

TOUR of ITALY, with a Map, 4s. 6d.

TOUR of SWITZERLAND,
Including M. De SAUSSURE's account of his expedition to the ſummit of MONT BLANC, which has been often attempted, but never before accompliſhed, with a Map, 2s. 6d.

Each

BOOKS printed for G. KEARSLEY.

Each of thefe TOURS contains all the information that can be ufeful to TRAVELLERS, and entertaining to READERS; among which are the expences upon the road, regulated by the mode of travelling. The different coins of each country are alfo explained.

The Fourth Edition, much enlarged,
(Ornamented with a confiderable number of new plates, containing feveral views in the newly difcovered iflands, fundry animals, an exact reprefentation of a Human Sacrifice, Captain Cook's head, from Pingo's medal, and a chart of the new difcoveries, with the tracks of the fhips)

A complete ABRIDGMENT of Captain COOK's VOYAGES round the WORLD;

Containing a faithful account of all the difcoveries, with the tranfactions at each place, a defcription of the inhabitants, with their manners and cuftoms, a full detail of the circumftances relative to Capt. Cook's death, and an account of his life by Capt. King.

Thofe who fuperintend the education of youth of either fex cannot put into their hands a more acceptable work, for the amufement of leifure hours, than thefe late voyages of difcovery, which abound with matter highly interefting and entertaining.

In two volumes. Price eight fhillings in boards.

₊ Either volume may be had feparate, Price four fhillings.

The following collection was compiled by a perfon of diftinguifhed abilities, for the ufe of young people, and as a guide to the curious traveller.

' A DESCRIPTION of SICILY and MALTA,
With an account of the late earthquake at Meffina; the eruptions of Mount Etna; the deftruction of Hybla; the prefent ftate of Palmyra; the cuftoms and manners of the Sicilians, their marriages, amufements, carriages, &c. Account of Syracufe, and the Knights of Malta; with a great variety of curious and fingular defcriptions, extracted from the travels of Brydone, Swinburne, Sir William Hamilton, and feveral other refpectable writers.

One volume. Price three fhillings and fixpence, bound.

A SHORT ACCOUNT of the MAHRATTA STATE,
Written in Perfian by a MUNSHY,
Who accompanied Col. Upton on his embaffy to Poonah.

Tranflated

BOOKS printed for G. KEARSLEY.
Tranflated by WILLIAM CHAMBERS, Efq; counfel at Fort William, in Bengal.
To which are added, the Voyages and Travels of M. Cæfar Frederic into and beyond the Eaft Indies.
Price two fhillings.

GRAY's SUPPLEMENT to the TOUR through GREAT BRITAIN.
Price two fhillings fewed.

ESSAYS on MODERN MANNERS.
Addreffed to PERSONS OF EVERY DENOMINATION, Particularly to PARENTS; and humbly dedicated to BEILBY, Lord Bifhop of LONDON.
By G. NEALE,
Curate of St. Margaret Pattens, Rood-lane, and Lecturer of St. Bennet, Gracechurch.
Nova vincendi ratio. CIC.

The VIRTUOSI's MUSEUM;
A Collection of elegant Views, in ENGLAND, SCOTLAND, and WALES; engraved from the drawings of
PAUL SANDBY, Efq; R. A.
With defcriptions to each plate; of which there are one hundred and eight.
Price Five Pounds Thirteen Shillings, half bound.

The following entertaining Selections by the Rev. JOHN ADAMS, A. M. are calculated for the inftruction as well as entertainment of youth. The whole feven volumes, one guinea; or they are fold feparately for three fhillings each.
Omne tulit punctum, qui mifcuit utile dulci. HOR.

The FLOWERS of ANCIENT and MODERN HISTORY,
Comprehending, on a new plan, the moft remarkable and interefting events, as well as ancient and modern characters; defigned for the improvement and entertainment of youth.
Two volumes.

The FLOWERS of MODERN TRAVELS,
Being elegant, entertaining, and inftructive extracts, felected from the works of the moft celebrated travellers; fuch as Lord Lyttelton, Sir W. Hamilton, Baron de Tott, Dr. Johnfon, Dr. Moore, Dr. Troil, Addifon, Brydone, Coxe, Wraxall, Savary, Topham, Sherlock, Douglas, Lady M. W. Montague, &c. &c. Intended chiefly for young people of both fexes.
Two volumes.

ANECDOTES,

BOOKS printed for G. KEARSLEY.

ANECDOTES, BON-MOTS, and CHARACTERISTIC TRAITS
Of the greateſt princes, politicians, philoſophers, poets, orators, and wits of modern times; ſuch as the Emperor Charles V. King of Pruſſia, Peter the Great, Henry IV. Charles XII. Lewis XIV. Voltaire, Dryden, Swift, Lord Mansfield, Garrick, and Dr. Johnſon.
One volume.

CURIOUS THOUGHTS on MAN;
Chiefly abridged or ſelected from the celebrated works of Lord KAIMES, Lord MONBODDO, Dr. DUNBAR, the immortal MONTESQUIEU, Dr. GOLDSMITH, and others, replete with uſeful and entertaining inſtruction on a variety of important ſubjects; including the reſemblance between the faculties of brutes and the human ſpecies, particularly the ORANOUTANG.

Social nature of Man, Population, Manners, Origin of Love, the Female Sex, Love in the Eaſt, Love in the North, Marriage Ceremonies, Cruelty, Unnatural Cuſtoms, Averſions, Coaches, Houſes and Furniture, Eating and Drinking, Commerce, Government, Agriculture, Peace and War, Muſic, Gaming, Luxury, &c. &c.

Deſigned to promote a ſpirit of enquiry in youth; and to make the hiſtory of the human ſpecies familiar to ordinary capacities.

" *The proper ſtudy of mankind is man.*"   POPE.
One volume.

The ENGLISH PARNASSUS.
Being a new ſelection of didactic, deſcriptive, pathetic, plaintive, and paſtoral poetry, extracted from the works of the lateſt and moſt celebrated Poets; ſuch as Doctors Beattie, Johnſon, Hawkſworth, Ogilvie, Goldſmith, and Young, Mrs. Barbauld, Miſs Falconar, Miſs More, Miſs Carter, Hon. C. J. Fox, Churchill, Cooper, Hayley, Warton, Crabbe, Fitzgerald, Burns, Thurſton, Pratt, Renwick, Hartſon, Skinner, Jerningham, Hudſon, Pope, Thomſon, Philips, Blair, &c. &c.
One volume.

In two volumes, 12mo.
An HISTORY of the CHRISTIAN CHURCH,
From the earlieſt periods to the preſent time; compiled from the beſt authors, principally with a view to the uſe of the younger Clergy.
By G. GREGORY, D. D. F. A. S.
Price ſeven ſhillings, boards.

The

BOOKS printed for G. KEARSLEY.

The POETICAL WORKS of DAVID GARRICK, Esq.
Now first collected, with explanatory notes.
With a complete list of his works, and the different characters he performed, arranged in chronological order; also a short account of his life, and the monody on his death, written by Mr. Sheridan, and spoken by Mrs. Yates, of Drury Lane Theatre.
In two volumes   Price seven shillings in boards.

The POEMS of Mr. GRAY.
With notes by Gilbert Wakefield, B. A. late Fellow of Jesus College, Cambridge.

*Ingenium cui sit, cui mens divinior, atque os
Magna sonaturum, des nominis hujus honorem.*   Horat.

Creative Genius; and the glow divine,
That warms and melts the enthusiastical soul;
A pomp and prodigality of praise:
These form the poet, and these shine in thee:

Price four shillings in boards.

A cheap and correct edition of the works of
GEORGE ALEXANDER STEVENS,
Containing a complete collection of his songs, printed verbatim from his last corrections; also his celebrated Lecture upon Heads, as delivered originally by himself, with additions, as spoken by Mr. Lee Lewes, at the Theatre Royal in Covent Garden, and the Royalty Theatre. To which is added, an Essay on Satire, by the late Mr. Pilon.

There are spurious and incorrect editions of Stevens's Works in circulation, against which it is necessary to caution the public. The songs may be had separate, price one shilling and sixpence, and the Lecture on Heads, price one shilling, or bound together, three shillings.

Illustrated by a great number of plates, which include above one thousand examples.
The sixth edition, including a variety of additions and improvements, both in the plates and letter-press,

A short and easy INTRODUCTION to HERALDRY.
In two parts.

Part I. The use of arms and armory, rules of blazon and marshalling coats of armour, with engraved tables upon a new plan, for the instruction of those who wish to learn the science.

Part II. A Dictionary of heraldry, with an alphabetical list of the terms in English, French, and Latin; also the different degrees of the nobility and gentry of England, with tables of precedency.

BOOKS printed for G. KEARSLEY.

The whole compiled from the moſt approved authorities.
By HUGH CLARK and THOMAS WORMULL.
Price four ſhillings in boards.

ESSAYS on SUICIDE, and the IMMORTALITY of the
SOUL.
By the late DAVID HUME, Eſq;
With remarks, intended as an antidote to the poiſon contained
in theſe performances.
By the EDITOR.
To which are added, Two Letters on Suicide, from Rouſſeau's
Eloiſa.
Theſe Eſſays have been for ſome time clandeſtinely circulated at a very extravagant price, without any comment. This myſterious mode of ſale, by rendering them an object of requeſt, has conſiderably enhanced their value. The notes which accompany and improve this edition, are written by a clergyman of the Church of England, and will appear to every ſerious reader of taſte and diſcernment, a ſatisfactory anſwer to every thing exceptionable in the text.
A new edition, with conſiderable improvements.
Price four ſhillings in boards.

OBSERVATIONS upon the FOUR GOSPELS.
Shewing their Defects, and how far thoſe Defects, together with the writings of St. Paul, have miſled the compilers of our Church Services, &c. thereby evincing the neceſſity of reviſing the whole by authority.
By a FRIEND to TRUTH.
" Wherever the religion of any ſtate falls into diſregard and
" contempt, it is impoſſible for that ſtate to continue long."
MACHIAVEL.
Printed at Geneva, and ſold by G. Kearſley in London for ten ſhillings and ſixpence.

PETER PINDAR's WORKS.
The firſt nineteen pieces, Price 2l. 7s. 6d. in boards.

The POETICAL WORKS of SAM. JOHNSON, LL. D.
Containing London, a Satire, and the Vanity of Human Wiſhes, both imitated from Juvenal; Irene, a tragedy; the Winter's Walk; Stella in Mourning; the Midſummer's Wiſh; an Evening Ode to Stella; Vanity of Wealth; the Natural Beauty; Tranſlation of Pope's Meſſiah, and ſundry other pieces.
A new edition. Price three ſhillings in boards.

The

BOOKS printed for G. KEARSLEY.
The WORKS of
ALEXANDER POPE, Esq.
In six volumes. Price eighteen shillings.

The PEERAGE of ENGLAND, SCOTLAND and
IRELAND.
With a new set of plates, neatly engraved, and an account of the present Peers ancestors, including three generations.
The whole in one pocket volume. Price six shillings.
These plates are new, and infinitely more elegant and accurately engraved than any extant.

Price 5s. in boards.
The LIFE of THOMAS CHATTERTON,
With CRITICISMS on his GENIUS and WRITINGS, and a concise VIEW of the CONTROVERSY concerning ROWLEY's POEMS.
By G. GREGORY, D. D. F. A. S.
Author of Essays Historical and Moral, &c.

Useful principally to Magistrates and Lawyers.
A new edition, corrected and enlarged, of
A COMPENDIOUS DIGEST of the STATUTE LAW,
Comprising the substance and effect of all the public Acts of Parliament in force from Magna Charta to the present time.
By THOMAS WALTER WILLIAMS, of the Inner Temple,
Barrister at Law.
Price thirteen shillings bound.

The FOURTH EDITION improved and enlarged, with a copious Index, containing above one thousand articles.
The GARDENER's POCKET CALENDAR,
On a new plan, alphabetically arranged, with the necessary directions for keeping a Garden in proper order, at a small expence, and for raising Flowers in every month of the year. Also, for cultivating Vegetables, for the use of an army in camp or garrison.
By RICHARD WESTON, Esq.
Price two shillings and sixpence sewed.

www.ingramcontent.com/pod-product-compliance
Lightning Source LLC
Chambersburg PA
CBHW030303240426
43673CB00040B/1042